THE CAMPAIGNS
OF

WALKER'S
TEXAS
DIVISION

Major General John G. Walker, C.S.A.

The Campaigns of

WALKER'S TEXAS DIVISION

by
Joseph Palmer Blessington

new introductions by

Norman D. Brown
&
T. Michael Parrish

State House Press
Austin, Texas
1994

Library of Congress Cataloging-in-Publication Data

Blessington, Joseph Palmer, 1841-1898.
The campaigns of Walker's Texas Division / by Joseph Palmer
Blessington ; new introductions by Norman D. Brown
& T. Michael Parrish.
p. cm.
Includes bibliographical references and index.
"First published in New York City in 1875 by Lange,
Little & Company" — P. xxiv.
ISBN 1-880510-04-9 (alk. paper)
ISBN 1-880510-05-7 (ltd. : alk. paper)
1. Blessington, Joseph Palmer, 1841-1898.
2. United States—History—Civil War, 1861-1865—Personal
narratives, Confederate. 3. Confederate States of America.
Army. Walker's Texas Division. 4. United
States—History—Civil War, 1861-1865—Regimental histories.
5. West (U.S.)—History—Civil War, 1861-1865—Campaigns.
6. United States—History—Civil War, 1861-1865—Campaigns.
I. Title. II. Title: Walker's Texas Division.

E580.5.W34B54 1994
973.7'82—dc20   93-43423

Printed in the United States of America

STATE HOUSE PRESS
P.O. Box 15247
Austin, Texas 78761

List of New Illustrations

center section of book

A BRIEF HISTORY OF WALKER'S TEXAS DIVISION

by Norman D. Brown

"Throughout the Civil War," Alvin M. Josephy Jr. writes in *The Civil War in the American West* (1991), "the military campaigns in the West were generally viewed by both Washington and Richmond as if through the reducing end of a telescope." Early Confederate reminiscences, which came predominantly out of the Atlantic coast states, followed the wartime focus of the Jefferson Davis administration and hinted that the war had been limited to Northern Virginia where Robert E. Lee and Stonewall Jackson won striking victories. South Carolinian John Haskell, an artillerist in the Army of Northern Virginia, dismissed the war west of the Mississippi, writing: "There was so much less fighting in the Trans-Mississippi area, that, like the one-eyed man in the country of the blind, anyone who was there was a great leader, and heroes were almost as cheaply made as in the Cuban [Spanish-American] War." Only when western Confederates began turning out war memoirs did the Army of Tennessee appear to have fought significant battles. Even further west, the Trans-Mississippi Confederates never had a very vocal booster club and produced only one outstanding hero—Richard Taylor, who won his first military laurels in Jackson's Valley Campaign.

If the Army of Tennessee defensively demanded acknowledgment of its courage despite winning fewer victories than the Army of Northern Virginia, the Trans-Mississippi veterans actually begged for recognition. "Am sorry to see so few items from this side the Father of Waters," W.L. Morrison of Hamilton, Texas, wrote the *Confederate Veteran* magazine in 1895.

> From reading the *Veteran*, one would almost conclude we had no war west of the Mississippi, while, in proportion to our numbers, we held as many Federals in check, when protecting Texas and western Louisiana, as any portion of the Confederate forces had to contend with. We also had as brave men, as noble women as ever lived on earth.

In an address to the Tenth Annual Meeting of the United Confederate Veterans in 1902, U.S. Senator James H. Berry of Arkansas, who had lost a leg in the war, pleaded: "All that we ask is that you who fought in the East should fully realize that your brothers in the Trans-Mississippi were Confederate soldiers also, equal in courage and self-sacrifice, equal in devotion to duty and love of country. . . ."

The vast Confederate Trans-Mississippi Department theoretically covered almost 600,000 square miles, embracing Missouri, Arkansas, the western four-fifths of Louisiana, Texas, the Indian Territory (Oklahoma) and the short-lived Confederate Territory of Arizona (roughly the southern two-fifths of the modern states of Arizona and New Mexico). It was never more than a peripheral theater of military operations, and its fate depended upon the shifting fortunes of the armies defending the Confederacy's heartland east of the Mississippi River. Historians have had relatively little to say about the war west of the river, especially after the fall of Vicksburg, Mississippi, on July 4, 1863. Yet, as Robert L. Kerby has pointed out,

> the Trans-Mississippi was the most extensive military department in the Confederacy; it was, at least potentially, a recruiting ground and a source of supply for

the East; its very existence was a factor which the Union high command had to weigh when planning campaign strategy; it did enjoy some unique advantages and encounter some unique problems; and its history does serve to complement and refine the history of the Confederate States.

In October 1862 Brigadier General Henry E. McCulloch was ordered to organize the Texas infantry then assembled at Camp Nelson, near Austin, Arkansas, into a division of four brigades, with a battery of artillery to be attached to each brigade. The First Brigade was commanded by Colonel Overton Young, the Second Brigade by Colonel Horace Randal, and the Third Brigade by Colonel George Flournoy. The Fourth Brigade under Colonel James Deshler was detached to Arkansas Post soon after its organization and was captured there on January 11, 1863. In early 1865 another Fourth Brigade was organized under Colonel Wilburn H. King.

On December 23, 1862, Major General John G. Walker, a forty-year-old Missourian who had served with distinction in the Army of Northern Virginia, was assigned to command the division; and it was known thereafter as Walker's Texas Division. The largest unit of Texans in the war, it made a reputation for long, forced marches from one threatened point to another in Arkansas and Louisiana and earned from the Union troops the complimentary sobriquet of "Walker's Greyhounds." "Where did they acquire these extraordinary powers of endurance, if not in their manifold journeyings beside their oxen?" suggested Stephen Powers, an Ohio journalist. "On the other hand, perhaps the slow motions of their oxen have had a hand in making them the laziest of all Americans."

The fighting was often as fierce in the Trans-Mississippi Department as it was east of the river, and Walker's Texas Division played a conspicuous part in four hard-fought battles:

Milliken's Bend, Sabine Cross Roads (called Mansfield by the Confederates) and Pleasant Hill in Louisiana, and Jenkins' Ferry in Arkansas. Three regiments—the 11th, 15th, and 18th Texas—also participated in the battle of Bayou Bourbeau, the largest clash between the contending forces in Union General Nathaniel Banks' "Great Texas Overland Expedition" through southern Louisiana in the fall of 1863. One past and two future governors of Texas were in the division: Edward Clark, Oran M. Roberts, and Richard B. Hubbard.

The men of the division long remembered Camp Nelson, because of the severe winter which caused much illness and many deaths. "Dysentery and fevers of various kinds made many victims," Joseph P. Blessington of the 16th Texas Infantry recalled. "The hospital was filled with sick. The sickness was owing a great deal to the impure water we had to use. Fully 1,500 men died at Camp Nelson." B.H. Carroll of the 17th Texas Infantry stated that the division "lost more men from measles and pneumonia in one winter at Little Rock than in all the battles in which it was engaged." "Thank god I am well and at my post again," Captain Elijah Petty of the 17th Texas wrote to his daughter Ella after a severe attack of typhoid pneumonia. "I resolved and swore that I would not die and sure enough I didn't. I didn't come to Arkansas to die—I think that God would never resurrect me here. If this was all the country in controversy in this war the winner would be ruined."

When the men were not dying like "rotten sheep" in camp, the departmental commander, General Theophilus Holmes, kept them marching and countermarching between Little Rock and Pine Bluff to counter real or imagined Federal invasions. "It was generally believed amongst the troops that General Holmes was advised by the Medical Board to give Walker's Division enough of exercise," grumbled Blessington. On January 11, 1863, the division took up the line of march to reinforce Arkansas Post, about fifty-five miles distant, which was under attack by a

Federal army and fleet; but the Post was surrendered before the Texans could get there and the division encamped on the river bank. Their camp was generally known as "Camp Freeze Out" because of the rain, snow, and freezing temperatures. Holmes, anticipating the Federal gunboats, backed by their army, coming up the Arkansas River, began fortifying some two miles from the river; but when it was learned that the Federals were on their way downstream, the Confederates marched back to Pine Bluff. The men had lost all confidence in Holmes. When it was learned that General Edmund Kirby Smith would replace Holmes as departmental commander, Captain Petty wrote his daughter: "I am truly glad of that. I look upon General H as a dilapidated old Granny and a drunkard besides. He has done no good nor ever will here. The confidence of the soldiery and people have departed from [him]."

In April 1863 Walker's Division was ordered to Monroe, Louisiana, so that it would be in a position to move to General Richard Taylor's assistance should he be compelled to fall back to Alexandria. Nathaniel Banks was advancing up Bayou Teche in southern Louisiana with sixteen thousand men. The last thirty-six-mile part of the trip, from Ouachita (or Washita) City to Monroe, was completed by boat. "On approaching Monroe, we passed through the camp of Walker's Division (8000) strong," Lieutenant Colonel Arthur Lyon Fremantle of the British army noted in his journal on May 10. "It was on the march from Arkansas to meet Banks. . . . The men were well armed with rifles and bayonets, but they were dressed in ragged civilian clothes." After arriving at Campti on the Red River, the division proceeded by boat to Alexandria, arriving on May 27. Banks had left Alexandria for operations against Port Hudson, Louisiana, in cooperation with Ulysses F. Grant's final push against Vicksburg from the south. After crossing the Mississippi Grant abandoned his communications and supply lines and pushed inland. First he struck at Jackson, the capital of Mississippi, driving back the small Confederate force General Joseph E. Johnston had collected there, and then turned on General John Pemberton's army, defeated it in two battles, and forced it into Vicksburg. After two ill-advised assaults the Federal army settled down to besiege the city, while gunboats kept up a bombardment from the river.

Early in June 1863 the Trans-Mississippi Confederates decided to attack Milliken's Bend on the Mississippi River, an assault destined to be their most serious threat from the west during the siege of Vicksburg. With Milliken's Bend taken, Young's Point, eleven miles below, would certainly fall, and thus Pemberton's army in Vicksburg would be covered if he chose to abandon the city and cross the river. In the meantime Kirby Smith instructed Taylor to keep Pemberton informed of his movements whenever practicable and "to spare no exertions in his efforts to throw supplies into Vicksburg from the west bank of the river."

Lying immediately above the town of that name, Milliken's Bend was a Federal camp fifteen feet above the right bank of the Mississippi. The camp, 150 yards wide, was sheltered by two levees, one on the riverbank and the other on its land side. In front of the forward levee the camp was protected by a thick hedge averaging fifteen feet in height. To the right and left were open fields, trailing off in each direction into densely wooded areas. Supporting gunboats could protect the camp's rear. The garrison, commanded by Colonel Hermann Lieb, consisted of the 23d Iowa Volunteer Infantry and the African Brigade (9th Louisiana, 11th Louisiana, 13th Louisiana and 1st Mississippi), numbering in all 1,061 men. The ex-slaves had been mustered in at Milliken's Bend on May 22.

By a roundabout route, on June 6 Walker's Division moved to the vicinity of Richmond, Louisiana. Five miles above this place, J.M. Hawes's brigade (formerly Young's) took the road leading to Young's Point to destroy the Federal camp there while

Henry E. McCulloch's brigade (formerly Flournoy's), numbering about fifteen hundred men, moved against Milliken's Bend.
Horace Randal's brigade remained in reserve at the intersection
of the roads.

McCulloch, encountering enemy skirmishers in considerable force under cover of a thick hedge, ordered a portion of his
command forward in line. The Confederates advanced from
hedge to hedge and ditch to ditch, through small running briars
and vines that made a regular military advance almost impossible.
Twenty-five paces from the first levee, on the Federal left flank,
three regiments—the 16th Texas Cavalry (dismounted), the 17th
Texas Infantry, and the 19th Texas Infantry—formed in line
under a heavy fire. The 16th Texas Infantry was behind and to
the right. The 16th, 17th, and 19th Texas charged the enemy
posted behind the levee with cries of "no quarter!" Some of the
Negro troops had only a few days of drill, many were inexperienced in the use of a gun and, according to the Federal district
commander Brigadier General Elias S. Dennis, their guns were
"very inferior." As the Texans charged up the first levee (which
was ten feet high and crowned with cotton bales), after one or
two volleys most of the white troops and some of the Negroes
in this line fled back to the second line of defense, leaving the
remaining Negro troops to defend the position. Hand-to-hand
fighting with bayonets and clubbed muskets broke out. "This
charge was resisted by the negro portion of the enemy's force
with considerable obstinacy, while the white or true Yankee
portion ran like whipped curs almost as soon as the charge was
ordered," McCulloch reported. "There were several instances in
this charge where the enemy crossed bayonets with us or were
shot down at the muzzle of the musket." E.P. Becton, a surgeon
in the 19th Texas Infantry, wrote his wife that "the Yankee force
at the Milliken Bend fight consisted principally of negroes and
the boys say they fought bravely for a little while but when the
charge was ordered they fled in confusion."

The Confederates drove the Federals into the open space between the two levees and through their camp to the riverbank, using their bayonets freely. "When we got to the top of the levee they bolted and ran to their gunboats," J.H. Pillow of the 17th Texas Infantry recalled many years later. "Then we put in our work. How many we killed I do not know, but there were dead ones all along to the river. I do not remember the number of men we lost. My only brother was killed." At the second levee nearest to the river the resistance stiffened. The gunboat *Choctaw* opened fire with a giant 100-pounder Parrott rifle and a nine-inch Dahlgren. "It was impossible for me to see the enemy on account of the high banks, and I could learn their position only by hailing our troops," reported Lieutenant Commander Frank M. Ramsay. McCulloch fell back to the first levee and took up a position there. The wounded were removed to the rear. An attempt against the extreme Federal right was checked by two companies of the 11th Louisiana posted behind cotton bales and part of the old levee.

McCulloch sent back some six miles to ask for reinforcements. At nine o'clock the gunboat *Lexington* came up and threw a few shells into the woods. Walker hastened forward just after noon with Randal's brigade but found that McCulloch had already withdrawn his troops out of range of the shells. His men were exhausted by the day's excessive heat and want of water. In the evening Walker withdrew the two brigades back toward Richmond.

In the meantime, General Hawes, who was to make a simultaneous predawn attack upon Young's Point while McCulloch assaulted Milliken's Bend, withdrew without making an attack or firing a shot when scouts reported three gunboats on the river (one of the vessels was actually a hospital boat). He left behind over two hundred stragglers. Confederate cavalry was sent to bring in these men. Taylor was quite severe on Walker's Division in his official report, writing: "Unfortunately, I discovered too late that the officers and men of this division were possessed of a dread of gunboats such as pervaded our people at the commencement of the war. To this circumstance and to want of mobility in these troops are to be attributed the meager results of the expedition. But "it was Taylor himself who was largely at fault," wrote historian John D. Winters. "By consolidating his forces he could have pushed over five thousand men against Milliken's Bend and Young's Point. As he did not trust his subordinate officers, he should have led his men into the field instead of remaining in the rear at Richmond." McCulloch's troops captured fifty Negro soldiers and two of their white officers ("unfortunately," according to Taylor) and brought back a number of horses and mules, commissary stores and some few small arms.

Confederate losses were significant: forty-four killed, 130 (or 131) wounded and ten missing—12.2 percent loss. Federal losses were reported to total 652. Of this number 101 were killed, 285 wounded, and 266 captured or missing. Some of the missing later straggled back into camp. Clearly, however, the Texans killed many wounded and otherwise defenseless blacks. Some of the Negro troops crouched below their works and were shot in the head. That afternoon Admiral David Dixon Porter arrived at Milliken's Bend in his flagship *Black Hawk*. What he saw he described in a letter to Grant.

> The dead negroes lined the ditch inside of the parapet, or levee, and were mostly shot on the top of the head. In front of them, close to the levee, lay an equal number of rebels stinking in the sun. Their knapsacks contained four days provisions. They were miserable looking wretches.

Walker's Division was in camp near Delhi, Louisiana, when news was received on the morning of July 7 that Vicksburg had surrendered on July 4. According to Blessington,

> a perfect storm of indignation burst forth among the
> troops. What! Surrender, and that too on the 4th of
> July, above all other days? Impossible. The men
> broke forth in bitter denunciation of Lieutenant-
> General Pemberton, boldly proclaiming that he had
> sold it to the enemy. Surrender on the 4th of July!
> Why should that day, of all others, be chosen for our
> humiliation?

But even more bad news was to come. On July 9 Port
Hudson, the last Confederate bastion on the Mississippi, surrendered to Banks after a six-weeks' siege. Federal gunboats could
now range up and down the entire length of the "Father of
Waters." The Trans-Mississippi states were isolated—for all practical purposes lost to the Confederacy. The men of Walker's
Division were plunged into gloom. "Since the fall of Vicksburg,
the men are very low spirited," Sam Farrow of the 19th Texas
Infantry admitted to his wife. "It is the opinion of a great many
that the war will soon close."

On July 11 the men boarded a train and rode the forty miles
to Monroe, where they remained until July 19 when they were
ordered to Alexandria on the Red River. Part of the trip was
made by water. En route General McCulloch was relieved from
command of the Third Brigade and ordered to Texas, and
General William R. Scurry was appointed to command the
brigade. The division remained encamped near Alexandria until
August 10, when it moved to Camp Green in the piney woods
about twenty miles southwest of Alexandria. "Released at length
from the swamps of the Tensas, where it had suffered from
sickness, Walker's division of Texas infantry joined me in the
early autumn, and was posted to the north of Opelousas," Taylor
wrote in his memoirs. "Seconded by good brigade and regimental

officers, he [Walker] had thoroughly disciplined his men, and made them in every sense soldiers; and their efficiency in action was soon established." It is evident that Taylor was trying to make amends for his earlier criticism of the division's behavior at Milliken's Bend and Young's Point.

In November, Walker's Division was ordered to the Mississippi River near its juncture with the Red River. Cannons were installed along the bank to harass enemy ships. Several transports were fired upon, but the only vessel to suffer severe damage was *Black Hawk*, which floated down the river and burned to the waterline. Gunboats shelled the troops, but only one man was killed. On December 15 Hawes' and Randal's brigades were ordered to Marksville, there to go into winter quarters. Scurry's Brigade remained behind to protect the Atchafalaya country. Captain Elijah P. Petty wrote his daughter from Simmesport on December 13: "You will see by the heading that I am at another place and so we go hither and thither and back again verifying the name that the feds gave us 'Walker's grey hounds.' I do reckon that Walkers Division has travelled more and fought less than any troops in the Confederacy." On February 11, 1864, Brigadier General Hawes was relieved from command of the First Brigade at his request and ordered to Texas. Thomas N. Waul (late of Waul's Texas Legion) was relieved from duty in Texas and given command of the First Brigade. He had surrendered with his legion at Vicksburg and was promoted to brigadier general after his exchange.

The high point of Walker's Division's service occurred during the early months of 1864 when it opposed Nathaniel P. Banks' invasion of western Louisiana by way of the Red River Valley. An estimated 150,000 cotton bales were scattered along or near the Red River's banks; and Shreveport, Kirby Smith's military headquarters, was the heart of a military-industrial complex that extended west to Marshall, Texas, and northwest to Jefferson, Texas.

On March 7 Banks advanced up the Teche with seventeen thousand men, while Admiral Porter's squadron and ten thousand infantrymen under General A.J. Smith captured Fort De Russy and Alexandria on the Red River in mid-March. On March 26 Banks pushed northwest, while Taylor gathered reinforcements from Texas. On April 8, at Sabine Cross Roads three miles southeast of Mansfield, he waited with 8,800 men for Banks to advance. As he rode along his line Taylor called out to General Camille Polignac. "Little Frenchman, I am going to fight Banks here, if he has a million men!" Shortly after 4:00 P.M., having completed his deployment, Taylor ordered a division under Alfred Mouton to charge the Federal right and Walker's Division to attack the left. Walker rode up in front of his troops and said, "Aim low boys, and trust in God." "Yelling like infuriated demons," the Texans brushed aside the Third Massachusetts Cavalry and swept up Honeycutt Hill, flanking and driving back the 67th Indiana and 23d Wisconsin, captured three guns, and turned them on the fleeing Yankees. The rout of the Federal left exposed the rear of the center, and disorderly flight followed.

Brigadier General Thomas E.G. Ransom, the commander of the Federal Thirteenth Army Corps, later described how the Confederates "came at him like the wings of a V, the open part covering his front and flanks, and that every time he attempted to form a line of battle the wings of the V enveloped his flanks and closed down on them like a nut-cracker." All semblance of order disappeared as the sole line of retreat—the Pleasant Hill road—was blocked by an abandoned wagon train hopelessly mired in a small creek. Seventeen more guns had to be abandoned. The Federals were driven back two miles until the First Division of the Nineteenth Army Corps made a successful stand at Pleasant Grove, checking the victorious Confederates in an action that lasted only twenty minutes before darkness fell.

Banks held a hasty council of war where it was decided—supplies, food and water all being in short supply—to fall back to Pleasant Hill, where A.J. Smith and his fresh troops could reinforce the army. All night long the retreat continued. Taylor granted his exhausted troops a well-deserved rest by a stream. Waul's Brigade occupied the front of the army during the night, only three hundred yards from the enemy's line. "The remainder of our infantry forces, 'watch-worn and weary,' truly slept upon their arms," wrote Colonel Thomas R. Bonner of the 18th Texas Infantry, "and silence—save the moans of the wounded and the groans of the dying—soon fell upon that field where late was heard the din and crash of battle."

Taylor hurried forward Mosby Parsons' Missouri Division and Thomas Churchill's Arkansas Division from their camp four miles above Mansfield. Kirby Smith had ordered these troops down from Arkansas. Taylor wrote Walker: "Your men and Polignac's will have some relief as Arkansas and Missouri have the fight in the morning. They must do what Texas and Louisiana did today." At the village of Pleasant Hill, Banks formed his eleven thousand effective infantry and artillery plus one thousand cavalry facing north to defend a low plateau. Taylor had just over twelve thousand men.

Taylor probed the Federal right with artillery and cavalry and sent Walker's, Parsons' and Churchill's infantry divisions against Banks' left and center, which was driven back into the village. Federal reserves under A.J. Smith counterattacked against the advancing Confederate right wing and drove it back. Taylor withdrew his troops and fell back six miles to a water supply. As the last Southerner disappeared into the woods, Banks rode up to A.J. Smith and took his hand. "God bless you, general," he said. "You have saved the army." After holding a council of war Banks retreated to Grand Ecore, where he could reunite his army with Porter's fleet, thus converting a tactical victory into a strategic defeat that sealed the fate of the Red River Campaign.

Banks suffered 3,692 casualties in the two battles; Taylor

gave his loss at Sabine Cross Roads as around one thousand men and 1,626 more at Pleasant Hill for a total of 2,626. Walker's Division casualty returns for the two battles, although incomplete, showed 69 killed, 404 wounded, and 141 missing—a total of 614.

After Pleasant Hill, Walker's Division was ordered back to Mansfield. The 3d Texas Infantry was attached to Scurry's Brigade to rebuild its strength. On April 15 the division crossed the Red River at Shreveport on a pontoon bridge and marched via Minden against General Frederick Steele's Federal force at Camden, Arkansas. The Texans arrived near Camden on April 26 and found that Steele had started back to Little Rock. About noon on April 30 the Federals were overtaken while crossing the Saline River at Jenkins' Ferry. It was here, in a sea of mud, that pursued and pursuers fought a battle novelist-historian Shelby Foote called "a miry nightmare of confusion and fatigue." Kirby Smith, in command of the Confederate army, committed his troops as fast as they arrived, first Churchill's Arkansans and then Parsons' Missourians. They made little headway, for the Federals had stout log breastworks in a position whose access was restricted on the left by Toxie Creek and on the right by an impenetrable swamp. Walker's Division came up about 9:00 A.M. and was ordered to turn the enemy's left flank. Committed piecemeal, just after Churchill and Parsons were thrown back for the second time, the Texans attacked furiously but did no better in the end than the Arkansans and Missourians before them. Both Randal and Scurry went down, mortally wounded; Waul was also wounded. "When Randal fell our command fell back," reported Confederate Surgeon Edward Cade, "and when they again advanced they found several of our wounded who had their throats cut from ear to ear by the Negroes." This was in reprisal for those wounded Federals of the 1st Kansas Colored Infantry who were shot and bayoneted where they fell during the battle of Poison Spring on April 18.

The Federals crossed the Saline and returned to Little Rock unmolested, ending the last real threat to Western Louisiana and Texas during the war. "Kirby Smith commanded in person and the general impression is that he didn't do any big things," Surgeon E.P. Becton wrote his wife. "The Feds continued their flight to Little Rock and supposed we might claim it as a victory." "It was a bloody little fight for us and nothing accomplished," an elderly veteran of Walker's Division wrote in 1910, "and I never could figure out why our commander ran up against such a hard proposition." The losses in Walker's Division, again incomplete, were 74 killed, 266 wounded and one missing, for a total of 341. Losses among the Missouri and Arkansas troops were reported as 542 killed, wounded and missing, bringing the total known Confederate casualties to 883.

On May 3 the Confederate army was ordered back to Camden, which was reached on the fifth. On May 9 Walker's Division started for Alexandria to rejoin Taylor, who was trying (unsuccessfully as it turned out) to trap Banks' army and Porter's fleet before they could reach the Mississippi River. The march was continued over muddy roads until May 22, when the Texans arrived at Pineville, opposite Alexandria. The division, from the opening of the campaign at Simmesport, Louisiana, to the time of its arrival at Alexandria, a period of about ten weeks, had marched seven hundred miles and fought three pitched battles. "Our Division has suffered more than all of them," Surgeon Edward Cade wrote his wife. "I consider it the finest Division West of the Mississippi and that it is not surpassed East." On June 17 the troops learned, much to their surprise and dismay, that Walker had been assigned to the command of the Department of West Louisiana, in place of the short-tempered Taylor who had been relieved from duty at his own request by Kirby Smith. Brigadier General Wilburn H. King took temporary command of the division.

In the latter part of July it was decided to send Walker's and

Polignac's divisions to the east side of the Mississippi River where they would form part of Taylor's new command, the Department of Mississippi and East Louisiana. Walker's men were moved near Harrisonburg, on the Black River, where they remained encamped for nearly a month. The order to cross created much dissatisfaction among the home-sick Texans. "As for my part I take crossing in stride although it is a bitter pill," one said. "I can't believe the present suffering of the soldiers will last long. This Hell roaring war can't exist long...it is rather cool for a man to leave his home exposed to the enemy and go to protect one that is already overrun though I can't tell what is best neither do I give a darn blew button." As a consequence, there were hundreds of desertions. "We learn today that because of our contemplated move, the infamous Texans have deserted in great numbers yesterday and last night," Louisianian Felix Pierre Poche fumed in his diary on August 19. "Two hundred out of Walker's Division returned of the four hundred that had deserted and one hundred thirty-five deserters of the Texas Brigade in our [Polignac's] Division." J.E. Harrison, the commander of the Texas Brigade, admitted that "there has been a great deal of excitement in my Brigade. I have lost 123 deserted, [who] won't cross the River. There are many others who dislike it extremely...." Taylor was satisfied that if he marched the two divisions any nearer the Mississippi he would lose by desertion "at least one-half the entire command." To intercept the deserters, at least two hundred of whom were armed, checkpoints manned by cavalry were established at various Red River ferries from Cotile to Grand Ecore.

In the meantime, Walker was ordered to assume command of the District of Texas, New Mexico and Arizona. Major General John Forney, who had commanded a division under Pemberton at Vicksburg, left Shreveport on August 12 to assume command of Walker's Division. Forney's arrival served further to inflame the Texans, who regarded him as too strict a disciplinarian. In view of their feelings he did not formally assume command of the division until September 4.

On August 18 Taylor issued orders cancelling the attempt to cross the Mississippi; he had received information from his scouts that the Federals had learned of the undertaking. Gunboats had taken position between Vicksburg and the Red River at intervals of about twelve miles, while other gunboats constantly patrolled between those points. A crossing under such circumstances would, in his opinion, be "impracticable"and would result "only in injury to the whole command. . . ." Kirby Smith concurred and ordered Taylor to cross the river alone. A few days later Taylor with his Negro servant and a guide made the crossing in a light canoe, the horses swimming alongside.

For the rest of the war Walker's Division was stationed at Monticello and Camden in Arkansas, and in the Shreveport-Minden area of Louisiana before returning to Texas, reaching Camp Groce near Hempstead on April 15, 1865. This was six days after Lee's surrender at Appomattox Court House. On May 12 Walker, displaced from his district command by Magruder, was ordered to relieve Forney in command of the Texas Division. But not even Walker, to whom the soldiers were "warmly attached," could hold them to their duty. Walker wired Kirby Smith that his infantry had mutinied on May 19, seized all transportation and supplies, and carried off to their homes everything they could get their hands on. "In a word," he announced, "there is not an animal, or wagon, or public stores of any description left in their track." By the time Kirby Smith arrived at his new headquarters in Houston on May 27, he was a general without an army and had no choice but to surrender.

Uncertain of the future, Walker unsuccessfully tried to persuade the officers and men of his division to go to Mexico with him and other senior Confederates. On June 6 he and five other men left Hempstead for San Antonio and from there the general continued his journey with a party of forty men which included Generals William Preston and Hamilton P. Bee.

Despite the inglorious conclusion to its military service, Walker's Texas Division was the backbone of the Confederate army in the Trans-Mississippi Department. Lester N. Fitzhugh's appraisal in the *Handbook of Texas* is a fair one: "The fighting service of Walker's Texas Division was less arduous than that of many similar commands in the Army of Northern Virginia and the Army of Tennessee. It operated efficiently, however, under peculiar difficulties unknown east of the Mississippi River, and it deserved major credit for preserving Texas from Federal invasion." Although made up of the same material that comprised Hood's Texas Brigade in the Army of Northern Virginia and Terry's Texas Rangers and Granbury's Texas Brigade in the Army of Tennessee, Walker's Division has been largely forgotten. Old myths die hard. The noted Civil War historian, William C. Davis, has written that by the spring of 1863 the "men in the ranks" of Kirby Smith's army "were hardly of the best. The cream of the Western soldiery had been drained away to the East." Fortunately, there has been a revival of interest in the Trans-Mississippi Confederates in recent years; and the "brave men" and "noble women" W.L. Morrison spoke of in 1895 are at long last beginning to receive the recognition for which they pleaded in vain during their own lifetimes. Yes, Virginia, there was a war west of the Mississippi.

JOSEPH P. BLESSINGTON AND HIS BOOK

by T. Michael Parrish

An Irishman born to a Catholic family in Belfast in 1841, Joseph Palmer Blessington immigrated to New York City at age sixteen. Three years later in 1860 he arrived in Texas where, at Eagle Lake on May 8, 1862, he joined Company H of the Sixteenth Texas Infantry commanded by Colonel George M. Flournoy. Serving effectively as a foot soldier but soon recognized for his intelligence, by early 1864 Blessington won promotion to corporal and assignment to the personal staff of Brigadier General William R. Scurry. During the critical battles of the Red River Campaign in the spring of 1864, Blessington shouldered a musket and saw action at Mansfield and Pleasant Hill in Louisiana on April 8 and 9. At Pleasant Hill he suffered a slight wound to the groin but managed to stay with Walker's Division during its rapid movement into Arkansas, where he participated in the tragic assaults at Jenkins' Ferry on April 30.

On June 27, 1865, Blessington was paroled by Federal occupation forces at Houston, and he apparently remained to marry Agnes Conaly there on June 25, 1868. During the early 1870s he and his wife moved to Austin, where he was employed as a salesman for the general merchandising firm of Sampson & Hendricks. Because a segment of his wartime experience had been with the hospital corps, Blessington worked during the early 1880s as part of the State Health Officer's quarantine efforts to control yellow fever epidemics along the Texas coast. Shortly afterward he moved his family (wife, four sons and a daughter) to Waco. After working for two years as a hatter, dyer and cleaner, in 1888 he was appointed a city sanitary inspector and held that position for all but one of the next ten years. On December 19, 1898, the fifty-seven-year-old Blessington died after a brief illness. The funeral and burial at Waco's Catholic cemetery were attended by prominent Waco city officials, comrades of the Pat Cleburne Camp of United Confederate Veterans, and fellow members of the Ancient Order of Hibernians.

Blessington's excellent book, *The Campaigns of Walker's Texas Division*, was first published in New York City in 1875 by Lange, Little & Company. Like most other chronicles of Civil War veterans who had served in the enlisted ranks, Blessington's memoirs were produced "at the author's expense" in a small number of copies. The book has since appeared in two reprint editions: in 1968 (Austin: The Pemberton Press) with Alwyn Barr's brief but incisive introduction which contains all of the biographical information known on Blessington; and in 1983 (Pine Bluff, Arkansas: B.R. Scallion). Both of these subsequent editions, each printed in only a few hundred copies, were soon out of print.

The remarkable value of Blessington's narrative—in which the most serious shortcoming is the rather erratic spelling of proper names—stems from the combination of vivid information from the diary he kept during the war, supporting testimony he obtained from former members of Walker's Division soon after the war, and original official battle reports by both Confederate and Federal commanders. Blessington's professionalism in corroborating his facts finds startling expression in his heavy plagiarism of entire paragraphs from Colonel Thomas R. Bonner's excellent article "Sketches of the Campaign of 1864," a dramatic account of the Red River Campaign by the commander of the Eighteenth Texas Infantry of Walker's Division. Although Blessington's original diary is now lost, its distinctive singularity can be recognized from the many passages published in the book wherein he is obviously quoting from the journal's daily entries, thus producing a veracity and immediacy too often missing from other postwar reminiscences by aging veterans.

The most important modern works on Walker's Texas Division are Norman D. Brown's superb edition of the letters of Captain Elijah P. Petty, and Thomas W. Cutrer's equally fine edition of the letters of Captain Virgil Sullivan Rabb, both cited in the bibliographical list that follows.

PUBLICATIONS CONTAINING INFORMATION ON WALKER'S TEXAS DIVISION

Anderson, John Q. *A Texas Surgeon in the C.S.A.* Tuscaloosa, 1957.

Barr, Alwyn. "The Battle of Bayou Bourbeau, November 3, 1863: Colonel Oran M. Roberts' Report." *Louisiana History* 6 (Winter 1965): 83-91.

Bears, Edwin C. *The Campaign for Vicksburg.* 3 vols. Dayton, Ohio, 1985-86.

Bearss, Edwin C. *Steele's Retreat from Camden and Battle of Jenkins' Ferry.* Little Rock, 1967.

Bonner, Thomas R. "Sketches of the Campaign of 1864." *The Land We Love* 5(October 1868): 459-66; 6(November 1868): 7-12.

Brown, Norman D. "John George Walker." In *The Confederate General.* 6 vols. Edited by William C. Davis, 6:88-89. N.p. 1991.

Brown, Norman D., ed. *Journey to Pleasant Hill: The Civil War Letters of Captain Elijah P. Petty, Walker's Texas Division, C.S.A.* San Antonio, 1982.

Campbell, Randolph B., and Donald K. Pickens, eds. "'My Dear Husband': A Texas Slave's Love Letters, 1862." *Journal of Negro History* 65(Fall 1980): 361-64.

Carleton, Fred. *Roll of Company G, 16th Texas Infantry.* Austin, 1899.

Carson, Geraldine Primrose. *From the Desk of Henry Ralph.* Austin, 1990.

Connor, Seymour V., ed. *Dear America: Some Letters of Orange Cicero and Mary America (Aikin) Connor.* Austin, 1971.

Cutrer, Thomas W., ed. "Bully for Flournoy's Regiment, We Are Some Punkins, You'll Bet: The Civil War Letters of Virgil Sullivan Rabb, Captain, Company 'I', Sixteenth Texas Infantry, C.S.A." *Military History of the Southwest* 19 (Fall 1989): 161-90; 20 (Spring 1990): 61-96.

Cutrer, Thomas W., ed. "'An Experience of Soldier's Life': The Civil War Letters of Volney Ellis, Adjutant, Twelfth Texas Infantry, Walker's Texas Division, C.S.A." *Military History of the Southwest* 22(Fall 1992), 109-172.

Durst, Leon, ed. "A Confederate Texas Letter: Bruno Durst to Jet Black." *Southwestern Historical Quarterly* 57(July 1953): 94-96.

Fitzhugh, Lester N. "Texas Forces in the Red River Campaign, March-May, 1864." *Texas Military History* 3(Spring 1963): 15-22.

Fitzhugh, Lester N. "Walker's Texas Division." In *The Handbook of Texas*. 3 vols. Edited by Walter Prescott Webb, H. Bailey Carroll, and Eldon Stephen Branda, 3:1078-79. Austin, 1952, 1976.

Glover, Robert W., ed. "The War Letters of a Texas Conscript in Arkansas." *Arkansas Historical Quarterly* 20(Winter 1961): 355-87.

Gravis, Peter W. *Twenty-Five Years on the Outside Row of the Northwest Conference*. 1892. Reprint. Brownwood, Tex., 1966.

Harrison, Jon, ed. "The Confederate Letters of John Simmons." *Chronicles of Smith County, Texas* 14(Summer 1975): 25-57.

Holder, Anne Thiele. *Tennessee to Texas: Francis Rochardson Tannehill, 1825-1864*. Austin, 1966.

Johnson, Ludwell H. *Red River Campaign: Politics and Cotton in the Civil War*. Baltimore, 1958.

Josephy, Alvin M., Jr. *The Civil War in the American West*. New York, 1991.

Kerby, Robert L. *Kirby Smith's Confederacy: The Trans-Mississippi South, 1863-1865*. New York, 1972.

Masterson, Ralph, ed. *Sketches from the Life of Dr. Horace Bishop*. [San Angelo?] ca. 1930.

Parks, Joseph H. *General Edmund Kirby Smith, C.S.A.* Baton Rouge, 1954.

Parrish, T. Michael. *Richard Taylor: Soldier Prince of Dixie*. Chapel Hill, 1992.

Richards, Ira Don. "The Battle of Jenkins' Ferry." *Arkansas Historical Quarterly* 20(Spring 1961): 3-16.

Smith, David P. "In Defense of Texas: The Life of Henry E. McCulloch." M.A. thesis, Stephen F. Austin State University, 1975.

Smith, Edmund Kirby. "The Defense of the Red River." In *Battles and Leaders of the Civil War.* 4 vols. Edited by Robert U. Johnson and Clarence C. Buell, 4:369-74. New York, 1887.

Taylor, Richard. *Destruction and Reconstruction: Reminiscences of the Late War.* 1879. Reprint. Edited by Richard B. Harwell. New York, 1955.

Weddle, Robert S. *Plow-Horse Cavalry. The Caney Creek Boys of the Thirty-fourth Texas.* Austin, 1974.

Winters, John D. *The Civil War in Louisiana.* Baton Rouge, 1963.

Wood, W.D., comp. *A Partial Roster of the Officers and Men Raised in Leon County, Texas. For the Service of the Confederate States . . .with Short Biographical Sketches of Some of the Officers, and a Brief History of Maj. Gould's Battalion.* N.p. 1899.

THE CAMPAIGNS
OF
WALKER'S
TEXAS
DIVISION

THE

CAMPAIGNS

OF

WALKER'S TEXAS DIVISION.

BY A PRIVATE SOLDIER.

CONTAINING A

COMPLETE RECORD OF THE CAMPAIGNS IN TEXAS, LOUISIANA AND ARKANSAS;
THE SKIRMISH AT PERKINS' LANDING AND THE BATTLES OF MILLIKEN'S
BEND, BAYOU BOURBEUX, MANSFIELD, PLEASANT HILL, JENKINS'
FERRY, &c., &c., INCLUDING THE FEDERAL'S REPORT OF THE
BATTLES, NAMES OF THE OFFICERS OF THE DIVISION,
DIARY OF MARCHES, CAMP SCENERY, ANECDOTES,
DESCRIPTION OF THE COUNTRY THROUGH
WHICH THE DIVISION MARCHED, &c., &c.

" When on the field of freedom bled,
I press the ashes of the brave ;
Marveling that man, should ever dread,
Thus to wipe out the name of slave ;
No deep-drawn sigh escapes my breast—
No woman drops my eyes distain ;
I weep not, gallant hearts, at rest—
I but deplore they died in vain."

NEW YORK:
PUBLISHED FOR THE AUTHOR
By LANGE, LITTLE & CO., PRINTERS,
108 TO 114 WOOSTER STREET.
1875.

LANGE, LITTLE & CO.,
PRINTERS, ELECTROTYPERS AND STEREOTYPERS,
108 TO 114 WOOSTER ST., N. Y.

DEDICATION.

THIS volume, with its many imperfections, is, with feelings of profound respect and admiration for officers and soldiers, and the cause for which they fought, dedicated to Major-General JOHN G. WALKER, and the dead and living of the gallant soldiers of his Division of the Confederate States Army, by one who has had the honor to fight under and with them, but whose rank never exceeded that of a

PRIVATE SOLDIER.

CONTENTS.

CHAPTER X.

CHAPTER XI.

CHAPTER XII.

CHAPTER XIII.

CHAPTER XIV.

CHAPTER XV.

CHAPTER XVI.

CHAPTER XVII.

CHAPTER XVIII.

CHAPTER XIX.

CHAPTER XX.

CHAPTER XXXIII.

CHAPTER XXXIV.

CHAPTER XXXV.

CHAPTER XXXVI.

CHAPTER XXXVII.

CHAPTER XXXVIII.

CHAPTER XXXIX.

CHAPTER XL.

PREFACE.

IN presenting the following pages to the public, I trust I am not ignorant of my presumption; and can only offer, as an apology, the neglect heretofore, of abler pens than mine, to rescue from probable oblivion the deeds and prowess of " Walker's Division " of Texas troops of the Confederate States Army.

To me the task has been a labor of love—still, one I would have preferred had been undertaken by some one more competent, who could in a measure do justice to the noble subject; for surely it would require the pen of a *Thucydides*, to give a full and graphic account of the battles, advances, and retreats, in which " Walker's Division " participated during the late civil war.

To the student of military science, the following pages will not be likely to afford much matter of interest, in a scientific point of view, as they are written by one whose position as a *private soldier* precluded a knowledge of the strategic reasons for the marches and battles which he merely chronicles.

That " truth is stranger than fiction " is an axiom as correct as it is right. Thus I claim for these pages of history a strict adherence to truthfulness in recording actual occurrences—facts gathered from the great and bloody drama of the late war, around which lingers the halo of imperishable glory, possessing all the fascination and interest of romance. This record has been jotted down on the long and weary march, in the quiet camp, before and after the fierce conflict of deadly strife. A correct record of events as they actually occurred, it is presented to the public. I have indulged in few fancies of the imagination, nor do I claim for this work any peculiar literary excellence. Simple in construction of sentences, unpretending in style of composition, it is given to the public for perusal, as one of the many bloody chapters in the history of the late revolution, when Southerners endeavored, by force of arms, to establish their independence, and preserve untarnished the principle of constitutional liberty bequeathed to them by their ancestors, and baptized and consecrated with their best blood, from the despotic domination of Radicalism.

Let the thousands of the loyal and true hearts that sleep beneath the blood-enriched soil of Louisiana and Arkansas answer. Let the glorious muster-roll of heroes and martyrs in our cause reply whether they were right or wrong in striking a blow for their freedom. The attempt has failed; and while the Southern people accept the issue of the struggle as the unalterable decree of a mysterious Providence, records of the past, as contained in this volume, will be regarded as priceless mementoes of heroic deeds and an imperishable epitome of gallant achievements, fierce conflicts, determined valor, and patient and long-enduring sufferings of those brave men who sacrificed their lives, and devoted their energies and efforts towards the establishment of long-cherished principles and institutions.

Mere history can furnish only a tittle of the vivid reality of warlike scenes. Perusing its pages, the reader gleans only the record of gallant achievements—lives in the midst of scenes befitting a romance, and not stern realities. Thus there is a strange fascination in such compilations. War has existed almost since the creation of the universe, and its records, from ancient days down to modern times, when Napoleon electrified the world with his brilliant victories, possess peculiar attractions and deep interest. Yet the reader gathers not from the pages of history, with its glowing descriptions, and all the attendant pomp and glory of the struggle, its attendant horrors, the deadly suffering, and unbearable anguish which accompany the dark side of the brilliant, fascinating picture.

'Tis well that it should be so. There are few, however, especially in this suffering, ruined Southern land, who do not understand, aye, know, from experience dearly purchased, what *war* means, in the fullest signification of the term.

This book is a chapter from its bloodiest record. The author has labored under peculiar disadvantages, being deprived of official records and documents, and has been compelled to rely on his present experience and information, and such notes and papers as could be obtained from the surviving members. In order to make my work acceptable to the general reader, I give a sketch of the battles in which the division participated, but making a diary of our marches the leading feature.

If I have failed in presenting as complete and interesting a work as the subject demands, it is a fault, not of the head or heart, but simply because my sources for obtaining necessary information have been, not only limited, but very meager.

I do not write this work from any mercenary motives, but with the sole desire of helping to rescue from obscurity the glorious military record " Walker's Division " earned during the late war.

I hope the history of every Texas regiment and brigade in the Confederate States army will be written, and thus preserve the material for some future *Bancroft* of Texas history. We have given too many Texas regiments and brigades to the late Confederate States service, to let their history sink into obscurity ; besides, their bravery and services are of such a nature as to cause a glow of pride to tingle through every Texan heart. As I have said, I hope other pens will write the histories of other organizations. If I have but contributed a correct record of Walker's Division to the general fund, I am satisfied. Imperfect as this record may be, it is given to the public, not for criticism, but as a compilation of facts, exhibiting some of the innumerable thrilling scenes through which they participated as votive actors.

Though vanquished in the final result, though the principle for which we fought and for which our comrades died seems to be forgotten in the blind passions of the hour, yet we have the proud satisfaction to know that our defeat was accomplished by an overwhelming foe, and they must and ever will do us the justice to say that they " met a foeman worthy of their steel."

I shall endeavor to give a graphic account of the organization of the 16th Texas Volunteer Infantry (Flournoy's), the regiment to which I had the honor of belonging until it was attached to a brigade, and this brigade with three others were formed into a division, the history of which division, from camp to field, I have endeavored to give as fully as possible, in the following chronicle

THE CAMPAIGNS

OF

WALKER'S TEXAS DIVISION.

CHAPTER I.

THE TEXAS SOLDIER.

> " Rebellion ! foul, dishonoring word,
>   Whose wrongful blight so oft has stained
> The holiest cause that tongue or sword—
>   That mortal ever lost or won.
> How many a spirit, born to bless,
>   Has sunk beneath that withering name,
> Whom but a day's, an hour's success
>   Had wafted to eternal fame ! "

ON the first day of February, 1861, Texas took sides with her sister States. The time had come when all the Southern States must "hang together" in one common cause, or else "hang separately." They hung together, cemented by the great principle that, "whenever any form of government becomes destructive of its ends, it is the right of the people to alter or abolish it."

As the news of the capture of Fort Sumter spread with the velocity of the hurricane, it roused the energies of the Southern people to the highest tone of patriotism, and to deeds of the most lofty action. The lawgiver left the senate-house, the lawyer the court, the judge the bench, the mechanic his shop, the husbandman his plough, and rushed forward to

the seat of danger, to join their Southern brethren on the
"tented field."

The bright star of victory led them onward through the
dark shades of war, casting light and hope athwart the path
of the war-worn Texas soldier.

Texas should be proud of the noble men who went forth for
her, to battle for right and liberty. They have taken a name
already famous, and made it the most glorious of the age.
They have borne aloft her banner—through toilsome marches,
through times of starvation, in rags, often shoeless and coatless—into the heart of danger, and planted it on the topmost
pinnacle of fame. The sons of the "Lone Star State" distinguished themselves on every battle-field, from the first battle of Manassas to the last one at Palmetto Ranch, on the
Rio Grande. And here I wish to note, that it is a singular fact
that the last battle of the war was, though the contending
parties did not number over fifteen hundred men, as decisive
a victory for the Confederates, in comparison with the numbers engaged, as the first battle of Manassas; but, alas! both
were unavailing offerings to the god of war.

The proud achievements of the troops of Texas are above
all praise. History furnishes us no nobler example of heroism
and constancy. I know of no battle where they have been
engaged, that they have not been chosen to bring on the fight.
What battery has stood the force of their resistless charge?
What retreat have they failed to cover? The flower of the foe
has been cut down by their determined valor. Patient and
enduring on the toilsome march, swift and certain in the surprise, and terrible as the tempest-blast in the charge, they
have proven themselves worthy of the name of Soldiers of
Liberty. If the world has ever known their superiors in valor,
history gives not the example.

Texans are born soldiers; from early boyhood they are
taught the use of the rifle and six-shooter. They know that
much depends on their skill in the use of arms—the safety
of themselves and their families from the murdering Lipau,
or the ruthless Comanche. They learn in early childhood

what has contributed so largely to the fame of the French soldier—perfect self-reliance at all times and under all circumstances. This, perhaps, is the most valuable quality a soldier can possess. Without it the most thorough bull-dog courage often ends in a worse than useless sacrifice of life. The Texan possesses another high quality of a soldier—power of endurance, and ability to march when suffering for food and water, that would prostrate men not trained to travel the immense prairies of Texas, where they are often for days without either.

*   *   *   *   *   *   *   *   *   *

The gallant dead—how fell they? Heroes! thousands of whom have no monuments save the memory of their everlasting valor. At the cannon's mouth, where the foe stood thickest, in the deadliest charge, with the forlorn hope, on the perilous scout, or at the first breach—there lay the Texan.

> "The soldier of liberty, who died for her sake,
> Leaving in battle not a blot on his name,
> He looked proudly to heaven, from the death-bed of fame."

May we not feel confident that the rising and coming generations of Texans will not attaint the holy halo that surrounds the name of the Texan soldier, but, on the contrary, try to emulate the deeds he has done and accomplished, not only on the tented field, but in the council chamber; and that, whether republican institutions on this American continent survive the present ordeal or not, the "Lone Star" of Texas shall ever remain the emblem of those who, like the immortal Bayard, are *sans peur et sans reproche?*

CHAPTER II.

THE PRIVATE SOLDIER.

" And while adversity's chill blast
  Sweeps like a besom o'er our land,
  And round her bleeding forms are cast
  The hated tyrant's chains at last,
  We still possess the glorious past—
  The victories of our patriot band—
  The memories of the fields of glory,
  Which aye shall live, in song and story,
  To cheer the brave and shame the coward.
  By that blue heaven bending o'er us,
  By that green earth spread out before us,
  By that dear fame of those who bore us,
  We are not whipped, but overpowered."

THE fortune of a private soldier is indeed an humble and, I might almost say, a penal one. Having to endure the sun-rays on the march, the blinding snows and chilling winds of winter, to plunge into the swollen torrent, or traverse the arid plains, nothing can possibly sustain him, unless it be a high and holy cause, or a sense of the rectitude of the purpose for which he has taken up arms, and for which he strikes. No glowing vision of a monument erected by a nation, or even by his comrades in arms, can allure him to the dangerous path. Of the private soldier of any army, but, above all, the private soldier of the army whose banners are consecrated to the laws which are the expression to us of the safeguard of popular rights, and the cause, in an eminent degree, of civilization and liberty pervading the soldiers of the armies everywhere, but especially the armies called together by such a cause—it may indeed be said of them, as an eloquent European said of those who fell before the walls of Buda, the consciousness of doing right impressed on their features, that "they were the nameless demigods of liberty." No monument rises up in his anticipations of the future ; he cannot expect that, when he returns from the war, either brave hands or fair hands can wreathe the bays upon his bent or aching brow, or even anticipate that he will be remembered by those who most heartily bade him leave the threshold of his home, and go forth and do his duty like a man. Nevertheless, there is a fame milder, and perhaps more sacred than that which descends in bounteous pleni- tude upon the head of the conspicuous officer, or upon those who have signally distinguished themselves in battle.

Among the private soldiers of the late Confederate army were men of culture, men of gentle training, men of intellect, men of several positions, men of character at home, men endeared to a domestic circle of refinement and eloquence, men of wealth, men who gave tone and character to the society in which they moved, and men who, for conscience' sake, made a living sacrifice of property, home, comforts, and who were ready to add crimson life to the holy offering. Many of these, if they would have surrendered honor, and their inde- pendence, could have remained in possession of all these elegances and comforts. But they felt like the Roman who said : "Put honor in one hand and death in the other, and I will look on death indifferently." Without rank, without title, without anticipation of distinction—animated only by the high- est and noblest sentiments which can influence our common nature—the private labors, and toils, and marches, and fights ; endures hunger, and thirst, and fatigue. Through watchings and weariness, sleepless nights and cheerless, laborious days, he holds up before him the one glorious prize—" Freedom to my country ;" "independence and my home."

I do not believe that there has been a private in the Con- federate army, who has been under the fire of battle, and has returned maimed or in the freshness of his vigor to his home, who will not enjoy the fame with which the loving wife, or venerable mother, or, prouder still, with which his children will remember his deeds. The private soldiers may not have municipal authorities to welcome them, after their onerous, tiresome, and exacting duties ; but with a love multiplied infinitely, multiplied by the dangers they have encountered, the labors they have resolutely and heroically performed, by the sacrifice of health and limbs that they have incurred for their country, that has given them shelter and has maintained for them a magnificent sanctuary—for all these the wife of their choice will clasp them, as I am sure she has done before, in hundreds of instances, still more dearly to her heart ; for all that she will still have a deeper sanctity. The waving hand of the old woman who nourished you at her breast will impart her welcome at the threshold, and perhaps her farewell benediction. With tears she may impart it, but ah ! they will be tears glowing with enthusiasm and with an old mother's love. This, I say, is the fame—the milder, the more obscure fame, if that be not a contradiction of terms—but nevertheless, by reason of this, the more sacred fame, which will be perpetuated for a generation or two, or more, in the household and amongst the relatives of the private soldier. I have often felt pained and annoyed at the flippant reference to the private, while the unreasoning speaker seemed to regard the officers as the prime and meritorious agents of all that is done. Why, in those ranks is an amount of intellect which would instruct and astonish the statesman ! The opinion of these men will be, and ought to be, omnipotent with the people and government of their country. The admiration of their devotion and heroism is without limit, and when the blind passion of our foes dies away, and harmony prevails throughout this continent, I hope our worthy foes will do us justice in acknowledging that the private soldiers of the Southern army were never whipped, but overpowered.

CHAPTER III.

THE ORGANIZATION OF THE 16TH TEXAS V. INFANTRY.—AT CAMP GROCE.—
DESCRIPTION OF CAMP GROCE AND CAMP HEBERT.—CAMP LIFE.—PRES-
ENTATION OF COLORS.—THE DEPARTURE.—RECEPTION AT HOUSTON.—
CAMP AT VIRGINIA POINT.—CAMP SCENES AND CAMP AMUSEMENTS.—
NIGHT ALARM.—SCENES ON PICKET.

HE 16th Texas V. Infantry was organized at " Camp
Groce," near Hempstead, Austin County, on the 25th
of March, 1862, with the following Field, Staff and
and Company officers, viz. :

Colonel—GEORGE FLOURNOY.
Lieut.-Colonel—JAMES E. SHEPARD.
Major—WILLIAM H. REDWOOD.
Quartermaster—W. H. D. CARRINGTON
Commissary—JOSEPH LEE.
Surgeon—U. G. M. WALKER.
Asst.-Surgeon—S. EWING.
Chaplain—R. H. TALIAFERRO.
Adjutant—R. L. UPHAW.

COMPANY A.

Captain, X. B. Sanders.
1st Lieut., J. M. White.
2d Lieut., J. F. Estes.
2d Lieut., Sr., Ishmael Kile.
Orderly Sergeant, D. A. Chamberlin.
75 men.

COMPANY B

Captain, W. H. Jerrell.
1st Lieut., A. Testard.
2d Lieut., H. L. Lewis.
2d Lieut., M. M. Murdock.
Orderly Sergeant, H. C. Surghuor.
74 men.

COMPANY C

Captain, M. H. Bowers.
1st Lieut., Joseph Bird.
2d Lieut., John R. Spann.
2d Lieut., J. L. Vaughn.
Orderly Sergeant, B. F. Lockwood.
83 men.

COMPANY D.

Captain, A. H. Chalmers.
1st Lieut., E. Taylor.
2d Lieut., W. L. McLaughlin.
2d Lieut., John Rumsey.
Orderly Sergeant, T. J. McLaughlin.
85 men.

COMPANY E.

Captain, G. T. Marold.
1st Lieut., A. E. Klaedon.
2d Lieut., C. H. Hanke.
2d Lieut., J. Groff.
Orderly Sergeant, F. Giesheke.
73 men.

COMPANY F.

Captain, Z. Hunt.
1st Lieut., Z. W. Matthews.
2d Lieut., B. T. Harris.
2d Lieut., C. M. Campbell.
Orderly Sergeant, S. Hayford.
84 men.

COMPANY G.

Captain, F. Moore.
1st Lieut., C. F. Millett.
2d Lieut., John Davidson.
2d Lieut., John Smith.
Orderly Sergeant, John O. Johnson.
89 men.

COMPANY H.

Captain, M. Quin.
1st Lieut., J. B. Good.
2d Lieut., J. McDonald.
2d Lieut., J. R. Coryell.
Orderly Sergeant, I. C. Bell.
51 men.

COMPANY I.

Captain, L. Moore.
1st Lieut., A. McDow.
2d Lieut., V. S. Rubb.
2d Lieut., W. H. Ledbetter.
Orderly Sergeant, James E. Wilkins.
111 men.

COMPANY K.

Captain, T. I. Peel.
1st Lieut., —— Peel.
2d Lieut., A. Ramer.
2d Lieut., James Donahoe.
Orderly Sergeant, J. M. Bennick.
64 men.

Camp Groce, so named in honor of Colonel L. W. Groce, the owner of the land, commanded a splendid panoramic view of a long extent of country, situated on a rising ground alongside of the Central Railroad, between three and four miles from the town of Hempstead, in Austin County. It was at first covered with trees and dense brush ; these being cleared away, except some of the trees left for shade, a pretty camp soon sprung up like a city. Here our regiment was pleasantly encamped, occupying the long wooden sheds that were built for our barracks. The bright fires that crackled and glowed around gave a cheerful appearance to the place, about which the men could be found grouped,—some cooking, some furbishing up their arms after return from drill, others pitching quoits, or collected together listening to some story-teller spinning his yarns. What a scene for one unaccustomed to witness a regular encampment! It was a spectacle both strange and new, to see young men, reared amid the luxuries and comforts of home, whose fair faces and white hands had never been soiled by contact with work, doing soldier's duty, bending over the camp-fire, preparing meals or boiling coffee —tears streaming from their eyes, caused by villainous smoke from those same camp-fires—carrying wood and water, and, when the day's duties were completed, lying down upon a board, with knapsack or a billet of wood for a pillow. Military discipline soon inducted us into the mysteries of camp-life, and in time we became accustomed to its daily routine, which was by no means light. At early dawn the reveille roused us from slumber. Roll-call being over, the companies were dismissed to put their quarters in order. Breakfast at 6 o'clock, A. M. In the mean time two men from each company were detailed to serve in the main-guard, to enforce discipline and guard the camp. A police guard was also appointed, who cleaned up all dirt and filth about the tents, brought water for the company, wood for the cooks, and, in fact, kept everything in order and cleanliness during the drilling of the troops.

There was a daily drill, three times a day, at the following hours, viz. :

> Company Drill, at 7 o'clock, A. M.,
> Company Drill, at 2 o'clock, P. M.,
> Battalion Drill, at 3½ o'clock, P. M.,

and "Dress Parade" every evening, at 5 o'clock ; at sundown, Company Muster, for roll-call and supper. Tattoo, at 9 P. M., when the men retired to their respective quarters ; fifteen minutes later, three taps of the drum was the signal for all lights to be extinguished, and the camp was in darkness and quietude. These duties were conducted with regularity and precision, and performed with a promptitude and cheerfulness surprising in men who had never known restraint, and were fresh from the business and luxuries of home. Everything necessary for the comfort and convenience of the troops was furnished, and laugh, jest, and song attested the general satisfaction and good feeling of the men.

Opposite "Camp Groce," on the left of the railroad, was

situated "Camp Hebert," named after Brigadier-General
P. O. Hebert, who then commanded the district of Texas,
New Mexico, and Arizona ;—here was encamped Colonel Carter's Brigade of Cavalry. From this position there was a magnificent view of the hills that gird the place, forming a sort of
natural amphitheatre; looking picturesque with their waving
forests of trees, and innumerable white tents. Look into the
cavalry officers' tents, and you will find that they don't fare
so badly in camp. Neat beds are contrived ; some are cots,
others saplings or frames covered with cotton, and plenty of
coverings. On one side is a table, with books and novels,
a box of cigars, and, most likely, a bottle of "commissary."
These, with a looking-glass, and the officers' equipments are
complete. Four flies form a mess-tent; and as the colonel
and staff are going to dine, we will just see what kind of fare
they have. It consists of stewed beef, boiled ham, mashed
potatoes, and a couple of chickens, which some of the Austin
County housekeepers were kind enough to raise for them—*at
least the officers' servants thought so ;* for dessert, a couple of
bottles of old rye, which some of the planters sent them—for
their especial benefit ; all these flanked by a respectable force
of negro waiters.

Officers and orderlies are always lounging or riding about
headquarters, which gave it a very gay and stirring appearance. At some distance from the colonel's headquarters are
the less pretentious headquarters of some of his subordinate
officers, while, a little further on, are the modest tents of the
rank and file, arranged in streets.

The men around these are collected in groups, wearing
their bell-spurs, while around each waist is dangling a huge
knife, made by some village blacksmith, giving them the
appearance of warriors, apparently ready for any emergency.
Some are playing cards, pitch and toss, or a thousand other
games known only in the army; others are dining, and grum-
bling at their rations, while dining, perhaps, on turkey. The
cooks are busy around a huge camp-kettle, placed on the fire,
in which a joint of bacon and some peas are bubbling and

bubbling around, as if they were patriotic enough to enjoy being eaten for the good of the soldier. A smaller vessel simmers near it; but, as the lid is on it, I cannot see its contents —most likely a brace of chickens under the wing of a fat turkey. This is the way the cavalry lived at "Camp Hebert." You might ask them where they got all these good things. They will tell you, as a matter of course, that their commissary furnished them. Follow their career through Arkansas and Louisiana, afterwards, and ask the ladies of those States about their chickens, when Carter's Cavalry was in their neighborhood.

Nothing of much interest transpired at "Camp Groce" (outside of the routine of camp duty), until the morning of the 25th of April. On that day the ladies of Austin County presented the regiment with a beautiful "flag." This appropriate present was received with hearty cheers. The address of the lady orator was one of peculiar force and unsurpassed eloquence. Her clear ringing voice was heard by all, and her manner and words sent a thrill of enthusiasm to every manly bosom, attested by frequent loud and prolonged bursts of applause. Colonel George Flournoy accepted the flag from the fair donors, and gave them assurance that, so long as a member of the 16th Regiment remained alive, it should never suffer a stain of dishonor. After the presentation of the colors, the regiment continued learning its A, B, C, of military tactics, until the 16th of May, when we bade adieu to the old camp, endeared to many by pleasant associations, and friendships formed to be severed only by death. We embarked aboard the railroad cars, bound for Virginia Point, and arrived at Houston about 4 o'clock, P. M. During our march from the Central to the Galveston Depot, the regiment was the recipient of one grand ovation, the balconies of the houses, banquettes, and streets being crowded with countless thousands of men, women, and children. Ladies waved their handkerchiefs, and flung bouquets on the marching column, bidding the brave boys farewell. Many knew that it was, perhaps, a last farewell to the enthusiastic and noble soldiers of this command, and they duly appreciated the heartfelt expression of sympathy showered upon them, and the emotion manifested upon many fair and lovely faces. As the regiment marched up Main Street, a gentleman remarked: "There goes a body of men who will make their mark on the battle-field." After arriving at the Galveston Depot, and finding no train ready to leave for Virginia Point, we encamped near the depot until the following day, when we went on board the train bound for Virginia Point, distant from Houston about forty-three miles. We arrived at Virginia Point about 2 o'clock, P. M. Our quartermaster was on hand to convey us. to our quarters, in a long row of wooden sheds, which had been previously occupied by Colonel Cook's Regiment of Artillery. They had left for Galveston a few days previous to our arrival.

Virginia Point commands a splendid view of Galveston Island. It was strongly fortified. Fort Nelson, at this place, had fine casements, an extensive esplanade, and mounted several guns of large caliber. The situation of the fort, on a jutting neck of land, was delightful. Here the troops spent their time pleasantly enough (except occasionally annoyance by musquitoes), reclining on the grass, watching the numerous vessels sailing by ; or, perched along the railroad bridge (connecting Galveston Island with the main land), rod in hand, awaiting a nibble from one of the finny tribe, or perhaps watching the declining sun gilding the prairies with its golden beams, while around was diffused the purple haze of an Indian summer. Here the troops were visited by their wives and children (such as were fortunate enough to have any), and many a pleasant day passed over in sweet forgetfulness of what had gone by, and with hopes of the future.

Nothing worthy of notice transpired in camp until the night of the 10th of June. Shortly after midnight we heard the "long roll" beat. This we knew was a token of danger. Presently, orderlies came galloping through camp, notifying company commanders to have their companies on the parade-ground in five minutes' time. Double-quicking to the parade-ground, some shoeless and hatless, we formed in line of battle. Presently the ordinance sergeant, assisted by several deputies, commenced issuing ammunition to the several companies. About the time each company had their ammunition, heavy cannonading was heard in the direction of Galveston. Many were the surmises and conjectures of the soldiers as to the cause. Apparently to keep up the excitement, one of the pickets stationed on the railroad bridge shouted aloud, "Who comes there?" followed by the report of a musket. The hands of every man clasped his gun tighter, and every preparation was made to resist an attack from the enemy— for, in the hurry and alarm, we could think of nothing else— but, on making inquiry about the sentinel's firing, it was ascertained that a cow, in attempting to cross the bridge, was shot by him. He reported to the officer of the guard that he saw, as he supposed, a "Live Yankee," creeping slowly towards him, with intent to kill him, and he fired in self-defence. His explanation proved satisfactory to the officer of the guard.

Another incident, I deem worthy to relate, occurred with another of the sentinels on the bridge. An officer, belonging to the regiment, was returning from Galveston. After passing by several of the pickets without any difficulty, he approached an Irishman (who was on picket). He halted the officer, and asked him for the "countersign." The officer informed him that he did not deem it necessary to avail himself of getting the "countersign," owing to the fact that he had supposed all the soldiers knew him. The Irishman replied that his instructions were, not to let any person pass without he had the "countersign." Moreover, he informed the officer, he knew no person while on duty ; and, if Jeff. Davis undertook to pass without having the "countersign," he would not allow him to pass. The officer, hearing those remarks, became very angry, and threatened to prefer charges against the Irishman. The Irishman became indignant, and, in order to punish the officer for his insulting remarks, ordered him to mark time, at the same moment presenting his bayonet to the officer's breast, and commencing to sing

> "I am monarch of all I survey;
> My right there is none to dispute."

After finishing his song, the officer asked him to call the officer of the guard, and have him released. He answered the officer by replying, that, if he wanted the officer of the guard, he could call him; but, for his part, he had no use for the officer of the guard. The officer hearing this, commenced calling for the officer of the guard. The officer of the guard hearing him, came and released the officer from his domicile.

Ever afterwards, when the officer took a trip to Galveston, he was pretty certain to have the countersign before he undertook to pass the bridge pickets.

It is a matter of fact that, several years afterwards, this same Irishman, while on picket in Louisiana, gave to a colonel of a cavalry regiment the same kind of treatment he had given to the infantry officer at Virginia Point.

After remaining on the parade-ground about half an hour, and seeing no enemy in sight, the command was given: "Right face," then "Countermarch, by file right," back again to our old quarters. In the mean time we were assured that the "stars and bars" still floated defiantly over Galveston Island.

We soon learned the cause of our being disturbed in our midnight slumbers. The cause of the heavy firing we heard was owing to the Steamer Rusk undertaking to run the blockade, which she did successfully. She was loaded with cotton for the government, and her destination was the ever-faithful "Island of Cuba." After the excitement died away, everything remained quiet in camp.

While encamped at Virginia Point, and, I might say, during the whole period of time we remained in Texas, there was a most improvident waste of beef, the regular rations being served out to each man. Those who could obtain choice luxuries from home, of course threw away the coarse and tough parts of the beef given them. These, however, soon found customers, for clouds of buzzards were continually hovering over and lighting within the lines, playing the part of most excellent scavengers.

Could we but have anticipated the horrible sufferings we were then bringing upon our heads, or rather stomachs, by the prodigality—had we thought the time was near at hand, when the poorest morsels we were throwing away so lavishly would be absolutely necessary to sustain life —a more provident course would have been adopted. Some of the old campaigners that had been in the Mexican War spoke of this waste of victuals at the time, remarking that the buzzards were fattening upon meat of which we should all feel the want before the close of the war; which proved, alas! too true. But by far the greater portion of the troops were inexperienced, and went on the principle of taking special good care of ourselves to day, and letting to-morrow look out for itself. We gained experience and wisdom afterwards, but we bought it at an enormous price.

Much as we all were pleased with our location at Virginia Point, our destiny was for a larger field to operate in. We soon learned that our services were required in Arkansas, to help drive back the invaders from her soil. General Hindman, Commander-in-Chief west of the Mississippi river, requested General Hebert, then in command of Texas, to send him all the Texas regiments he could spare. Consequently, on the 1st of July, Colonel Flourney received orders from General Hebert, to hold his regiment in readiness to march at a moment's notice. On the evening of the 6th of July, the order for the regiment to march to Little Rock, Arkansas, was read at dress parade. The ensuing night was accordingly spent in various avocations by officers and men. Nearly all wrote home to their friends the exciting news, while the balance gave way to fun and jollification; very little sleep was enjoyed by any one. The morning of the 7th dawned, and the preparations for the march were made; blankets were rolled up, haversacks filled with rations, guns and equipments were highly polished up, awaiting for the regiment to form, in order to take a final adieu of Virginia Point.

CHAPTER IV.

MARCHING ORDERS.—RETURN TO CAMP GROCE.—STORM IN CAMP.—PART-
ING SCENES.—EN ROUTE FOR LITTLE ROCK.—ON THE MARCH.—A
REVIEW.—SPECIAL ORDER.—CAMP TEXAS.—MARCH THROUGH LITTLE
ROCK.—DESCRIPTION OF LITTLE ROCK.

N the 7th of July, under the heat of a scorching sun, the regiment marched aboard the railroad cars. After a ride of about five hours, we arrived in Houston. As we marched through the town, to the Central Depot, the same greeting was extended to us by the ladies as they had done previously. There is something solemn, yet soul-stirring, in the solid tramp of a body of armed men, as they depart for some scene of deadly strife, with ensigns fluttering in the breeze, and the strains of martial music, or the roll of the stirring drum. Shortly after our arrival at the depot, we went aboard the cars, bound for our old camp-ground, viz., Camp Groce, where we were to remain a few days, to make the necessary preparations for the forthcoming long and tedious march to Little Rock.

Nothing unusual transpired on our trip from Virginia Point, worthy of notice. On our arrival at Camp Groce, we were much surprised to find Colonel Elmore's Regiment of Infantry occupying our old barracks; consequently, we had to take possession of Camp Hebert, then vacated by Carter's Brigade of Calvalry. We remained at this camp several weeks, for the purpose of making tents, and making preparations for our journey to Arkansas. The morning after our arrival in camp, our quarters were visited by one of those terrific storms so prevalent during this season of the year, and which the open nature of the country rendered all the more furious in its force and grandeur. About nine o'clock, huge masses of clouds, inked in their darkness, gathered in the northwest in fantastic forms; they were piled up like a succession of jagged mountain peaks, their rough edges tinged with a pale yellowish light. How a vivid flash of lighting would dart its forked tongues, athwart the blackness, followed by the rumbling thunder-roll! The storm drove down with furious speed upon our encampment. The men hurried hither and thither, driving down the tent-pegs, and tightening the cords. From experience, they knew what to expect. It burst at last upon the camp with tenfold fury. The lightning's blinding flash was followed by the thunder's peal, crash upon crash, in rapid succession. The trees groaned and shivered with the wind-king's mighty power. Then came the rain, first in large pattering drops, succeeded finally by a deluge of water, as if all the flood-gates of heaven had been loosed. Cries, shouts, and laughter were heard on all sides, according to the nature of the men's mishaps; tents tumbled upon their occupants, from beneath which the men would emerge like drowned rats, much to the amusement of their more fortunate comrades. Such scenes as these were of no rare occurrence and formed a part of the soldier's experience at Camp Hebert.

Many of the troops had become impatient at the delay, as the regiment had to remain at this camp until the 31st of July. Previous to our taking up the line of march, the regiment was inspected by Colonel George Flournoy. A neat and appropriate address was delivered by him. About 2 o'clock, P. M., we went aboard the train, bound for Navasato, our wagon train having been sent ahead of us the day previous. On our arrival at Hempstead, the platform was filled to its utmost capacity with citizens of both sexes, from different portions of the State. The scene that ensued beggars all description. Language grows weak and impotent in the attempt to portray these early parting scenes of the war. The warm embrace, the streaming eyes, agonizing expressions of sorrow, loving words of cheer and advice, the whispered prayers for their loved ones' safety, the tokens of love and remembrance, are memories as ineffaceable as the foot-prints of time. Regardless, in the abandonment of the excitement and deep feelings of the moment, the members of the different companies kissed and embraced their sweethearts indiscriminately. Those soft, encircling arms, and the warm pressure of loving lips, linger with the soldier to his dying hour, and often come back, with irrepressible influence, to the hearts of those who survive the dread carnage of battling hosts.

Fair countrywomen! 'twas but the expression of your woman's sympathy, deep affection, and abiding hope in the cause which your loved ones had espoused. Many of those warmly-throbbing hearts now mouldering lie 'neath the green sod of distant States, in the soldier's humble grave ; but the survivors cherish the memory of those bygone scenes with deep reverence and holy affection.

At the expiration of the given time, the men promptly returned to the cars. Cheer after cheer was given to the ladies of Hempstead, as we took our departure for Navasoto.

On our arrival at Navasoto, scenes similar to those at Hempstead took place, wherever the regiment had friends and relations, while every farm, hamlet, city, and village, poured forth their inhabitants at the roadside to wave an adieu to the men. Such enthuasism, unanimity of sentiment and feeling was never before exhibited.

As we marched through the town to our camp-ground, bouquets of flowers were continually lavished upon us by the fair donors of Navasoto. We encamped in the rear of the town, and had dress-parade, in order to please the ladies of Navasoto. We remained here until the morning of the 2d of August, awaiting the arrival of our wagons, from Camp Groce.

Aug. 2d. Early this morning, the regiment took up their line of march for Little Rock, Arkansas. During the march, the troops were compelled to carry their knapsacks, in order to break them in to the harness of old veteran soldiers. After marching five miles, we struck camp, selected for us by our quartermaster.

Aug. 3d. At two o'clock this morning, the reveille aroused the men from their slumbers. After cooking breakfast, we took up the line of march once more. What a day of severe experience it was for all who participated therein ! Shoulders grew sore under the burden of supporting knapsacks, limbs wearied from the painful march, and feet grew swollen and blistered as the men marched along the dusty road. The country we marched over was rocky, especially around the town of Anderson. The troops, however, soon became accustomed to marching, and bore its hardships with fortitude and courage, keeping up their spirits with songs and jokes, as they passed along. After marching twelve miles, we arrived at a small creek, and reposed on its banks for the night.

Aug. 4th. Marched ten miles. Passed by several well-cultivated farms, with

> " Dress-waving fields and pastures green,
>   With gentle groves, and slopes between. "

Aug. 5th. Marched five miles, and camped on Bead-Eye creek. The country here was beautiful, being an open, rolling prairie land, extending as far as the eye could reach, in gentle undulations. In former ages this section of country was inhabited by a tribe of Indians called the Bead-Eye tribe; consequently the creek derived its name from the tribe of Indians. Tired and weary as the troops were, they had little spirit to examine the beauties of nature. We remained encamped at this creek until the morning of the 8th. In the mean time, our camps were continually visited by fair ladies from the surrounding neighborhood. Many were the bright smiles on their fair faces, and also loving glances from their bright eyes. Aye, and cheering words from their fair lips, to the brave defenders of their firesides, were conclusively bestowed on the brave soldiers, showing how beauty appreciated valor. On the morning of the 8th, the march was once more resumed, much to the satisfaction of the men. Soldiers are proverbial for their restlessness, and, strange as it may seem, infinitely prefer the tedious and toilsome march to the quietude of camp life for any length of time. Arrived at the town of Madisonville, and marched by platoons through the town, to the tune of

Dixie. The town was thronged with ladies from the surrounding country, eager to look at the soldiers and hear the music of the band.

This town is built on a sand-hill, which makes it look desolate and bleak. After passing the town, we marched two miles, and camped on the bank of a small running stream, marching the distance of ten miles.

Aug. 9th. Marched eight miles. Crossed the Trinity river at Robbins' Ferry, and camped on its banks until the morning of the 11th inst. While resting here, the troops enjoyed themselves by bathing their sore and wearied limbs.

The morning of the 11th dawned a bright and beautiful one; a lovely harbinger of those dreamy days when the soul drinks in with intoxicating pleasure every scene of beauty. At daylight the troops were in line, ready for the march. Marched eighteen miles, and arrived at Colonel Bennet's old camp-ground. It is situated west of the town of Crockett.

Aug. 12th. Marched twelve miles, over a dusty road, and through a section of country almost devoid of water.

Aug. 13th. Marched ten miles, over a deep sandy road. The heat was suffocating, the thermometer stood at 110°, and the breeze was as refreshing as steam from an escape-pipe.

Aug. 14th. Marched eight miles, and camped at a tan-yard. This may look like slow travelling, but it is accomplishing a great deal when we take into consideration the effect of the sun, the heat being terrible. The nights were somewhat pleasant, but the days perfectly awful with their suffocating atmosphere. If you wish to imagine yourself in this country, just get into a hot oven, and if there be any difference, it will be in favor of the oven.

Aug. 15th. At daylight this morning, we took up the line of march. Passed through the town of Palestine, and camped two miles east of the town, after marching eight miles. The crops in this section of country apparently were good; the farmers seemed highly pleased with the prospect before them; peaches were in abundance—delicacies which the men made the most of, and greatly enjoyed. Palestine is situated on

3

rolling hills, and distinguished for no particular beauty, either of location or building.

Aug. 16th. Marched fourteen miles. The day, as usual, was sultry and warm. We camped near a spring of cool water, which proved to be refreshing. It was the first water we had met on our day's march.

Aug. 17th. Marched nine miles, and camped on the banks of the Angelina river, where we remained until the morning of the 20th inst. While encamped here, the troops enjoyed themselves in swimming.

Aug. 20th. Crossed the Angelina river, and marched fourteen miles. The general appearance of the country, after crossing the river, was hilly, interspersed with rich valleys of great fertility, covered with a dark mulatto soil.

Aug. 21st. Marched two miles, and encamped near the town of Tyler. We remained at this camp until the morning of the 23d inst. On the evening of the 22d, there was a review of the regiment by General H. E. McCulloch and staff. The affair was grand and imposing, and attracted an immense concourse of people. Although there were present no "knights of the quill," to write about the manly appearance and military bearing of the men, the general seemed very much pleased with their discipline and cleanliness. After the review, he made a patriotic speech to the troops.

Aug. 23. About 7 o'clock, A. M., we took up the line of march again. Marched through Tyler, to the tune of Dixie. The morning was clear and beautiful. The gorgeous sunrise, viewed from the hills, the evidence of divine handiwork bursting upon us at every step, swelled our hearts with unutterable emotions. As we proceeded on our journey, climbing hill after hill, the men would stop and gaze, as they arrived on the summit of the various hills, apparently with breathless admiration upon the grandeur of the scenery. We bivouacked about 11 o'clock, at a spring in the piny woods, after marching nine miles.

Aug. 24th. Marched nine miles. The march to-day was very tiresome, up and down hill. The day was warm, almost to suffocation. We halted for about fifteen minutes in every hour to rest.

Aug. 25th. Crossed the Sabine river. It was so shallow that the men were able to wade through the water, which was very transparent and intensely cold. After crossing the river, our road was up the river for a few miles, when it turned into the hills, where we had a beautiful view of the adjacent scenery. We encamped at a running creek, after marching fifteen miles.

Aug. 26th. Marched nine miles. This day's march brought us over a very hilly country. Our encampment was very well selected, being at the base of a range of hills, where wood and water were abundant.

Aug. 27th. Marched fourteen miles, and camped near the town of Gilmer. This was one of the severest day's marches we experienced. It was excessively warm, without the least air. The hills on each side seemed, as it were, to reflect the rays of the sun so as to strike us with double force, until it became almost insupportable.

Aug. 28th. Passed through the town of Gilmer, in Upshur County. Gilmer, apparently, looks rather the worse for wear. It is built on a sandy soil, and as we marched through the town, the sand would rise around us in perfect clouds. We marched ten miles through a thickly-timbered country.

Aug. 29th. Marched thirteen miles, and camped near the town of Dangerfield, where we rested until the first of September. The men spent their time principally in washing their clothes.

On the 1st of September we were on the march again. Passed through the village of Dangerfield, noted for the rocky and hilly country around it. You could discover the iron ore on several hills, and I have no doubt but there is iron enough in these ridges or hills to meet all the wants of the State, if properly worked. We camped in a valley between two high hills. The distance we traveled to-day was seven miles.

Sept. 2d. Marched twelve miles over a rocky and mountainous country.

Sept. 3d. Marched ten miles ; in two days' march we crossed many gorges, or deep ravines, that were very much broken and very difficult to travel over.

Sept. 4th. Marched twelve miles ; crossed the Sulphur Fork River and encamped on its banks : the width of the river where we crossed it did not exceed fifteen feet.

Sept. 5th. Marched seventeen miles. The section of country we traveled over to-day, apparently was very fertile ; corn, wheat, oats, and rye matured well.

Sept. 6th. Marched ten miles ; crossed the State line, dividing Texas from Arkansas. The only difference by which we recognized that we were in Arkansas was a sign-board with the learned inscription, " Ark-Saw." The schoolmaster had likely been lately abroad when this was written. After crossing the imaginary line, three hearty cheers were given for Texas. We passed through a little village named Rondo. Near this place we encamped alongside of the camp of Waterhouse Regiment for the night. They did us the honor of presenting arms as we passed their camp.

Sept. 7th. Early next morning we bade adieu to Waterhouse Regiment and proceeded on the march. Marched thirteen miles and encamped on the bed of Red River, nearly opposite the town of Fulton. It was cloudy through the day and drizzled a little ; during the night it rained hard. At ten o'clock no biped walks outside the tents, save sentinels marching the lonesome rounds through wet and darkness.

Sept. 8th. Crossed Red River on a ferry-boat drawn by oxen ; the teamsters had considerable difficulty in getting their wagons up the high bluff at Fulton. It continued drizzling rain, making our marching laborious through the stiff clay. We arrived in camp late in the evening, after marching twelve miles. After our arrival in camp the following order was read to us on " dress-parade " :

Head-Quarters, Trans-Mississippi Department,
LITTLE ROCK, ARKANSAS,
Sept. 6th, 1862.

SPECIAL ORDER, No. 19.

Brigadier-General Henry E. McCulloch having reported to these head-quarters, is hereby assigned to the command of the Division composed of Colonels Randall and Clarke's Brigades. He will, immediately on assuming command of the Division, report to these head-quarters the true rank of each of the field-officers of the several regiments of his Division, lately arrived from Texas.

By command of Major-General HOLMES.

On the morning of September 9th we passed through the town of Washington, a pleasant-looking town, having a population of about three thousand inhabitants. It is situated in the midst of a fine farming-country. Some of its residences are very fine, principally built of brick. Delightful gardens, tasteful lawns, and spacious streets, give the whole place an air of comfort and elegance. We encamped about a mile north of the town, where we remained until the morning of the 13th, when we took up the line of march, traveling through a beautiful section of country. In fact, I might term it a perfect garden, and though not literally teeming with milk and honey, it was teeming with something better —farm-yards, well stocked with hogs and poultry, stacks of corn-fodder, corn-houses and bins filled with corn and grain ; and sweet potatoes seemed to grow spontaneously. We arrived in camp early in the day, after marching ten miles.

On the morning of the 14th we waded the Little Missouri River, and marched sixteen miles.

Sept. 15th. Marched sixteen miles; passed through the village of Okolona, noted for having a ten-pin alley and blacksmith's shop.

Sept. 16th. Marched twelve miles ; passed through the town of Arkadelphia, the band playing the "Bonny Blue

Flag." Crossed the Washita River, two miles below town, and encamped on its banks.

Sept. 17th. Marched twelve miles up the river bank.

Sept. 18th. Marched twelve miles and camped at the village of Rockdale. This place is provided with a hotel, grocery store, and blacksmith's shop.

Sept. 19th. Marched twelve miles over a rocky road, destitute of water.

Sept. 20th. Marched nine miles and encamped on the right bank of the Saline River, about two miles from the town of Benton. The river at this point looks more like a creek than a river. We remained at this point until the morning of the 22d, for the purpose of washing our clothes, in order to be clean and neat in dress previous to entering Little Rock.

Sept. 22d. Early this morning we passed through the town of Benton, and continued our march until we arrived in sight of the spires of Little Rock, about four miles distant. All of a sudden the regiment made a flank movement, from the road into the woods on the right of the road. After marching through the woods for about a mile, we arrived at an old camp-ground, known by the name of " Camp Texas," where all Texas troops had to go through the etiquette of military tactics, previous to paying their respects to the " Grand Mogul" of the Trans-Mississippi Department, namely, General Holmes.

Sept. 23d. About eight o'clock this morning we took up the line of march for Little Rock ; about half-past nine we arrived in the suburbs of the city ; stacked arms and rested about half an hour to make preparation for the grand triumphal march through the city. As we marched through the city we did full justice to "Hardee's Tactics." As we passed the State House, General Holmes and the Governor of the State, and their respective staff-officers, took their position on the steps of the State House to witness our marchings. The regimental flag was dipped through respect for them. The men were in fine spirits, and marched through the streets of Little Rock with a firm and regular step. They attracted universal attention and received a perfect ovation, the streets being crowded with men and fine ladies, who greeted them most enthusiastically. There was the fluttering of innumerable handkerchiefs, and showers of bouquets greeted us on our march. In passing through the city we observed officers of all grades loitering about the city. There seemed to be no scarcity of gold lace and brass buttons. If they had been organized into a corps, they were so numerous that they would be able to defend the city against any force that the enemy might bring to bear against it, provided they remained, without the assistance of the *private soldiers.*

After marching through the principal streets of the city we took the road leading to St. John's College, distant from town about two miles ; the college was used as a hospital. We camped near the college. On the following day all of our wagons, with the exception of six, were taken from us ; shortly afterwards our transportation was reduced down to one wagon for the regiment. All surplus baggage was sent to Little Rock for *safe keeping,* never to be returned.

The city of Little Rock is built on the banks of the Arkansas River. It is the capital of the State of Arkansas. The country surrounding it is rich and productive. At the commencement of the war it had a population of 11,000 inhabitants. It is adorned with many fine buildings ; among the most noted are the State House, Arsenal, Penitentiary, St. John's College, and Gas-works. It is famed likewise for its beautiful churches ; also for its magnificent private residences, with their lovely flower-gardens, which savored of Oriental ease and luxury. It is hard to conceive a city more beautifully situated or more gorgeously embellished, with splendidly shaded walks and drives, with flowers, shrubberies, and plantations. Most of its stores and public buildings were of brick, while most of the private residences were framed, neatly painted, with piazzas hanging with plants and creepers. A spell of ease and voluptuous luxury seemed to pervade the place. The river is navigable at all seasons of the year.

CHAPTER V.

ON the morning of September 25th, we took up the
line of march for White River. We crossed
the Arkansas River at Little Rock, on a pontoon
bridge; after marching fifteen miles we arrived at our camp-
ground.

Sept. 26th. Marched fifteen miles, and camped near the town
of Brownsville. Near this place were encamped a great many
Texas troops, both cavalry and infantry; the former commanded by Brigadier-General H. E. McCulloch, and the latter
by Brigadier-General Nelson. We remained encamped at
this place until the 2d day of October, when we took up our
line of march for Clarendon Heights, on White River. The
cavalry and infantry commanded by Generals McCulloch
and Nelson were ordered to report to General Hindman, at
Duval's Bluff. The infantry command was afterwards ordered
to report to General Roune, at Clarendon Heights. After
marching twelve miles, we arrived in camp. Shortly after
our arrival it commenced pouring down rain.

Oct. 3d. Still raining. It looks as if the windows of heaven
had opened abruptly; the rain descends like a deluge. After
marching twelve miles, through mud and water, over Grand
Prairie, we arrived at camp. Our wagons failed to arrive
until late in the evening. When they arrived, commenced the
great strife of tent-pitching, or rather, blanket-stretching, in

an overflowed prairie; deep floundering of mules and commissary wagons; swift going to and fro of quartermaster sergeants; terrible objurgations of truculent teamsters; curses not low of company caterers, over drenched "corn bread" and ruined rations, with no fires to cook them withal. But at last night-shadows fall; "tattoo" is beaten, and somnolent "taps" resolve our motley crowd under our blankets, supperless.

Oct. 4th. Sunrise, or rather the hour for sunrise, sees us stirring, seeking a more eligible site for another camp. Here we are, all afloat in Grand Prairie, and likely to remain so if these pluvial skies continue over us. Casting your eye across the prairie, you behold the flags of the different regiments and battalions of Texas. Ploughing through the mud and water knee-deep, advancing towards us, some few miles in our rear was Churchill's Division, composed of one brigade of Arkansians, and one brigade of Texans, trying their muscular strength as to which would get to Clarendon Heights first. After marching twelve miles we arrived in camp, near Clarendon Heights, where we remained until the 9th inst. After all the troops had arrived, there was a temporary organization of an army corps. The entire number of our forces at this point amounted to about 25,000 troops, of all arms. For what purpose they were concentrated here I am unable to explain; I doubt if any officer beside the general commanding the Trans-Mississippi Department knew. Several rumors were afloat about the advance of the enemy; but, with the exception of some of Colonel Parson's Cavalry stampeding and giving a false alarm, there was no enemy nearer to us than the garrison at Helena, on the Mississippi River, some fifty miles distant. At Clarendon Heights were assembled the bone and sinew of Texas and Arkansas, all dressed in their home-spun suits. Alas! but few of that gallant band are now left to tell their sufferings in crossing and re-crossing Grand Prairie. Our camp at Clarendon Heights was situated in a deep wood of lofty pines, which, being stripped of their foliage, afforded little shelter, while the ground was saturated and muddy from rain. The troops not being allowed any tents to protect them from the wintry blast, officers and men had to sleep beside the camp-fires, and cover themselves with their blankets the best they could. To add to our misery, General Holmes ordered fortifications to be built. A detail of fifty men from a regiment was every day employed. The rainy weather having set in they were prevented from making much headway. Occasionally the "long roll" would beat, as it were to excite the minds of the troops for battle ; then again, a reckless cavalryman would ride through our camp, informing us that the enemy were landing from their transports. Rumors about the enemy were continually spreading throughout the camps. Many of our troops were armed with the old flint-lock guns, with a buckskin pouch, resembling the backwoods hunter. The fever and ague, having broken out amongst the troops, spread to an alarming extent; more than half of the Division was confined with them, and amongst the members of several regiments there was not a sufficiency of men well enough to do guard duty.

On the morning of the 9th we took up the line of march back towards Little Rock. It was currently reported in camp, that the enemy was about to play a "*coup de main*," by coming up the Arkansas River, thereby cutting off our communication with Little Rock. General Churchill's Brigade of Arkansians, and Garland's Brigade of Texans, were ordered to the Arkansas post. After marching seventeen miles we arrived in camp, late in the evening. During the night a heavy hail-storm occurred.

Oct. 10th will be long remembered by the members of the Division that participated in the march re-crossing Grand Prairie. It rained, sleeted, and froze. The bleak north wind swept over the prairie, and struck, with benumbing force, our thin and straggling lines. Men lost the step, and, swerving from the line, dropped by the wayside, to rest on the few mounds in the prairie that were not covered with water. Completely chilled through—even their senses were benumbed—they would beg to be left behind, to sleep and to perish. A stupor, a perfect indifference for life, came over many of them.

The exhausted mules sank down in their harness, and were left as they fell. All were left who could not help themselves. Each man, wrapped in his own misery, cares not for his comrade's wretchedness, but as the reflection of his own increases its intensity. But the men are patient; accustomed as they are to long marches, they make little complaint. Yet there was one thing that did not seem fair: that we should be marched on a line of railroad, and the said railroad (Memphis and Little Rock) chartered by the government, and not be carried over it. Perhaps it would have made our heads swim to have been put through so fast. Even the sick were not allowed to ride. We arrived in camp late in the evening, after marching fourteen miles, the rain still pouring down in torrents.

And without any tents or shelter to be found,
But by the rain we were all drowned,
To cheer our hearts for Arkansas.

Having no shelter to protect us from the elements, we made large fires to keep us warm. Around the fires were groups of sick, huddled together to protect themselves from the wind's fierce charge. Boys, do you remember it all now, without the aid of this notice? We do distinctly and most emphatically remember the 10th of October, 1862.

On the morning of the 11th, we took up the line of march, without being able to cook breakfast, owing to the incessant rains. Marched seven miles, and encamped near the village of Brownsville, where we remained until the morning of the 13th. We discovered that the alarm about the enemy getting in our rear proved false. Colonels Roberts' and Speight's Regiments, and Edgar's Battery, were ordered to the village of Austin. Could a correct daguerreotype view have been taken of us, at any point on the march between Clarendon Heights and Brownsville, I know not whether it would excite more pity than mirth; in fact, I am inclined to believe it would occasion a little of both.

On the morning of the 14th, the balance of the troops were ordered to Austin, distanced about thirteen miles. On our arrival near the village we encamped near some springs. We were given to understand that this camp was to be our winter-quarters, and to be known by the name of Camp Nelson, in memory of General Nelson, who died a few days previous to our arrival at this place.

Camp Nelson was located about two miles east of Austin, in a belt of woods skirting the valleys running east and west, shut in by high acclivities. The country here is a succession of high, rocky hills, and deep, dark, narrow defiles, surrounded on all sides by these frowning hills. The camp was protected from the cold, piercing, wintry winds; yet it also seemed like imprisoning the men to winter them here, far distant from any communication with friends at home. Occasionally the mail-carrier from Little Rock would arrive in camp, bringing glad tidings from the loved ones at home. He was welcome to all alike. Occasionally, curses were showered upon him for not bringing letters to all. He would console them by telling them he would bring them a letter the next time. While we were encamped here there was a great deal of sickness amongst the troops. Dysentery and fevers of various kinds made many victims. The hospital was filled with sick. The sickness was owing a great deal to the impure water we had to use. Fully 1,500 men died at Camp Nelson. It was a sad and silent affair to follow a comrade-in-arms to his final resting-place; gloomy thoughts arose in many a manly bosom. How mournful thus to die, among rough but sympathizing comrades, with no soft hand to wipe the death-damp from the clammy brow; no loved one's voice to whisper words of hope and consolation to the departing spirit! Yet such was "the beginning of the end" to many a sorrowful scene through which the soldier is destined to pass. Now, scenes of suffering and death have not blunted the feelings or familiarized the mind with human agony, and the heart must needs go out in tender sympathy toward the far-distant relatives of the buried volunteer. Ah, those graves of our dead!—what memories come back at the thought of them!

> " As softly as starlight melts into day,
> On pinions of angels their souls passed away.
> Strong men are bound—in anguish they weep
> O'er the dead still so dear, in death's quiet sleep.
> But ah! far away o'er mountain and glen
> Lie the homes that they ne'er shall enter again;
> Where loving ones wait to welcome, in joy,
> Back to their sunlight their own soldier boy.
> But above them now sweeps the blue azure dome;
> Ne'er shall parents or friends welcome them home.
> Dear comrades, farewell! your battles are o'er;
> Together in conflict we'll rally no more.
> Farewell! life is o'er; earth fades from your sight;
> Around you has closed death's long dreamless night;"

Agreeable to orders from Lieut. General Holmes, commanding the Trans-Mississippi Department, Brigadier-General Henry E. McCulloch was assigned to the duty of making a general organization of the Texas Volunteer Infantry, that were encamped at Camp Nelson, into a division. This division consisted of four brigades. A battery of light artillery was attached to each brigade.

The following-named officers comprised General McCulloch's staff, with their respective rank, viz. :

> Major WM. KING, *Quartermaster*
> " J. H. EARLE, *Commissary of Subsistence.*
> Captain WM. A. PITTS, *Ordnance Officer.*
> 1st Lieut. A. McCULLOCH, *Aid-de-Camp.*
> Captain B. E. BENTON, *Asst. Adjt. General.*

After the organization of the division, it was officially known as McCulloch's Division. Major Gen'l John G. Walker relieved General McCulloch from command of the same, about three months after the organization. General McCulloch was assigned to the command of the 3d Brigade, relieving Colonel George Flournoy from command of the same. The division assumed the name of Walker's Division, and was known by that name until the close of the war, notwithstanding several changes took place in the division commanders. The division was known to Confederate troops, as well as to many of the Federals, by the very appropriate name of "Walker's Greyhounds."

I deem it necessary to remark to my readers, that the muster-rolls of the various regiments are based upon the rolls of the year 1863, as a fair standard of the company and staff officers then on duty. Some of the officers' names are omitted from the list of names, owing to the fact of failing to receive the necessary information. In order to avoid unnecessary expenses, I deemed it fair and just to avoid giving the names of officers that were promoted, or killed, or those who died, and those who resigned from the cause of sickness or otherwise, etc.

The 1st Brigade of the Division was commanded by Colonel Overton Young, of the 8th Texas Volunteer Infantry, and consisted of the following regiments, viz. :

> The 8th T. V. Infantry, commanded by Lieut. Colonel B. A. Phillpot,
> 13th T. Dismounted Cavalry " " Colonel J. H. Burnett,
> 18th T. V. Infantry " " Colonel W. B. Ochiltree,
> 22d T. V. Infantry " " Colonel R. B. Hubbard,

and Captain Halderman's Battery of Light Artillery, numbering four guns. This brigade was afterwards commanded by Brigadier-Generals Haws, Ward, and King. The following are the lists of the company and regimental officers belonging to the brigade, viz. :—

NAMES OF OFFICERS OF THE 8TH TEXAS V. INFANTRY.

Colonel OVERTON YOUNG.
Lieut. Col. B. A. PHILLPOT.
Major—J. W. RAINE.
Surgeon—J. R. BEAUCHAMP.
Asst. Surgeon—U. HAYNIE.
Quartermaster—L. H. DUICHAM.
Commissary—J. E. COOK.
Adjutant—VOLNEY ELLIS.

COMPANY A.

Captain, Wm. Clark.
1st Lieut., A. G. Nolan.
2d Lieut., Henry Holtzclaw.
2d Lieut., W. C. Dilrell.

COMPANY B.

Captain, F. Voight.
1st Lieut., M. G. Thomas.
2d Lieut., E. G. Grayson.
2d Lieut., E. S. Dickson.

COMPANY C.

Captain, E. Smith.
1st Lieut. Jas. Weltman.
2d Lieut., T. M. Price.
2d Lieut., B. F. Scott.

COMPANY D.

Captain, A. D. Story.
1st Lieut., J. G. Searcy.
2d Lieut., G. D. Campbell.
2d Lieut., Thomas H. Graves.

COMPANY E.

Captain, L. H. Durham.
1st Lieut., W. R. Turner.
2d Lieut., A. J. Ball.
2d Lieut., J. C. Holman.

COMPANY F.

Captain, Jas. Jeffries.
1st Lieut., J. A. Holt.
2d Lieut., H. Peudarves.
2d Lieut., S. S. Edney.

COMPANY G.

Captain, A. T. Simpson.
1st Lieut., S. S. Smith.
2d Lieut., Jeff. Campbell.
2d Lieut., W. H. Harris.

COMPANY H.

Captain, A. V. Green.
1st Lieut., M. A. Fuller.
2d Lieut., Clay Robertson.
2d Lieut., C. R. Claybrook.

COMPANY I.

Captain, Wm. Peck.
1st Lieut., W. B. Waldron.
2d Lieut., L. T. Epps.
2d Lieut., Clay Robertson.

COMPANY K.

Captain, W. M. Nunn.
1st Lieut., John H. Yarbo.
2d Lieut., H. H. Jones.
2d Lieut., A. Bugbee.

JAMES OF OFFICERS OF THE 18TH TEXAS V. INFANTRY.

Colonel—W. B. OCHILTREE.
Lieut-Col.—D. B. CULBERTSON.
Major WM. H. KING.
Surgeon—F. D. HALOWGUEST.
Assistant Surgeon—J. N. B. GWINN.
Quartermaster—WM. COLBY.
Adjutant—D. D. WALTON.

COMPANY A.

Captain, M. A. Gaston.
1st Lieut., D. A. Gates.
2d Lieut., J. W. Richardson.
2d Lieut., J. K. Mathews.

COMPANY B.

Captain, R. Z. Buckner.
1st Lieut., W. T. Davenport.
2d Lieut., R. Beaty.
2d Lieut., H. F. O'Neil.

COMPANY C.
Captain, Thos. R. Bonner.
1st Lieut., A. A. Cameron.
2d Lieut., G. M. Martin.
2d Lieut., H. McKnight.

COMPANY D.
Captain, John K. Cocke.
1st Lieut., G. W. Martin.
2d Lieut., J. W. Gillian.
2d Lieut., J. H. Bonner.

COMPANY E.
Captain, R. Kunningham.
1st Lieut., John R. Ferguson.
2d Lieut., A. W. Henderson.
2d Lieut., J. J. Davanay.

COMPANY F.
Captain, J. G. Wood.
1st Lieut., J. Cherry.
2d Lieut., T. B. Coplin.
2d Lieut., V. Evans.

COMPANY G.
Captain, J. Dansby.
1st Lieut., C. G. Graham.
2d Lieut., H. L. Holt.
2d Lieut., S. E. Newsom.

COMPANY H.
Captain, J. W. Duncan.
1st Lieut., L. W. Stephens.
2d Lieut., T. S. Skeen.
2d Lieut., B. A. Jones.

COMPANY I.
Captain, W. W. Thompson.
1st Lieut., J. C. Maple.
2d Lieut., Wiley Mayers.
2d Lieut., M. Farley.

COMPANY K.
Captain, W. H. Lovelady.
1st Lieut., T. S. Skeen,
2d Lieut., J. M. Castle.
2d Lieut., Thos. E. Vick.

NAMES OF OFFICERS OF THE 13TH TEXAS DISM. CAVALRY.

Colonel--JOHN H. BURNETT.
Lieut.-Col.—W. A. CRAWFORD.
Major—C. R. BEATY.
Surgeon—THOS. H. HOLLIS.
Assistant Surgeon—J. R. CORNISH.
Quartermaster—R. J. BLAIN.
Commissary--
Adjutant—J. PAT. HENRY.

COMPANY A.
Captain, G. W. Nash.
1st Lieut., J. H. Noble.
2d Lieut., B. Durst.
2d Lieut., H. Dursh.

COMPANY B.
Captain, J. F. Smith.
1st Lieut., John Long.
2d Lieut., J. B. Young.
2d Lieut., F. A. Bickham.

COMPANY C.
Captain, C. J. English.
1st Lieut., E. D. Cruddock.
2d Lieut., W. H. Crease.
2d Lieut., T. B. Payne.

COMPANY D.
Captain, Jas. S. Hawks.
1st Lieut., J. C. Oldham.
2d Lieut., R. W. Smith.
2d Lieut., G. W. Hudson.

COMPANY E.

Captain, Jas. Eastland.
1st Lieut., J. E. Jennings.
2d Lieut., E. E. Jessup.
2d Lieut., J. B. Rouncervil.

COMPANY F.

Captain, S. B. Thomas.
1st Lieut., W. J. Reynolds.
2d Lieut., J. B. Wright.
2d Lieut., M. V. Miller.

COMPANY G.

Captain, Thos. F. Frunth.
1st Lieut., W. F. Seale.
2d Lieut., M. McAllister.
2d Lieut., W. H. Crawford.

COMPANY H.

Captain, S. Stark.
1st Lieut., Thos. J. Bruck.
2d Lieut., John D. Williams.
2d Lieut., W. T. Hare.

COMPANY I.

Captain, S. A. Fairchild.
1st Lieut., G. W. Haynes.
2d Lieut., F. A. Davis.
2d Lieut., H. G. Clure.

COMPANY K.

Captain, John F. Beam.
1st Lieut., C. H. Jones.
2d Lieut., E. G. Gercloff.
2d Lieut., W. P. Hicks.

NAMES OF THE OFFICERS OF THE 22D TEXAS V. INFANTRY.

Colonel—R. B. HUBBARD,
Lieut.-Colonel—J. J. CANNON.
Major—P. F. PARKS.
Surgeon—E. P. BECTON.
Assistant Surgeon—W. M. HAMILTON.
Quartermaster—F. N. GARY.
Commissary— —— DILITUMITY.
Adjutant—BIRD HOLLAND.

COMPANY A.

Captain, E. A. Brown.
1st Lieut., J. L. Brown.
2d Lieut., V. A. Paul.
2d Lieut., Jun., G. W. Traylor.

COMPANY B.

Captain, John T. Nelson.
1st Lieut., E. Baker.
2d Lieut., B. F. Rogers.
2d Lieut., Jun., Jóseph Henry.

COMPANY C.

Captain, S. S. Coizine.
1st Lieut., Wm. Boyd.
2d Lieut., A. M. Barnes.
2d Lieut., Jun., F. M. Tidwell.

COMPANY D.

Captain W. R. Anderson.
1st Lieut., J. L. Ewing.
2d Lieut., J. C. Swagerty.
2d Lieut., Jun., S. L. Shopner.

4

COMPANY E.

Captain, A. D. Renshaw.
1st Lieut., B. C. Stone.
2d Lieut., B. W. Browning.
2d Lieut., B. P. Stout.

COMPANY F.

Captain, John Gaynes.
1st Lieut., G. S. Shotwell.
2d Lieut., H. W. Vinson.
2d Lieut., Jun., John R. Oats.

COMPANY G

Captain, J. M. Jones.
1st Lieut., A. M. Glover.
2d Lieut., J. Ables.
2d Lieut., O. N. Shelton.

COMPANY H.

Captain, J. J. Carter.
1st Lieut., J. H. Rambo.
2d Lieut., J. R. Wright.
2d Lieut. B. W. Lee.

COMPANY I.

Captain, E. Sharp.
1st Lieut., R. C. McKinly.
2d Lieut., J. W. Wood.
2d Lieut., Jun., Wm. Masterson.

COMPANY K.

Captain, P. E. Freeman.
1st. Lieut., J. P. Huddleston.
2d Lieut., J. W. Ewing.
2d Lieut., Robert Good.

NAMES OF THE OFFICERS OF "HALDERMAN'S BATTERY."

Captain—HORACE HALDERMAN.
1*st Lieut.*—A. R. GRAVES.
1*st Lieut.*—G. P. BASS.
2*d Lieut.*—CHAS. SPANN.
2*d Lieut.*—W. P. ALLEN.
Assistant Surgeon.—G. W. BOYNTON.

ORGANIZATION OF THE 2D BRIGADE BY COLONEL H. RANDALL, OF THE 28TH T. D. CAVALRY.

The 2d Brigade comprised the following regiments :

The 28th T. D. Cavalry, commanded by Lieutenant-Colonel E. H. BAXTER.
" 11th T. V. Infantry, " Colonel O. M. ROBERTS.
" 14th " " Colonel ED. CLARKE.
Gould's Battalion, " Major E. S. GOULD.
And Captain Daniel's Battery of Light Artillery.

The Second Brigade was commanded by General McClay after the death of Colonel (afterwards General) Horace Randall.

The following officers comprised Colonel H. Randall's staff.

Colonel RANDALL, *Commanding Brigade.*
Major B. HARDEMAN, *Quartermaster.*
Major J. M. DOUGLAS, *Commissary of Sup.*
Capt. J. M. JESSUP, *Aid-de-Camp.*
Lieutenant L. RANDALL, *Ordnance Officer.*
Capt. J. B. HARDEMAN, *A. A. General.*

NAMES OF THE OFFICERS OF THE 28TH T. D. CAVALRY.

Colonel—HORACE RANDAL.
Lieut.-Col.—ELI H. BAXTER.
Major—H. G. HALL.
Surgeon—W. P. SMITH.
Asst.-Surgeon—E. W. CEADE.
Quartermaster—N, P. WARD.
Commissary—
Adjutant—GEORGE T. HOWARD.

COMPANY A.

Captain, W. A. Jemison.
1st Lieut., J. W. Fuller.
2d Lieut., J. H. Claidy.
2d Lieut., John B. Dormon.

COMPANY B.

Captain, P. Henry.
1st Lieut., James H. Cannon.
2d Lieut.. I. P. Smith.
2d Lieut., I. K. Dolby.

COMPANY C.

Captain, A. W. D. Berry.
1st Lieut., P. W. Clements.
2d Lieut., G. O. Thomas.
2d Lieut., E. I. Newton.

COMPANY D.

Captain, J. M. Scott.
1st Lieut., D. Skinlock.
2d Lieut., James B. Allen.
2d Lieut., A. L. Adams.

COMPANY E.

Captain, O. M. Doty.
1st Lieut., Wiley J. Thomas.
2d Lieut., S. G. Wolfe.
2d Lieut., William A. Muckleroy.

COMPANY F.

Captain, Theop. Perry.
1st Lieut., John McLemore.
2d Lieut., I. L. Wagnor.
2d Lieut., R. Fitzpatrick.

COMPANY G.

Captain, W. F. Roberts.
1st Lieut., Geo. B. Campbell.
2d Lieut., James H. Gee.
2d Lieut., H. M. Warren.

COMPANY H.

Captain, J. C. Means.
1st Lieut., Jesse Sheffield.
2d Lieut., W. G. Blain.
2d Lieut., W. A. Hobb.

COMPANY I.

Captain, J. A. McLemore.
1st Lieut., W. B. Vaughn.
2d Lieut., Morgan Rye.
2d Lieut., T. N. Garmer.

COMPANY K.

Captain, W. H. Rumsey.
1st. Lieut., M. M. Sample.
2d Lieut., T. M. Lumsbright.
2d Lieut., J. M. Trosper.

NAMES OF THE OFFICERS OF THE 11TH T. V. INFANTRY.

Colonel—O. M. ROBERTS.
Lieut.-Col.—JAMES H. JONES.
Major—N. J. CARAWAY.
Surgeon—A. G. V. DONEY.
Quartermaster—W. M. ROSS.
Commissary—JOHN H. DOUGLAS.
Adjutant—W. H. CHRISTIAN.

COMPANY A.

Captain, M. Mast.
1st Lieut., John C. Fall.
2d Lieut., H. H. Cawthon.
2d Lieut., L. B. Polk.

COMPANY B.

Captain, Thomas Smith.
1st Lieut., J. L. Tipps.
2d Lieut., James W. Welch.
2d Lieut., O. M. Auh.

COMPANY C.

Captain, W. G. Engledow.
1st Lieut., W. W. Hill.
2d Lieut., J. C. Tarbutton.
2d Lieut., G. W. Stephens.

COMPANY D.

Captain, T. H. Rountree.
1st Lieut., E. W. Giles.
2d Lieut., D. Scanlock.
2d Lieut., W. H. Lenke.

COMPANY E.

Captain, A. F. Jordon.
1st Lieut., J. H. Ross.
2d Lieut., George T. Harrison.
2d Lieut., W. H. Wooton.

COMPANY F.

Captain, R. P. Sibley.
1st Lieut., J. H. Oliphant.
2d Lieut., W. T. Eddington.
2d Lieut., W. T. Nurris.

COMPANY G.

Captain, G. T. Walker.
1st Lieut., W. D. Thompson.
2d Lieut., J. B. Johnson.
2d Lieut., N. J. Cates.

COMPANY H.

Captain, A. H. Johnston.
1st Lieut., R. B. Roberts.
2d Lieut., James Matthews.
2d Lieut., F. W. Harper.

COMPANY I.

Captain, T. B. Smith.
1st Lieut., Thomas J. Foster.
2d Lieut., E. R. Kaykendall.
2d Lieut., C. Coulson.

COMPANY K.

Captain, O. E. Roberts.
1st Lieut., J. J. Fain.
2d Lieut., J. A. Derrick.
2d Lieut., W. W. Edwards.

NAMES OF THE OFFICERS OF THE 14TH T. V. INFANTRY.

Colonel—EDWARD CLARKE.
Lieut. Col.—WILLIAM BYRD.
Major—A. H. ROGERS.
Surgeon—W. E. SAUNDERS.
Asst. Surgeon—W. S. FOWLER.
Quartermaster—JOHN BRYAN.
Commissary—
Asst. Adjutant—R. R. JONES.

COMPANY A.

Captain, N. S. Allen.
1st Lieut., J. H. Van Hook.
2d Lieut., B. C. Rain.
2d Lieut., J. L. Buchan.

COMPANY B.

Captain, W. L. Pickens.
1st Lieut., J. L. Thompson.
2d Lieut., P. G. Nebhut.
2d Lieut., J. C. Harcrow.

COMPANY C.

Captain, W. I. Smith.
1st Lieut., J. D. G. Adrain.
2d Lieut., B. W. Boren.
2d Lieut., B. P. Batey.

COMPANY D.

Captain, R. F. Wiley.
1st Lieut., C. B. Russell.
2d Lieut., S. M. Sears.
2d Lieut., Moses Pace.

COMPANY E.

Captain, J. J. Flinn.
1st Lieut., W. E. Shipley.
2d Lieut., H. C. Hollis.
2d Lieut., W. W. Noble.

COMPANY F.

Captain, E. B. Gassaway.
1st Lieut., G. W. Davis.
2d Lieut., W. H. Farris.
2d Lieut., William Davis.

COMPANY G.

Captain, D. C. Laird.
1st Lieut., William Gibson.
2d Lieut., W. M. Seeton.
2d Lieut., L. A. Denson.

COMPANY H.

Captain, P. G. Nebhut.
1st Lieut., J. F. Buchan.
2d Lieut., Mileno McKing.
2d Lieut., Jesse Woodward.

COMPANY I.

Captain, J. M. Spratt.
1st Lieut., B. F. Hart.
2d Lieut., W. A. Nieth.
2d Lieut., S. H. Cox.

COMPANY K.

Captain, Sam. J. Lyle.
1st Lieut.,
2d Lieut., K. H. Lockhart.
2d Lieut., A. D. Spratt.

NAMES OF THE OFFICERS OF GOULD'S BATTALION.

Major—ROBERT S. GOULD.
Surgeon—W. E. SAUNDERS.
Quartermaster—HENRY D. PATRICK.
Adjutant—C. T. BANNMAN.

COMPANY A.

Captain, P. I. Holly.
1st Lieut., W. R. Hulett.
2d Lieut., S. S. Strong.
2d Lieut., E. W. Womack.

COMPANY B.

Captain, William W. Veser.
1st Lieut., Neil McMillan.
2d Lieut., J. T. Glass.
2d Lieut., T. I. Camp.

COMPANY C.

Captain, James McClean.
1st Lieut.,
2d Lieut., D. B. Grigsby.
2d Lieut., R. H. Grigsby.

COMPANY D.

Captain, Thomas J. Thorn.
1st Lieut., J. D. Polk.
2d Lieut., L. D. Goodwyn.
2d Lieut., Sam. Hanna.

COMPANY E.

Captain, A. G. Rogers.
1st Lieut., T. J. Nison.
2d Lieut., I. R. Barbee.
2d Lieut., C. G. Wooten.

N. B.—On Nov. 12th, 1864, Companies A and B of the squadron of Cavalry attached to the Division, was dismounted and attached to Gould's Battalion. Major Gould was promoted Lieut.-Colonel, and Captain Veser to Major of the same.

NAMES OF THE OFFICERS OF " DANIEL'S BATTERY."

Captain—J. M. DANIEL.
1st Lieut.—
1st Lieut.—
2d Lieut.—
2d Lieut.—J. J. WILSON.
Assistant Surgeon—G. W. BRYAN.

ORGANIZATION OF THE THIRD BRIGADE BY COLONEL GEORGE FLOURNOY, OF THE 16TH TEXAS V. INFANTRY.

The 3d Brigade comprised the following regiments, viz.:

The 16th Texas V. Infantry, commanded by Lieut.-Colonel J. SHEPARD ;
" 16th " D. Cavalry, " Colonel WM. FITZHUGH ;
" 17th " V. Infantry, " " R. T. P. ALLEN ;
" 19th " " " " R. WATERHOUSE ;
And Captain Edgar's Battery of Light Artillery.

The 3d Brigade was afterwards commanded by General H. E. McCulloch, General Tom Scurry, and General R. Waterhouse.

NAMES OF THE OFFICERS OF THE 16TH T. V. INFANTRY.

Colonel—GEORGE FLOURNOY.
Lieut.-Colonel—JAMES E. SHEPARD.
Major—W. H. REDWOOD.
Surgeon—U. G. M. WALKER.
Assistant Surgeon—I. W. COCKE.
Quartermaster—A. F. FLOWERS.
Commissary—A. C. McNEELY.
Adjutant—R. L. UPSHAW.

COMPANY A.
Captain, X. B. Sanders.
1st Lieut., J. M. White.
2d Lieut., J. F. Estes.
2d Lieut., Ishmael Kile.

COMPANY B.
Captain, W. F. Jerrell.
1st Lieut., A. Testand.
2d Lieut., H. L. Lewis.
2d Lieut., M. M. Murdock.

COMPANY C.
Captain, M. H. Bowers.
1st Lieut., Joseph Bird.
2d Lieut., John R. Spann.
2d Lieut., J. S. Vaughn.

COMPANY D.
Captain, A. H. Chalmers.
1st Lieut., E. Taylor.
2d Lieut., W. S. McLaughlin.
2d John Rumsey.

COMPANY E.
Captain, G. T. Marold.
1st Lieut., A. E. Klaedon.
2d Lieut., C. H. Hanke.
2d Lieut., J. Groff.

COMPANY F.
Captain, Z. Hunt.
1st Lieut., Z. W. Matthews.
2d Lieut., B. T. Harris.
2d Lieut., C. M. Campbell.

COMPANY G.
Captain, Fred. Moore.
1st Lieut., C. F. Millet.
2d Lieut., John Davidson.
2d Lieut., John O. Johnson.

COMPANY H.
Captain, M. Quin.
1st Lieut., J. B. Good.
2d Lieut., J. McDonald.
2d Lieut., J. R. Coryell.

COMPANY I.
Captain, Alex. McDow.
1st Lieut., V. S. Rubb.
2d Lieut., W. H. Ledbetter.
2d Lieut., N. Franklin.

COMPANY K.
Captain, —— Peel.
1st Lieut., T. J. Peel.
2d Lieut., A. Ramer.
2d Lieut., James Donahoe.

NAMES OF THE OFFICERS OF THE 16TH T. D. CAVALRY

Colonel—WM. FITZHUGH.
Lieut.-Colonel—E. P. GREGG.
Major—W. W. DRUMOND.
Surgeon,—W. P. HEAD.
Assistant Surgeon ——— BIRDSONG.
Assist. Quartermaster—DAVID RHINE.
Assistant Commissary ——— ———.
Adjutant—T. H. HUDSON.

COMPANY A.

Captain, F. M. Dougherty.
1st Lieut. G. T. Bird.
2d Lieut., H. Coppage.
2d Lieut., Hugh Cox.

COMPANY B.

Captain, R. C. Coffey.
1st Lieut., G. W. Fitzhugh.
2d Lieut., James M. Tucker.
2d Lieut., James A. Poindexter.

COMPANY C.

Captain, James D. Woods.
1st Lieut., George W. McGlothlen.
2d Lieut., George A. Dickeman.
2d Lieut., W. A. Anderson.

COMPANY D.

Captain, John H. Talbert.
1st Lieut., W. D. McDonald.
2d Lieut., C. S. Dwining.
2d Lieut., A. Clark.

COMPANY E.

Captain, W. T. G. Weaver.
1st Lieut., J. K. P. Russell.
2d Lieut., D. M. Waddill.
2d Lieut., F. Kilgore.

COMPANY F.

Captain, W. H. Taylor.
1st Lieut., T. J. Taylor.
2d Lieut., E. M. Young.
2d Lieut., J. M. Cope.

COMPANY G.

Captain, M. W. King.
1st Lieut., G. M. Hobson.
2d Lieut., T. H. Batsell.
2d Lieut., J. W. Connolly.

COMPANY H.

Captain, G. H. Fitzhugh.
1st Lieut., L. Walker.
2d Lieut., J. J. Miller.
2d Lieut., W. H. McDaniel.

COMPANY I.

Captain, Thos. F. Mosbey.
1st Lieut., W. B. Sargent.
2d Lieut., S. J. Hodges.
2d Lieut., W. J. McAnew.

COMPANY K.

Captain, Fred. L. Gates.
1st Lieut., August Buimer.
2d Lieut., J. W. Kulfin.
2d Lieut., J. M. Morrill.

NAMES OF THE OFFICERS OF THE 17TH T. V. INFANTRY.

Colonel—R. T. P. ALLEN.
Lieut.-Colonel—GEORGE W. JONES.
Major—J. W. TABOR.
Surgeon—D. PORT. SMYTHE.
Assistant Surgeon—R. H. LEWIS.
Assistant Commissary—CYRUS COFFY.
Adjutant—T. M. HUNT.

COMPANY A.

Captain, R. D. Allen.
1st Lieut., John E. Martin.
2d Lieut., O. H. P. Garrett.
2d Lieut., I. C. Douglass.

COMPANY B.

Captain, I. Z. Miller.
1st Lieut., Ciceo Nash.
2d Lieut., Samuel Fleming.
2d Lieut., Chas. Keton.

COMPANY C.

Captain, Thomas H. Gutlin.
1st Lieut., B. T. Middleton.
2d Lieut., Geo. G. Tucker.
2d Lieut., I. M. Fort.

COMPANY D.

Captain, H. Ryan.
1st Lieut., A. J. Ridge.
2d Lieut., A. Boyce.
2d Lieut., L. T. Duson.

COMPANY E.

Captain, Seth Mabey.
1st Lieut., J. M. Young.
2d Lieut., Geo. W. Miller.
2d Lieut., W. Rice.

COMPANY F.

Captain, E. P. Petty.
1st Lieut., J. S. Cunningham.
2d Lieut., H. N. Little.
2d Lieut., H. McLester.

COMPANY G.

Captain, W. J. Maltby.
1st Lieut., C. M. Smith.
2d Lieut., D. V. Grant.
2d Lieut., O. W. Wimberly.

COMPANY H.

Captain, C. A. Sabath.
1st Lieut., E. Kollmaner.
2d Lieut., J. C. Douglas.
2d Lieut., W. B. Rover.

COMPANY I.

Captain, John Smith.
1st Lieut., J. Jalonick.
2d Lieut., R. H. Taylor.
2d Lieut., Jno. W. Houston.

COMPANY K.

Captain, S. J. P. McDowell.
1st Lieut., J. B. Long.
2d Lieut., E. H. Rogan.
2d Lieut., B. F. Luce.

NAMES OF OFFICERS OF THE 19TH TEXAS V. INFANTRY.

Colonel—R. WATERHOUSE.
Lieut.-Colonel—E. W. TAYLOR.
Major—W. L. CRAWFORD.
Surgeon—J. P. HERVEY.
Assistant Surgeon—J. E. KIRLEY.
Quartermaster—A. C. SMITH.
Commissary—
Adjutant—J. B. JONES.

COMPANY A.

Captain, W. J. Clarke.
1st Lieut., J. H. McDermott.
2d Lieut., W. N. Covey.
2d Lieut., R. W. Hill.

COMPANY B.

Captain, B. A. Baker.
1st Lieut., W. B. Rountree.
2d Lieut., H. W. Mahoffey.
2d Lieut., Jasper Thomas.

COMPANY C.

Captain, A. C. Allen.
1st Lieut., G. W. Smith.
2d Lieut., L. P. Moughan.
2d Lieut., John Punkhurst.

COMPANY D.

Captain, C. S. Marshall.
1st Lieut., M. M. Deerson.
2d Lieut., T. B. Yarborough.
2d Lieut., W. R. Hoover.

COMPANY E.

Captain, A. R. K. Northrop.
1st Lieut., J. R. Jones.
2d Lieut., J. G. Lee.
2d Lieut., J. E. Kirkley.

COMPANY F.

Captain, F. D. Sedberry.
1st Lieut., K. D. Bateman.
2d Lieut., W. H. Mason.
2d Lieut., C. C. Coppedge.

COMPANY G.

Captain, L. M. Ferguson.
1st Lieut., J. J. Bradley.
2d Lieut., O. C. Connor.
2d Lieut., I. J. Arberry.

COMPANY H.

Captain, H. A. Wallace.
1st Lieut., J. R. K. Brooks.
2d Lieut., W. M. Wallace.
2d Lieut., W. E. Barksdale.

COMPANY I.

Captain, J. A. Piques.
1st Lieut., A. M. Ewing.
2d Lieut., W. K. Hoover.
2d Lieut., P. P. Robinson.

COMPANY K.

Captain, S. A. Minter.
1st Lieut., T. H. Pogue.
2d Lieut., J. S. Minter.
2d Lieut., S. S. Bromley.

NAMES OF OFFICERS OF EDGAR'S BATTERY.

Captain, Wm. Edgar.	2d Lieut., H. Hall.
1st Lieut., J. M. Ransom.	2d Lieut., N. R. Gomey.
1st Lieut., John D. Grumbus.	Assistant Surgeon, T. C. Thompson.

The 4th Brigade, commanded by Colonel Deshler, consisted of his own regiment, the 18th T. D. Cavalry, commanded by Lieut.-Colonel Darnell, and the

10th T. V. Infantry, commanded by Colonel R. Q. MILLS.
15th T. D. Cavalry,   "   "   "   —— SWEET.
25th T. D.   "   "   "   "   —— GILLESPIE.

The 4th Brigade, commanded by Colonel Deshler, might be said to be only temporarily attached to the division, from the fact that they left the division shortly after it was organized. Shortly after their withdrawal from the division, they were captured at the Arkansas Post. After they were exchanged, they remained east of the Mississippi River.

Shortly after the organization of the division, Lieutenant-General Holmes arrived in camp from Little Rock, to review each brigade of the division separately. He was well pleased with the discipline of the troops. After the review, everything remained quiet in camp until the night of the 20th of November, when we were aroused out of our slumbers by hearing the "long-roll" beat. As this was the recognized signal of danger, there was rolling, tumbling, and jumping out from our berths or bunks; a general scramble for clothing, intermingled with all kinds of cries and exclamations : "Where are my shoes?" "Who has my pants?" "Where in the devil is my coat?" etc. We arrived on the parade-ground, some clothed, others *deshabille*, hatless and shoeless—a motley crowd indeed—only to find a pleasant moonlight morn and nothing astir.

We had been incontinently "sold" by some staff-officer, who gave the alarm to ascertain how long a period of time it would take us to form in line of battle. After remaining in line of battle for half an hour, another staff-officer rode

along the line, and directed regimental commanders to allow
their men to return to their quarters again. Many of the men
enjoyed the joke, while others used the king's English in a
manner not taught in the Bible. The excitement soon died
away, and we remained in camp till the morning of the 24th,
when we took a final adieu of camp Nelson.

CHAPTER VI.

LEAVE CAMP NELSON.—ARRIVAL AT BAYOU METOR.—GRAND REVIEW
OF THE DIVISION.—THE DIVISION ORDERED TO VICKSBURG.—EN
ROUTE FOR VAN BUREN.—CAMP NEAR LITTLE ROCK.—SPENDING
CHRISTMAS IN CAMP.—SPECIAL ORDER.

N the morning of the 24th of November, we took up the line of march for Bayou Metor, distant about eleven miles from Camp Nelson; marched eight miles and camped.

Nov. 25th. Marched three miles. It took us until late in the evening to get our wagons over a shaky and boggy bottom; each regiment was engaged in corduroying the road to get their wagons over. For the information of the uninitiated, I must tell them that corduroying a road is placing two or three tiers of trees along like a railroad-track, and then across those others are laid, and the interstices filled in with earth. We made several miles of such in our campaigns through Arkansas and Louisiana. After we got our wagons over safely, we shortly arrived at our camp on Bayou Metor, where we remained until December 1st.

The following day, after our arrival at Bayou Metor, we received orders to make preparations for a "grand review," to be held by General Holmes, on the morning of the 27th. The troops were busily engaged in cleaning themselves, as well as their arms and accouterments, so as to make a good appearance before their department-commander.

About 8 o'clock, A. M., on the morning of the 27th, the division, accompanied by their respective batteries of artillery, proceeded to the parade-ground, distant about three miles from our camp. The ground selected was quite extensive, and very well suited for the formation and inspection of troops. Shortly after our arrival on the parade-ground, General Holmes, accompanied by his respective staff-officers, arrived on the ground, from Little Rock. Several carriages, with citizens, accompanied him, to witness the review. As he rode rapidly along the line to examine the condition of the troops, the bands struck up the tune of "Hail to the Chief." After taking his position, the column passed in review. At the head of the column was General McCulloch and staff, followed by Young's Brigade, then Randall's, next Flournoy's, and their respective batteries. This review—the first real review of the Division—presented a dazzling sight. There they are, before you—the columns extending for about two miles marching along with their guns and bayonets glittering in the morning sun, and the gay flags and banners flaunting in the breeze—there they are, infantry and artillery; brigade and regimental commanders, dressed in gorgeous uniforms, and riding prancing steeds richly caparisoned; staff officers gay and sparkling, full of ambition and the hope of winning an honored name. After the review we returned to camp. Had dress-parade at 5 o'clock, P. M. Orders were announced for company commanders to make out their pay-rolls. On presentation of the pay-rolls to the regimental quartermasters, the troops received two months' pay. After receiving their pay, the officers had gay times, going to parties given by the citizens in the neighborhood. Doubtless, to this day the buxom Arkansas ladies in that vicinity remember the Texans, with their manly bearing, good looks, polished ease and elegance of manners, and graceful movements. The majority of these men were gentlemen, once moving in refined society at home, and nothing more delighted them than to exhibit their accomplishments to the astonished gaze of these same plain, honest, country people.

The soldiers enjoyed themselves in dancing and singing during the evening, filling the quiet air with their harmonious voices; the pleasant songs floating away in the quietude, in soft, echoing refrains.

Nov. 28th. Orders were read at dress-parade for company drills four hours each day. There was a very alarming increase of sickness. Drill! what, and give up all other schemes? Verily, no! The life of ease and pleasure which had made the hours pass away, had undoubtedly incapacitated the men from doing soldier's duty. Was it really so? Let us see how the sequel proves.

Dec. 1st. Moved camp five miles further up the bayou. Nothing worthy of notice transpired in camp until the evening of the 4th inst., when it commenced to snow, continuing to do so all night. Next morning we awoke to find the ground hidden 'neath winter's white mantle, while the light, feathery flakes were rapidly descending from the dark clouds overhead. On the morning of the 6th, the sun rose on a wintry scene of dazzling beauty, such as the eye seldom gazes on. The air was sharp and biting, the ground beautiful in its smooth whiteness; while the limbs, twigs, and boughs of the trees glittered and glistened as the sun shown upon their crystal covering of ice, as if incased in diamonds.

It was one of winter's most magnificent pictures, calling forth unbounded expressions of admiration from those who had never witnessed such a spectacle. It was, indeed, something new to those who had been accustomed only to the softly-smiling skies and balmy atmosphere of Texas.

On the morning of the 10th, General H. E. McCulloch was ordered by General Holmes to hold his division ready to move to Vicksburg, Miss.

On the morning of the 13th we took up the line of march to Vicksburg, marching 18 miles. After our arrival in camp, a courier arrived with dispatches from General Holmes to General McCulloch, countermanding the Vicksburg march, and ordering the division to march to Van Buren, Arkansas.

Dec. 14th. Marched eight miles, through mud and water. The "iron horse" on the Memphis and Little Rock Railroad blew his whistle, as much as to say: if we came to Arkansas with the expectation of riding on railroads we would find ourselves mistaken.

Dec. 15th. Marched nineteen miles. On our line of march Major C. F. Morgan's Squadron of Cavalry passed us on their way to reinforce General Hindman, who was reported retreating in the direction of Fort Smith, followed by a large force of Federals, commanded by General Curtis. After getting about four miles above Little Rock our route of march was again countermanded. The division was ordered to camp nearly opposite Little Rock.

On the evening of the 16th, Colonel Speight's Regiment was ordered to the Indian Nation.

We remained encamped opposite Little Rock long enough to spend Christmas, and anything but a merry Christmas. Many of us had intended to keep Christmas somewhat after the manner of our home style, but we could purchase neither eggs nor whisky in Little Rock, to make an egg-nog. We were, therefore, compelled to make our Christmas dinner of a piece of corn bread and some blue beef. On Christmas night the citizens of Little Rock could witness fully 15,000 camp-fires, that glowed and sparkled like the gas-lights of a city.

The imagination can easily picture such a Christmas night-scene in camp. The sentinel's challenge, and the strains of the regimental bands, ring clearly and musically on the night-air. Around the fires that glow and flame, the men were grouped, singing, joking, laughing with a light-hearted ease, as if they never knew "dull care." Most of them were full of practical jokes, light and sparkling as champagne, and had a gay faculty of taking the sunny side of everything. No wonder if, amid such scenes, the soldier's thoughts fled back to his home, to his loved wife, to the kisses of his darling child, to the fond Christmas greeting of his parents, brothers, sisters, friends, until his eyes were dimmed with the dews of the heart. The exile feels a longing desire, particularly at Christmas time, for the pleasant, genial fireside and loving hearts of home. How many of that group will, ere another Christmas comes, sleep in a bloody and nameless grave?

Dec. 26th. Left camp at sunrise ; re-crossed the Arkansas

River at Little Rock, and camped three miles from town, on the Pine Bluff Road. In the evening the following order was read, on "dress-parade," to each regiment in the division :

SPECIAL ORDER NO. 121.

1st. Major-General John G. Walker, having reported to these headquarters, in obedience to Special Order No. 264, Adjutant and Inspector-General's Office, is assigned to the command of the Division of Texas troops now commanded by Brigadier-General McCulloch. On being relieved by Major-General Walker, Brigadier-General McCulloch will assume command of Flournoy's Brigade, same Division.

2d. Major-General Walker, with his Division, will move without delay, and take post at Pine Bluff.

By command of Major-General HOLMES.

CHAPTER VII.

MARCH FROM LITTLE ROCK TO PINE BLUFF.—COUNTER-MARCHING.—GEN-
ERAL WALKER ASSUMES COMMAND OF THE DIVISION.—HOG STEALING.
—DESCRIPTION OF PINE BLUFF.—EN ROUTE FOR ARKANSAS POST.—
DISPATCHES FROM GENERAL CHURCHILL TO GENERAL WALKER.—SUR-
RENDER OF THE ARKANSAS POST. — CAMP "FREEZE OUT." — PICKET
DUTY.—ARRIVAL OF GENERAL HOLMES.--FORTIFYING AT CAMP "FREEZE
OUT."

ON the morning of December 27th we took up the line
of march for Pine Bluff.   About four miles from Little
Rock, the Pine Bluff road leaves the river; consequently the scenery, marching through the Pine Hills, is not
very interesting. We struck camp on the side of a hill, after
marching fifteen miles.

Dec. 28th. Marched eleven miles, over a rocky and hilly
country.

Dec. 29th. Marched eleven miles, over the same kind of
road as yesterday.

On the 31st of December we took up the line of march,
back by the road we came, to Little Rock. Marched fifteen
miles.

The year '62 went out amid a blustering storm. The wind
blew almost a hurricane, shrieking forth a watchful requiem
over the dying year. The gloom was indicative of the dark
storm-cloud of war, that hung like a funeral pall over the
land, bringing sorrow and woe to thousands of once happy
households. The mind involuntarily winged a thought toward the coming year, and sadly questioned, "Will 1863 still
find the land the scene of bloodshed and fierce strife?" It
trusted not; and looked forward to the day-spring of brighter
hopes. The Confederate soldiers, the patriot sons of the
South, were thought of amid their terrible sufferings in Ten-

nessee and Virginia, as they nobly endeavored to roll back the swift tide of invasion.

We remained at this camp until the morning of the 2d of January, 1863; in the mean time the following order was read on dress-parade, announcing the change of commanders of the division:

GENERAL ORDER No. 1.

In accordance with instructions from the head-quarters of the Trans-Mississippi Department, the undersigned hereby assumes command of the division of Texas troops lately commanded by Brig.-General McCulloch.

The following officers are announced as comprising the Division Staff.

Signed,   JOHN G. WALKER,

Major-General Commanding.

Major R. P. McCLAY, Chief of Staff.
Major A. H. MASON, Commissary.
Major WILLIAM M. STONE, Quartermaster.
Major THOMAS B. FRENCH, Major Artillery.
Surgeon E. J. BEALL.
Surgeon E. L. MASSIES.
Captain J, A. GALT, Assist. Adjutant-General.
Captain THOS. COX, Assist. Quartermaster.
1st Lieut. COMPTON FRENCH, Aid-de-Camp.
Captain W. A. Smith, Assist. Adjutant-General.
A. FAULKINER, Captain commanding Cavalry Squadron.

The first day of the new year opened bitter cold. It froze all day. In commemoration of the new year we marched twelve miles.

Jan. 2d. Marched six miles, and camped within four miles of Little Rock. We remained at this camp until the ꞌ morning of the 5th, when we were ordered about face, and marched back again to Pine Bluff. Marched ten miles and camped.

Jan. 6th. Marched fifteen miles. It was generally believed amongst the troops that General Holmes was advised by the Medical Board to give Walker's Division enough of exercise.

This may be the object of our marching and countermarching between Little Rock and Pine Bluff.

Jan. 7th. Marched eight miles.

Jan. 8th. Marched twelve miles and camped five miles west of Pine Bluff. We remained at this camp until the morning of the 11th. At this camp the division was formed in line of battle to witness three soldiers belonging to McCulloch's Brigade, drummed out of camp for " hog-stealing." The bands played " The Rogue's March " along the line. The three soldiers marched along the entire line, followed by a file of soldiers, with fixed bayonets. This kind of punishment, inaugurated by General McCulloch, seemed to be a novelty to the Texas boys, and it created roars of laughter amongst the troops. Boys, ask yourselves if you were ever guilty of " hog-stealing " during the late unpleasantness ?

The town of Pine Bluff is the county-seat of Jefferson County. The town is built on the west bank of the Arkansas River, situated about fifty miles south of Little Rock, in the midst of a fine cotton-growing country. At the commencement of the war, it had a population of about four thousand inhabitants. Some of the residences were very fine, and built of brick. Delightful gardens, tasteful lawns, and spacious streets, give the whole place an air of comfort and elegance. The river was navigable to this place at all seasons of the year.

While encamped near Pine Bluff, we learned that the enemy had been badly repulsed at Vicksburg; and, in all probability, part of their forces would ascend the Arkansas River, for the purpose of capturing the place. On the night of the 10th, General Walker received dispatches from General Churchill, stating that eight gunboats and twenty-five transports had arrived near the Arkansas Post, and he expected to be attacked every moment. He asked for reinforcements.

On the morning of the 11th we took up the line of march to reinforce General Churchill's command, distance about fifty-five miles. Passing through the town of Pine Bluff, we continued our march down the river-bank. After marching twenty-five miles we camped for the night. During the march, couriers bearing dispatches were continually passing to and fro from General Walker to General Churchill. The following dispatch was received by General Walker from General Churchill, about 8 o'clock, P.M. :

Head-Quarters, Arkansas Post,
JAN. 11th, 1863, 7.30 A.M.

GENERAL WALKER :

I am now occupying my inner line of intrenchments. I have strong hopes of success. If I am not overpowered by numbers shall fight to the last, and should I be compelled to leave these works I will withraw into the " fort " with two thousand men, and still fight, until every gun is dismounted. The enemy are now drawn up in line of battle in front. I expect them to attack me every moment. My infantry has not been engaged. The enemy has a great deal of artillery. I have but one field-battery.

T. J. CHURCHILL,
Brig.-General Commanding.

The next dispatch received was dated ten o'clock, notifying General Walker that the infantry pickets were engaged, and that he, General Churchill, was still hopeful of holding out until reinforcements arrived.

At daylight on the morning of the 12th, we continued the march about five miles in the direction of the Post, and camped on the river-bank. News was received by General Walker that General Churchill had surrendered, with all his forces (about daylight). General Churchill's command con- sisted of one Brigade of Arkansians and Colonels Deshler's and Garland's Brigade of Texans. From stragglers who made their escape from the Post, it was learned that, after a few hours' fighting, a white flag was displayed from a promi- nent point, unexpected to General Churchill and many of the troops of his command, as they were confident of holding the place until Walker's Division arrived. Alas! the traitor's name is screened from history; but enough is known that no private soldier had anything to do with this traitorous act. Reader, pause and reflect for a moment. An army of some six or seven thousand well-disciplined troops, strongly fortified, with plenty of provisions, ammunition, etc., surrendering after a few hours' fighting, no matter how great the enemy's strength might be, when, by holding out a few hours longer, sufficient force would be on hand to render them assistance! With Hindman's forces on the left bank of the river, and Walker's on the west bank, the enemy would evidently vacate the post, and take shipping on their boats, bound for some other point outside of the Arkansas Post. We remained encamped on the bank of the river until the morning of the 19th, awaiting the advance of the enemy. In the mean time, General Holmes arrived in camp from Little Rock, to assume command in person. On the morning of the 13th we awoke out of our slumbers to behold the ground covered with snow, which was still falling, with no prospect of its clearing away soon. During the day all our tents were taken away from us. This camp was generally known by the name of "Camp Freeze Out."

In the evening it commenced to freeze, until our wet garments were stiff. The cold increased. "It was winter in its most savage mood. The wind howled like a wounded monster through the frozen wood." The wide waste of snow and ice concealed the treacherous pits and fallen timber of the forest from our unpracticed eyes. We expected every moment to meet the enemy's fleet and forces; for the river, swollen by the rain, hurried its dark flood along with drift and foam, sweeping masses of snow from the banks, and seemed conspiring with the elements to hasten his advance. But the dark flood knew better the secrets of fate.

Jan. 14th. To-day six prisoners, escorted by Captain Morgan's Company of Cavalry, passed through the camps on their way to Pine Bluff. They were captured while foraging for some delicacies that Uncle Sam didn't furnish them with,

From them we learned that, after the surrender of the Arkansas Post, our troops were put aboard transports bound for St. Louis, and from there they would be conveyed to Camp Douglas, Illinois.

On the morning of the 15th, General Holmes, anticipating the gun-boats up the river, backed by their land forces, commenced fortifying some two miles from the river bank (a pretty safe distance). A detail of twenty men from each regiment in the division commenced fortifying. The position selected by General Holmes was a pretty secure one, for once inside of the fortification, the enemy could not see us from the river bank, nor we them.

On the 16th it commenced snowing at noon-time; by sunset some four or five inches had fallen. During the night it commenced to freeze, which was pretty severe on the troops that were on picket. Picket duty is the most dangerous and least cheering part of the service. It has not the excitement of battle, the presence of comrades, the charge, the cheer of the wild huzza of victory and triumph; it has no such stimulating influences. No matter how cold the weather may be, even in the depth of winter, the advanced pickets are not allowed fire, and dare not walk about to warm themselves.

The morning of the 17th dawned with the elements still against us. Worse than ever, it commenced to rain in the morning; at noon it ceased for a short period of time; it then commenced to snow, and during the evening it commenced to freeze, with the wind blowing from the north. Parsons' Brigade of Cavalry arrived in camp: they relieved the infantry pickets from duty for the time being. During the night we learned that the enemy's fleet had withdrawn from the Arkansas Post, and were on their way to the Mississippi River. On the evening of the 18th we received orders to be ready the following morning, to take up the line of march back again to Pine Bluff.

CHAPTER VIII.

BIOGRAPHICAL SKETCH OF GENERAL WALKER.

MAJOR-GENERAL John G. Walker, was born in Cole County, State of Missouri, in the year 1825. His father, the Hon. J. G. Walker, was State Treasurer for many years. At the age of twenty-one years, he was appointed by President Polk 1st lieutenant of Company K, Colonel Persifer F. Smith's regiment of mounted rifles, in which he bore his part in the campaigns of Mexico. Afterward he served with the same command in California, Arizona, New Mexico, and Oregon, having attained the rank of Captain in the United States service. At the beginning of the late war he was on duty at Fort Union, New Mexico, and his affections being with the South, he lost no time in resigning his Federal commission and making his way to the Confederate seat of government. On tendering his services to President Jefferson Davis, he received the commission of Colonel, and as such commanded the 2d Regiment of Virginia troops in the army of General Beauregard, then in Virginia. He was shortly afterward promoted to the rank of Brigadier, and distinguished himself in the bloody battles of that State, and was in due time made a Major-General. While in command of a division in Lee's army, he took a prominent part in the capture of Harper's Ferry, and the next day reached the field of Sharpsburg, just in time to save the fortunes of that battle. President Davis, on hearing of the number of Texas troops that had arrived at Little Rock, Arkansas, subsequently ordered General Walker to Little Rock, to take command of the Texas troops at that point, then commanded by Brigadier-General H. E. McCulloch.

General Walker, after taking command of the Texas troops, soon became very popular with them—his presence was always hailed with the wildest enthusiasm by both officers and soldiers. His masterly retreat before Banks' army, and his gallant and desperate charge at Mansfield and Pleasant Hill, where he was seriously wounded, evince his capacity and bravery as a commander.

Notwithstanding his sufferings from his wound, he begged to be carried on a litter to command his men.

He gave us our first lesson in the field in the face of an enemy, and of all the generals in command of the Confederate troops, he was the most untiring, vigilant, and patient. No commander could surpass him. Devoid of ambition, incapable of envy, he was brave, gallant, and just. At Jenkins' Ferry he arrived just as the battle commenced, although in a feeble state, suffering from his wound. At the sight of him, many of the troops were so enthusiastic that they placed their hats upon their bayonets, and gave him hearty cheers. It was a touching and fitting compliment to the gallant chieftain.

Nor did he escape the attention of the department commander, for his gallantry and services on the battle-field. He was assigned to the command of the District of Louisiana, and afterward to the command of the Department of Texas, New Mexico, and Arizona, a position he filled with honor to himself and the department he commanded.

I deem it proper to copy from the *Houston Telegraph* newspaper the appropriate remarks relating to the discharge of his duties while in command of the department, as follows:

" The administration of the duties of the commander of this district by Major-General Walker have added to the high reputation of that gallant officer. As a commander in the field, he had won the best distinction of a soldier, that of well-fought battles, honorable wounds, and the confidence and devotion of his soldiers. We have never heard an officer or private from General Walker's old Division but spoke of him in terms of admiration and attachment. Accustomed to and preferring service in the field, we understand it was in opposition to his own feelings and taste that General Walker entered on the command of a district so extensive, important, and responsible as this.

" We believe that he leaves it having impressed all who have had any opportunity of seeing him in the exercise of his duties, with the conviction of his ability, his conscientious devotion to duty, and the equity and justice of his character.

"Laborious, systematic, painstaking, unostentatious—working himself according to a rigid standard of duty, and exacting the like from others, confidence had gathered strongly around the sound judgment and propriety of his general business administration of our military affairs. We are very sure he will carry with him, we hope to more honorable fields, the sincere respect and confidence, and the warm good wishes of the people of Texas."

General Walker, in giving up the command of the district, was assigned to the command of a cavalry corps that was encamped near Hempstead. In taking command of the cavalry, he issued the following masterly and patriotic address, although forlorn, and while negotiations were pending for the surrender of the Trans-Mississippi Department :

"Soldiers : In assuming command in the field at this dark hour in the history of the war, I confidently appeal to your patriotism to sustain me in the discharge of the responsible duties I have assumed. The disastrous events, the intelligence which has just reached us, point to some decisive crisis of the war, which our limited knowledge of those events does not yet permit us fully to appreciate.

" Every instinct of manhood, however, calls upon us to bear the great disaster that has overtaken our arms with fortitude, resolution, and patriotism. Let us so conduct ourselves that, whatever may be the result of this war, we may be able to point with honorable pride to the part we have sustained in upholding the honor of the South.

"We cannot yet determine what line of policy it may become necessary for the Trans-Mississippi army and people to pursue in view of recent events, but let us bear in mind that nothing but eternal infamy, individually and nationally, will result from abandoning the field at present. Remember, be true to your duty! Stand by your colors and your generals, and treat those who advise differently as your worst enemies, and traitors to your country.

CHAPTER IX.

RETURN TO PINE BLUFF.—CAMP MILLS AND CAMP WRIGHT.—DESCRIPTION
OF CAMP WRIGHT.—CARD PLAYING.—GENERAL HAWS ASSUMES COM-
MAND OF THE 1ST BRIGADE.—MARCHING ORDERS.—GENERAL HOLMES'
FAREWELL ADDRESS TO THE DIVISION.

N the morning of January 19th we bade adieu to Camp "Freeze Out,' and took up the line of march back again to Pine Bluff. The road being impassable to travel, we marched through the deserted plantations, weary, foot-sore, hungry, and cold. Yet, the troops marched with buoyant spirits, joking, laughing, and singing as they marched along. After marching twelve miles, we arrived at camp.

Jan. 20. Marched fourteen miles. The troops continued to travel through mud, ankle deep ; yet, cold and drenched as they were, they marched cheerfully forward, shouting forth, with stentorian voices, the chorus of the "Bonnie Blue Flag," and other patriotic songs. It seemed as if they were determined their spirits should not succumb to their accumulated sufferings, hardships, and trials. It appears almost incredible that men could exhibit such reckless indifference, such strength of will and determination, after such a week of bitter experiences as these men underwent. The war, however, developed and decided some strange theories as to the amount of physical powers which the human frame contained—powers of enduring fatigue, hunger, thirst, heat and cold—which would scarcely have been believed before, if asserted. We arrived at camp, situated northwest from Pine Bluff. This camp was known by the name of Camp Mills, after Colonel R. Q. Mills, of the 10th Infantry. He was captured at the Arkansas Post.

We remained at this camp until the 9th of February, drilling and cleaning our camp-ground. General Walker issued orders that two men from each company in the division should be granted furloughs for a reasonable period of time. This order gave general satisfaction throughout the division. In the mean time, while remaining at this camp, the weather changed to bright, clear, and pleasant days. Tents sufficient to shelter, and blankets to make the troops comfortable, soon arrived, when we were ordered to move camp to a more suitable location, on the banks of the Arkansas River, about four miles north of the town of Pine Bluff. Our camp at this location was known as Camp Wright, receiving the name from the owner of the land that it was located on.

Our situation here was a good one, and, for the first time since we had been in the State, the troops were comfortably situated. And they appreciated it very much; for, if ever there was an army that had been harassed and "used up" to accomplish nothing so far, it was this army. At this camp, it was an imposing sight to see a long stretch of country, rich and beautiful as the sun ever shone upon; the deep pine forests; belts of wood, whose dark green foliage contrasted strongly with the white tents. Fields lately luscious with vines are drooping with amber-colored corn, all of them covered over wifh white tents, arranged with street-like precision, with regiments or battalions on parade or review, with martial music echoing along the river-bank, from splendid bands. Add to this the Arkansas River, flowing on in majestic grandeur, on its bosom numerous transports steaming up and down. Such was our encampment at Camp Wright.

The nights were surpassingly fine, considering the season of the year. No fairy tales of magic wonder, no genii power of Aladdin's wonderful lamp could produce anything so sublimely grand. Here, in the southern clime, the nights are superb. The moon floats grandly through a clear, azure sky of the deepest blue. The white tents glow, and the bright arms stacked on the parade-ground, glimmer in the moonshine, while the river looks like a sea of molten silver, quivering under the soft moon-beams. In this fair and fertile land, marred by man but blessed by God, the days and nights passed merrily. At night the tents resounded with laughter, music, and fun ; by day, the leisure hours were spent in visiting each other, or playing the fascinating game of " bluff." When the cry of " lights out!" ran from mouth to mouth along the line of sentinels, the camp became shrouded in darkness; but suppose we step into a tent, and see if the lights are really "out." Lifting the "fly," upon the inside of which a blanket is pinned, we enter. Sergeant ———— and privates * * * and 0 0 0 (whom many of our readers would recognize without the aid of a magnifier), and others are seated comfortably upon a blanket, each mouth adorned with a pipe from which clouds of smoke are emanating, while their minds are all intent upon the cards before them. The light is well shaded, so as to be invisible on the outside, and the game goes on under the whispers of the players. Corn grains are spread around, each representing a specific amount, not greater than a dollar.

From the players, who are steeped in tobacco-smoke, we catch the sentences : " I'll raise you two." " I'll go five better." " Can't see it." " Three queens," etc., etc., etc. Thus was the game of " Bluff" often played in our camp, and seldom was it finished until the early morning reveille startled the players from their sport. While remaining at this camp, many of the troops received sixty days' furlough, and renounced camp-life *pro tem.*, to visit distant friends in Texas. We remained at "Camp Wright" until the 24th of April, without anything unusual transpiring, with the exception of the appointment of Brigadier-General Haws to the command of the 1st Brigade. Colonel Young, on being relieved from command of the brigade, resumed command of his regiment. The following-named officers comprised General Haws' staff, viz :

Major C. McCLARTY, *A. A. General.*
Major R. H. DYER, *Quartermaster.*
Major R. S. SEMAN, *Commissary of Subsistence.*
Captain J. L. ROBERTSON, *Adjt. and Inspector-General.*
1st Lieut. A. J. WALKER. *Ordnance Officer.*
1st Lieut. S. N. HAWS, *Aid-de-Camp.*

Brigadier-General Haws was formerly a United States officer, but, like many of his old comrades in arms, he offered his
services to the Confederate government, which were cheerfully
accepted. He was commissioned by President Davis to the rank
of Brigadier-General, and assigned to a brigade of cavalry
under command of Major-General Hindman. He participated
in many of the cavalry raids throughout Arkansas. He arrived
in time to lend his aid to Walker's division, in the anticipated
attack of the enemy, near the Arkansas Post, with his command
of cavalry.

On the evening of April 23d, at dress-parade, the following
address or order from General Holmes was read to each
regiment in the division previous to our departure for Louisiana.

"Major-General J. G. Walker will proceed with his division
without delay to Monroe, Louisiana. On his arrival he will
report for orders to Lieut.-General Kirby Smith, commanding
the department.

"In taking leave of Walker's Division, the commanding
general of the district expresses his sincere regret. It was
instructed and disciplined under his supervision ; and, having the fullest confidence in its strength, patriotism and
valor, he hoped it would be his proud privilege to participate
in the honor in store for it when it meets the enemy. Better
officers and men no division can boast of. The Confederacy
may well be satisfied with the security of its interests entrust-
ed to them.

By command of Lieut.-General HOLMES."

CHAPTER X.

THE DIVISION MOVES TO LOUISIANA.—ARRIVAL AT OUACHITA CITY.—
A NEW MODE OF TRAVELING.—EXCURSION TRIP ON THE WASHITA
RIVER.—OVERLAND ROUTE TO ALEXANDRIA.—A FREE RIDE.—DESCRIP-
TION OF ALEXANDRIA.

THE morning of April 24th was clear and beautiful, such as we often experience in the spring. We left camp at daylight, bound for Alexandria, Louisiana. Reports had reached us from Louisiana, that General Dick Taylor was retreating from before the enemy, who was advancing on Alexandria. Marched fourteen miles, and camped.

April 25th. Marched ten miles. The country we traveled over resembles the lands of Northeastern Texas. The soil is very fertile, and produces large crops of corn, oats, and wheat.

April 26th. Marched fifteen miles. The country we marched over was thickly settled.

April 27th. Marched twelve miles, and camped near the town of Monticello.

April 28th. Marched twelve miles. As we passed through Monticello, the ladies were on the sidewalk, waving their handkerchiefs as a token of admiration for the Texas boys.

April 29th. Marched eleven miles ; passed through the villages of Lacy and Fountain Hill.

April 30th. Marched ten miles, and encamped near the town of Hamburg. On the morning of May 1st we continued our march. After crossing the State line dividing Arkansas from Louisiana, we camped in the midst of a small prairie, having marched only three miles.

May 2d. Early in the morning we continued our march, traveling in a southwesterly direction. The day was excessively warm, and water along our route was very scarce.

After a hard and laborious march of sixteen miles, we arrived at a running stream of clear water, where we camped for the night.

May 3d. Marched sixteen miles, and camped on Bayou Bartholomew, a tributary of the Ouachita River.

May 4th. Marched twelve miles, down the bank of the bayou, and camped about three miles from Ouachita City.

May 5th. Marched three miles, and arrived at the mouth of Bayou Bartholomew, where it empties into the Ouachita River. Opposite the mouth of Bayou Bartholomew is located the famous City of Ouachita (or Washita), consisting of a store and warehouse. It is situated on a high bluff. The river is navigable to this point at all seasons of the year. On our arrival at the mouth of the bayou, we witnessed about a dozen transports awaiting to carry us to the town of Trenton, nearly opposite the City of Monroe. After everything was in readiness we got aboard ; shortly afterwards, we found ourselves rapidly steaming down the crystal-like Washita river, at the expense of the government. This ride on the transports was unexpected on our part. We arrived at Trenton about 4 o'clock, P. M., distant from Bayou Bartholomew about thirty-six miles. Our division quartermaster kindly paid our fare by giving a check on the Confederate Government. After disembarking at Trenton, we marched two miles, and camped in the rear of the town. We remained at this camp until the morning of the 9th. While encamped near Trenton, various rumors were currently afloat in camp about Banks' army advancing on the town of Alexandria, and the capture of the same. These rumors proved, alas ! too true. We waited anxiously to hear from our army under the command of General Dick Taylor—how they were progressing with the enemy. General Hebert, then commanding the Northern District of Louisiana, endeavored to obtain a brigade of the division, to assist him in driving back, or rather to capture, a brigade of the enemy that was encamped on the banks of the Mississippi River, making raids all over the country. As General Walker's orders were imperative to proceed to Alexandria, he could not accommodate General Hebert, but promised to do so as soon he drove Banks' army back. The sequel will show how he fulfilled his promise.

May 9th. About sunrise we embarked on board of the same transports that conveyed us from Washita City; our destination this time was Alexandria. Our wagons the day previous went overland. About 8 o'clock, A. M., the signal whistle was blown for "all aboard." Shortly afterwards, the boats moved out into the current of the river, and took their position in line,—General Walker's boat taking the lead, under a full head of steam. When passing by the town of Monroe, the inhabitants appeared to have turned out in mass to witness us passing by. The ladies waved their handkerchiefs as a token of friendship, and the bands played some of their favorite pieces of music, to please the ladies.

The troops were highly pleased with the trip; they experienced that it was a much easier mode of travel than taking it afoot, with their knapsacks on their backs. Nothing worthy of notice transpired on our trip down the river, until we were near the town of Harrisonburg, when a courier, from General Dick Taylor's head-quarters, hailed General Walker, and handed him a dispatch informing him that the enemy had crossed Red River at Alexandria, and were likely to attack Fort Beauregard at Harrisonburg in the rear; and that four gunboats had left Alexandria for the purpose of making an attack by water. He sent a dispatch to Colonel Logan, commanding the fort, to burn his last cartridge in its defence. Colonel Logan replied that he had as much force as he wanted, and that he would hold the fort with "God's blessing."

General Walker at once ordered his boats to "about ship" on hearing the news from Colonel Logan. So we took the back track once more for Trenton, where we arrived about 3 o'clock the next morning, after an excursion of one hundred and twenty-five miles. We remained on board until daylight, when we went ashore, and camped four miles west of the town, where we remained until the morning of the 16th, waiting to hear further news from the enemy. If they suc-

6

ceeded in capturing Fort Beauregard, it was expected they would advance on the town of Monroe or Trenton. General Walker, in the mean time, kept his communication open with Colonel Logan.

On the morning of the 13th, four gun-boats, under command of Commodore Woodworth, arrived about two miles below the fort, and demanded the surrender of the same. Colonel Logan replied, that as long as he had a cartridge left, his command would never surrender. Shortly after the " truce " had expired, the gun-boats commenced shelling the fort with a vengeance, and kept up the cannonading until late in the evening, without doing any damage to the fort or garrison. The next morning they opened their fire again. Colonel Logan and his garrison were not idle. During the night, he sent a company of sharpshooters in the vicinity of the gun-boats, for the purpose of picking off their gunners. In this they were very successful, as they compelled the gun-boats to withdraw some distance down the river, from their original position. The cannonading continued throughout the day, without doing much damage. About sunset two dispatch-boats of the enemy joined the fleet, after communicating with Commodore Woodworth. The gun-boats shortly afterwards retired, as, for the present, they had abandoned any further attack on the fort.

Before retiring, they buried six of their men on the river-bank. As they were descending the river, they continued throwing up signal rockets. Quantities of cotton and broken timber, evidently torn off by our shot and shell, floated down the river in their wake. Thus, with a very small force, Colonel Logan had accomplished his design in compelling the enemy to withdraw, notwithstanding their guns were of a heavier caliber than his, and with only the loss of one of his men, who was killed early in the action.

During the bombardment of the fort, General Walker received a dispatch from Colonel Bartlett, commanding at Delhi, that the enemy, numbering about 1,000, had crossed Bayou Macon, and were advancing on Monroe. This news, and the delay of our wagon-train, retarded our march in any direction in pursuit of the enemy. In the mean time, news was received that the enemy had recrossed Bayou Macon, and, for the present, had abandoned their raid on Monroe. Our wagon-train having arrived, we took up the line of march on the morning of the 16th, for the town of Campti, on Red River. Marched seventeen miles, and camped for the night.

May 17th. Resumed our march this morning, and marched fourteen miles. Passed through the town of Vernon.

May 18th. Marched fifteen miles, and passed through the village of Woodville.

May 19th. Marched nineteen miles. The country we passed over is of light, rich soil, rolling enough to make it fine for cultivation, and is covered with timber of the largest kind, which extends from the Washita to Red River. Grain is raised in abundance, consisting of corn, oats, barley, and wheat.

May 20th. Marched nineteen miles. Passed through the town of Sparta, situated on top of a sand-hill.

May 21st. Marched seventeen miles through a pine forest.

May 22d. Marched sixteen miles, and encamped at a large lake, two miles to the right of the town of Campti. On our arrival at this place, we learned that Banks' army, hearing of our approach, had evacuated the town of Alexandria, and was falling back towards the Mississippi River. We remained encamped at the lake, awaiting boats to carry us to Alexandria, until the morning of the 26th, when we marched to Campti, there to take passage on the boats that had arrived during the night, for Alexandria.

Nothing worthy of notice transpired on our trip down the river. We arrived at the Alexandria Falls, about two miles from the town of Alexandria, on the morning of the 27th. The distance from Campti to this point is 150 miles. Randall's Brigade continued down the river, expecting to overtake the enemy before they got to the Mississippi River. In this they were unsuccessful. They returned the following day to camp, near Alexandria. After ascertaining that the enemy had crossed the Mississippi River, on their way to attack Port Hudson, we remained encamped near the Falls of Alexandria, for the purpose of cooking rations, previous to taking a trip to Perkins' Landing, on the Mississippi River. The town of Alexandria is built on the right bank of Red River, about 200 miles from its mouth. The river is navigable to this point at all seasons of the year. The town is beautifully located in the midst of a cotton and sugar-cane country. It is unrivaled, in the State of Louisiana, for its healthy and pleasant situation, and the grandeur of the surrounding scenery. Its principal street, about one mile in length, is built on the bank of the river, and, parallel to this street and river is located the Planters' Railroad, running through the town, and extending south a distance of about twenty-five miles. The sidewalks are thickly covered with stately shade-trees, overlapping themselves in many places. Opposite, and across the river, is one range of pine hills. Another lies about twelve miles southwest from the town. It seems of an irregular formation, and extends to the Sabine River, on the border of Texas.

Picturesque views, of great beauty, are obtained from the surrounding hills. At a distance of two miles up the river are situated the rapids of Alexandria (better known as Alexandria Falls). These rapids or falls have become historical, from the fact of Commodore Porter's building a dam across them, in the year 1864, in order to enable him to get his fleet over them, on his cotton expedition up Red River.

The town of Alexandria has several fine public and private buildings; among the most noted is the Ice-house Hotel; also the Court-house and Market-house. The town is also adorned with many fine churches, of all denominations. Across the river, about four miles from the town, stands the famous Military Institute that General Sherman presided over at the commencement of the war.

CHAPTER XI.

EXPEDITION UP THE TENSAS RIVER.—A NIGHT MARCH TO PERKINS'
LANDING.

N the evening of May 28th we left camp near Alexandria for Little River, distance about twenty miles. Marched ten miles through a pine and hilly section of country.

May 29th. Marched ten miles and arrived at Little River; here several transports were waiting to carry us up the Tensas River. Previous to going aboard of them, we cooked two days' rations. It would shame a lazy cook to see with what expedition we cooked our meals. The moment we stacked arms, fires were lit of rails or branches, and the knapsacks thrown off. Then we took a slice of bacon or a piece of beef, and roasted it before the fire on the end of a stick. In this way a soldier cooked his hasty meal in about fifteen minutes. About two o'clock we were all aboard; lines and stage-planks were hauled in.

The boat that General Walker and staff were aboard of led off, followed by the balance of the transports, all loaded with troops. On they went, ploughing through the waters of Cathoulia Lake. Nothing unusual occurred during the trip. We arrived at the mouth of Black River during the night, ascending the same until we arrived at the mouth of the Tensas River. Previous to ascending the same, the utmost caution for the safety of the troops was adopted by General Walker. To prevent a surprise from the enemy, sentinels were placed upon the hurricane deck of all the transports to keep watch, lest the enemy should be lurking about. We were only twenty-five miles from the Mississippi River. The country between the two rivers was invested with the enemy's pickets. On our way up the river, a Federal soldier was taken prisoner; he was foraging amongst the negro cabins. A few miles further up the river, from where we captured the Federal soldier, is Buck's plantation, the head of navigation. We arrived at this place on the evening of the 30th inst. The distance from Little River to this point is about 250 miles. We went ashore on the right bank of the river, and camped. After supper we received orders to be ready to march at a moment's notice.

At 9 o'clock, P. M., McCulloch's Brigade took up the line of march for Perkins' Landing, on the Mississippi River. This landing is near the town of New Carthage, and about fifteen miles from Vicksburg, and distant about twelve miles from Buck's plantation. Randall and Haws' Brigades followed after. At this place the enemy was encamped, and supposed to be in heavy force. While on the march we passed by farm after farm all deserted and the buildings going to decay.

After leaving the river, the route of the troops was through a cane-brake, dark and dismal, and as desolate and dreary as the imagination could picture, and highly musical with croaking of frogs; to these add reptiles of every hue and species, and you have some idea of the ground. It was difficult for the troops to march over. Tramp! tramp! tramp!—firm and undaunted, the brigade proceeded on its perilous journey, like a band of dark spirits, over the hard and uneven road, accompanied by the dull rumbling of the artillery carriages. That was a night that tried men's souls. Although moving slowly forward, in momentary expectation of being attacked, nothing special occurred. As the first roseate hues of morn tinged the eastern horizon, we discovered the smoke arising from the enemy's camps.

CHAPTER XII.

SKIRMISH AT PERKINS' LANDING.—A NEGRO'S DESCRIPTION OF THE CANNONADING.—OFFICIAL REPORT OF THE SKIRMISH.

ON the morning of the 31st of May, McCulloch's Brigade formed in line of battle, in a skirt of timber adjoining Perkins' plantation, and commenced to advance on the enemy's camp. They were followed soon after by Haws' and Randall's Brigades. On the arrival of McCulloch's Brigade at the enemy's camp, they discovered, much to their surprise, that the enemy had withdrawn, under the protection of their gun-boats. The enemy seemed not to anticipate our coming until a few minutes previous to our arrival, as they left precipitately, leaving behind them their provisions and cooking utensils. Our troops helped themselves to the enemy's "hard-tack" and coffee. The coffee they found very palatable, and more nourishing than corn-meal coffee. After they had satisfied their appetites, McCulloch's Brigade advanced in search of the enemy. After passing the enemy's camp about half a mile, their skirmishers were fired upon from the direction of the woods that were on the right. Our skirmishers quickly returned the fire, and advanced in the direction of the woods, where the enemy was formed in line of battle. On their arrival at the woods, they discovered, much to their surprise, that the enemy was in full retreat, double-quicking towards the levee that was in front, and about half a mile from where our troops were fired upon. After ascertaining that the enemy was formed in line of battle behind the levee, and under the protection of their gun-boats, they fell back and joined their respective commands. In the mean time one of the enemy's gunboats opened fire upon them, without doing much harm, their shots being fired at random, as it were, to fire the woods. General McCulloch immediately ordered Captain Edgar's Battery of Light Artillery to the front. After taking their position, they at once opened fire on the gun-boats. Their battery was ably supported by Allen's and Waterhouse's Regiments, while Flournoy's and Fitzhugh's regiments supported the flanks. A regular artillery duel now ensued. The intervening valley was one dense cloud of smoke, which rose in floating canopies over it. We could behold the sheets of flame, followed by volumes of smoke, jump out from the mouths of the brazen monsters, while the loud reverberating sounds echoed through the river valley. Captain Edgar and his lieutenants handled their brave veterans with skill: they worked their guns with alacrity. It might not be amiss to mention that Perkins' Landing is situated about twenty-five miles south of Vicksburg, between Carthage and Ashwood Landings.

Several of our artillery shots must have evidently taken effect on the gun-boats, as they soon dropped down the river, out of the range of our guns.

After the withdrawal of the gunboats, the entire division was formed in line of battle, expecting to draw the enemy out from under cover of their gun-boats. After remaining in line of battle about half an hour, our pickets returned and reported that the enemy got aboard of their transports, destroying a large amount of stores that were intended for Grant's army at Grand Gulf.

Shortly afterwards we took up the line of march back again to the Tensas River. We arrived at camp on the Tensas River late in the evening, after marching twenty-four miles.

Our loss at Perkins' Landing was one killed and six wounded. The loss of the enemy must have been greater.

* * * * * *

A good story was told of a negro cook, named Sam, belonging to one of the officers, who helped himself to the enemy's goods while the cannonading was going on. While he was engaged in making a thorough examination of the enemy's camp, it was visited occasionally by a round-shot or shell. It was getting too hot for Sam; so he removed to what he thought a safe place, when a shell comes right bang near him. Sam jumped up like an acrobat, and grinned like a gorilla. "Oh, Sam, are you scared?" asked a soldier who was calmly looking on. "Golly, massa, I can put up with dem black fellows," meaning round-shot, "but them damn rotten fellows dat burst so, dey play de bery debil—you don't know where dey strike you," said Sam, alluding to the shells. He could not stand that, nor did he understand it. He threw awāy his plunder, and hastened to discover some place of concealment. He ran, and ran, until he was completely exhausted; he knew not where to go. He lay down behind a log. A shell exploded near the spot. That was no safe place. He espied Captain Edgar's Battery busy at work handling their guns, and thought that would be a good place for protection. After reaching the spot, he discovered that it was anything but safe. In hunting about, he found a place to hide in. Glory! Alas, he found one of his fellow-servants stove into the hollow log so firmly that he was unable to extricate himself. Poor Sam for two long hours was running from place to place, but nowhere could he find a spot free from those awful bombs that followed him with such pertinacity. Everything must have an end—the fighting closed. Old Sam found himself safe and sound. He afterwards remarked, that if there were any more battles, he would stay out of the way of the bombs.

OFFICIAL REPORT OF THE SKIRMISH AT PERKINS' LANDING.

Major R. P. McCLAY, *Asst.-Adjt. and Insp.-General:*

SIR,—At one o'clock this morning, I moved with my brigade from this camp to attack the enemy at Perkins' place, on the Mississippi River. Had two bridges constructed over Bayou De Russy (one of timber, the other of cotton bales and

plank). Marched ten or twelve miles; drove the enemy's
outposts in, and attacked him by opening a fire of shot and
shell from one section of Captain Edgar's Batteries, directed
against his transports and encampment, both of which were
too closely under the cover of his gun-boats to admit of an
infantry attack without endangering too great a loss to us,
with no a prospect of receiving corresponding benefit to our
cause.

The principal portion of my infantry were kept under cover
of a small levee and mots of timber skirting a lake, which hid
them from the enemy's view, while the section of the battery and Colonel Waterhouse's Regiment were thrown forward in the open field, the battery opening fire upon the
enemy's transports, which was instantly returned by the
enemy's gun-boats. This fire was kept up by Captain Edgar
for one hour and twenty minutes, during which time he threw
ninety-six shot and shell into the enemy's camp, and at his
transports, upon which he was embarking his land forces.
Having witnessed the conduct of officers and men of the battery
and Colonel Waterhouse's Regiment, it is gratifying to say, that
they did their duty nobly. Captain Edgar commanded his
men and guns, causing them to be ably and effectually
handled. Their fire was energetic and efficient; nearly every
shot and shell well directed. Himself, and his officers and
his men, behaved most gallantly during the engagement, exposed to heavy fire from the enemy's transports during the
whole time. Colonel Waterhouse was in front of his regiment, exhibiting coolness and courage worthy of imitation
by all officers and men. His major (Taylor) and company
officers were alike calm and at their respective posts, ready
to execute with promptness any order that might be given,
while their men stood up under the fire like a wall of mason-
ry, until ordered by me to lie down, in order to expose them
as little as possible to the balls and fragments of shell that
were constantly flyingly thick about them.

Major Redwood, who was placed in charge of the skirmishers (aided by Captain Flowers, quartermaster of Colonel

Flournoy's Regiment, his adjutant), managed them with ability and courage which showed him fit for the duty to which he had been assigned, while the officers and men under his command behaved in the most commendable manner.

Captain Pitts, of my staff, was put in command of a few men mounted as cavalry, and used as a corps of observation or reconnoitering party. He was in advance of all; obtained and furnished me valuable information as to the position and movements of the enemy, without which my own movements would have been conducted at great disadvantage. The services of this party were indispensable to me, and were gallantly performed. The balance of my command, though hidden as far as possible, most of the time, from the enemy, were nevertheless exposed to his shell, which were thrown from his gun-boats wherever he suspected we might be posted; and not an officer or man, so far as I could perceive, failed to do his duty, or showed the least disposition to avoid a full participation in the conflict. Upon the contrary, all seemed anxious to go fully into the fight, and when ordered to form line of battle in the open field, within six hundred yards of the bank of the river, in full view of the gun-boats, the movement was executed with as much promptness, coolness, and courage, as it could have been done by the best troops the world has ever produced.

The enemy fired over two hundred shot and shell at my command, with less effect than I supposed the same number could have been fired at the same distance. My loss was one killed, two wounded, and two missing.

The loss of the enemy could not be ascertained, but must have been considerable, as several of Captain Edgar's shots were known to take effect upon the transports; besides the many well-aimed shells that exploded in the timber which covered their encampment, as well as many favorable opportunities which presented themselves to our skirmishers, of picking off individuals during the fight. I learn from unofficial sources, that the enemy had eleven killed and several wounded on the land, besides those which must have suffered similarly on the transports.

It is not in the number killed and wounded of the enemy that the loss or the benefit to our cause chiefly consists, but in the fact that they were compelled to remove or destroy their stores, abandon their camp, and break up their depot on the bank of the Mississippi River, directly under the cover of their gun-boats, which is well calculated to distract the movements of General Grant, and cause a diversion in favor of Vicksburg, by compelling him to send a force to their side of the river, to prevent his communication from being cut off from his source of supplies on the Upper Mississippi River.

Signed,   General HENRY E. McCULLOCH.

CHAPTER XIII.

THE DIVISION CROSSES THE TENSAS RIVER.—MARCH TO MILLIKEN'S BEND
AND YOUNG'S POINT.—SCENES BEFORE THE BATTLE.

N the morning of June 1st, we commenced crossing the Tensas River. After crossing, the division camped on the river-bank.

On the morning of the 2d, Haws' and Randall's Brigades took up the line of march for Flowers' plantation, on Bayou Macon. After marching twelve miles, they camped on the banks of the bayou, waiting for McCulloch's Brigade. On the morning of the 3d, McCulloch's Brigade took up the line of march for Flowers' plantation.

On the 4th, the entire division marched up the banks of Bayou Macon some thirteen miles. Bayou Macon is a deep, dirty, sluggish stream, stocked with a variety of fish and alligators. The river bottoms on both sides of the bayou are wide, well-timbered, and of the greatest fertility, admirably adapted to either cotton or corn. Clear of the bottoms, you meet with undulating prairies, affording nutritious grass for pasturage. The country is subject to bilious fevers, and others of a debilitating type.

June 5th. Marched fifteen miles. On our march through the swamps we beheld several large rattlesnakes, that had been killed by our advance guards. Very frequently, in the swamps of Louisiana, a soldier wakes up in the morning and finds that he has a rattlesnake for a sleeping partner; but there is one excellent trait in the character of these reptiles: they never bite unless disturbed, and will get out of the way as soon as possible, except in the month of August, when they are said to be blind, and will snap at anything they may hear about them.

June 6th. Marched ten miles, and camped near the village of Richmond on Roundaway Bayou. We remained here long enough to cook rations, previous to advancing on Milliken's Bend and Young's Point, on the Mississippi River. After cooking two days' rations we remained in camp about four hours, to rest. In the evening we received orders to get ready for a night-march. All the troops realized the hardship of a night-march, and the forthcoming battle ; yet not a man quailed or was found missing from his place. Many of the men delivered letters to those detailed to remain with the wagons, for the loved ones at home, in case they died on the battle-field. In sections four abreast, and close order, the troops took up the line of march, in anticipation of meeting almost certain death, but with undaunted, unquailing spirits. In breathless silence, with the high and glittering stars looking down upon them, through dark and deep defiles marched the dense array of men, moving steadily forward ; not a whisper was heard—no sound of clanking saber, or rattle of canteen and cup.

After crossing Roundaway Bayou at Richmond, nothing unusual transpired until we arrived within six miles of Milliken's Bend (the same distance from Richmond), where the road forks ; the right-hand road leads to Young's Point (some twenty-two miles distant), and the left leads to Milliken's Bend. Haws' Brigade proceeded to Young's Point for the purpose of breaking up the enemy's camp, and McCulloch's Brigade proceeded to Milliken's Bend for the same purpose ; while Randall's Brigade remained at the forks of the road, to reinforce either of the two brigades in case of emergency.

CHAPTER XIV.

THE BATTLE OF MILLIKEN'S BEND.—OPERATIONS OF HAWS' BRIGADE AT
YOUNG'S POINT.—GENERAL M^cCULLOCH'S REPORT OF THE BATTLE.—
GENERAL WALKER'S REPORT OF HIS DIVISION AT MILLIKEN'S BEND
AND YOUNG'S POINT.—FEDERAL REPORT OF THE BATTLE.

> "Oh, few and weak our numbers were—
> A handful of brave men ;
> But to their God they gave their prayers,
> And rushed to battle then."

BOUT four o'clock, on the morning of June 7th, 1863,
McCulloch's Brigade, after a tedious night's march,
had arrived within a mile of Milliken's Bend, on the
Mississippi River, for the purpose of attacking the enemy,
who were encamped in heavy force at this place. Milliken's
Bend is a level plateau, free from timber and traversed by
several roads. It was well capable of defense, for the levee
protected the front, while burdock hedges extended all around
it, making it, as it were, a naturally-fortified place.

Owing to the position and circumstances, it was reasonable
to suppose that the enemy would have artillery placed in
position to sweep the roads leading to their fortifications.—
They relied on their gun-boats principally, to protect them
from any flank movement. Their infantry pickets extended
about half a mile from the main levee, and were concealed behind the hedges. Our cavalry scouts, belonging to Colonel Harrison's Louisiana Regiment, had advanced to within half a mile
of the levee, when they were fired upon. The effect of so sudden and terrible a fire, from an invisible foe, was very startling
and disheartening. No wonder the simple-minded cavalry
scouts were broken, and that many of them hurried to the rear,
in utter confusion, with and without muskets, hats, or coats !

As they rushed headlong from under fire, down the road, our men were led to suppose it was the enemy ; consequently they were fired upon by our infantry pickets, and it was not until two of their horses were killed that we discovered the mistake ; fortunately, none of the men got hurt.

General McCulloch, having to rely on his infantry pickets after the cavalry abandoned him, brought forward his heavy lines of skirmishers, who were met with a galling fire of musketry. The enemy's skirmishers soon fell back.

"McCulloch's Brigade, advance!" is heard in a bold, distinct voice above the roar and clamor of battle. "Forward, double-quick, guide center!" and onward the gallant heroes dash into the face of the most invulnerable point of the enemy's works.

They are greeted by a murderous fire of minie balls. Gaps are opened in the ranks, but they close again and move still onward ; thus fighting from hedge to hedge, and ditch to ditch, to the main levee, where the enemy took position. It was impossible for our troops to keep in line of battle, owing to the many hedges we had to encounter, which it was impossible to pass, except through a few gaps that had been used as gates or passways ; so we had to get out the best way we could. The 16th Dismounted Cavalry, under command of Colonel Gregg, the 17th Infantry, under command of Colonel Allen, and the 19th Infantry, commanded by Colonel Waterhouse, took position on the left of the road, while the 16th Infantry, under command of Colonel Flournoy, took their position on the right of the road.

With the first streak of daylight visible through the light mist that ascended from the river, the battle became general. The enemy opened a terrible fire of musketry. After firing a volley at the enemy, we were ordered to charge them with the bayonet. Without stopping to reload, the troops on the left of the road rushed upon the enemy. The enemy gave away and stampeded pell-mell over the levee, in great terror and confusion. Our troops followed after them, bayoneting them by hundreds. After the enemy got behind their breastworks, composed of cotton-bales, they made a stubborn fight. When our troops got into close quarters with them (the troops of the enemy were composed principally of negroes), bayonets were crossed, and muskets clubbed, and the struggle indeed became a close and deadly one.

The enemy repeatedly attempted to hold their position behind their cotton-bales, but were met each time by the ringing cheer and charge of the gallant Texans; so much so, that their heroic commander, General McCulloch, exclaimed, "Bravo, bravo!" in ecstasy of admiration and delight. Nothing could sucessfully resist the fighting of our troops. Our officers and men did all that men could do; they fought like so many tigers over their prey. When our troops gained the bloody field, they could see how desperately they had fought for its possession.

Dead bodies were found lying in every direction. Let us take a look along the shattered ranks. An awful sight! See that number of brave fellows now stretched in their gore, who, but an hour ago, were the personification of life, strength, and manliness; who had marched up with stout hearts to the fray—a march only from earth to eternity. They will never march again! Our gallant troops were led by such men as the gallant and brave Colonel Dick Waterhouse, ably assisted by his mild and heroic Lieutenant-Colonel Taylor; the tactician, Colonel R. T. P. Allen, assisted by his indefatigable Lieutenant-Colonel Wash. Jones; so, too, the bloody 16th Dismounted Cavalry, still without their veteran Colonel Fitzhugh, but in good hands when led by the chivalric Lieutenant-Colonel Gregg, aided and assisted by the intrepid Major Diamond.

As I previously announced, the 16th Infantry was on the right of the road when the charge over the levee was undertaken. The commander of the 16th Infantry, the brave statesman Colonel George Flournoy, was entirely ignorant of the plan of attack; consequently, under the circumstances, he had to rely on his own judgment—ordering his men to cut their way through the burdock hedge in their front. Once

7

through the hedge, he gave the command to fix bayonets; in the meantime he gave instructions to his officers, that as soon as the regiment had crossed the levee, the regiment should move, by the right flank, towards the enemy's quarters. After giving the command "Double-quick!" in a loud and sonorous voice, the regiment commenced to advance towards the levee, and, apparently, the greatest vivacity and enthusiasm prevailed among his men. Already a rattling fire on the right plainly announced that the work of destruction had commenced; but, alas! as the 16th Infantry was on the eve of climbing the levee, General McCulloch's adjutant arrived with orders, from General McCulloch to Colonel Flournoy, to double-quick his regiment to the left of the brigade, to prevent the enemy from flanking his left wing. The calm and cool perception of Colonel Flournoy in undertaking to attack the enemy on their flank instead of their front, showed a great deal of skill and wisdom. An attack made on either the right or left flank of the enemy's works, could have easily been accomplished, without any serious loss to our troops, while an attack coming from any other source was hazardous and dangerous to the attacking party, owing to the fact that the enemy had their cotton-bale breastworks to cover them. Colonel Flournoy directed the adjutant to tell General McCulloch that his regiment would be able to capture the enemy's camp if he would allow him. The adjutant informed him that his orders were imperative, and must be obeyed. Colonel Flournoy immediately ordered his regiment to double-quick to the left of the brigade. Away they go, pell-mell, along the foot of the levee, led by their colonel, erect and precise in his saddle, towering above his men, calm as a summer morn. It was cheering and inspiring indeed to observe his men, calm and with such determined air, and the unbounded confidence with which they followed him. The strong voice of his lieutenant-colonel, Shepard, the Ney of the division, conspicuous on his iron-gray charger, is heard urging his men forward with a velocipede speed. As he passes by the various regiments of the brigade, with sword in hand, cheer after cheer greets him. As a token of gratitude towards them, he uncovers his head, showing his gray hair, and announcing to them the fact that it wasn't a safe place to make them a speech ; he would do so after the battle was over. Here I will state, that of all the field officers of Walker's Division none was more highly respected by the troops of the division, than Lieutenant-Colonel James E. Shepard. The 16th Regiment having arrived at the position assigned to them, and with celerity formed in line of battle, to await further orders, General McCulloch shortly afterwards came along, and ordered a detail from each company of the regiment to act as sharpshooters, and to take their position near the top of the levee, to harass and annoy the enemy as much as possible. In the mean time, Colonel Flournoy, hearing some firing in his rear, ordered a company to ascertain where the firing came from. The company sent out by him soon returned with six prisoners that were lying in ambush.

General McCulloch, while riding along the line, was fired upon by a stray Yankee, who had evidently been cut off from his command. Carrying always a carbine when in action, he returned the fire, and killed the Yankee, proving to be a better marksman than his opponent.

During the firing across the levee by our sharpshooters an incident occurred worthy of notice, which I will relate : A musician, belonging to the band of the 16th Infantry, who was detailed to aid and assist the infirmary corps, was sent to a house in rear of the command for the purpose of getting some water for the wounded. Arriving at the house, he found himself in the middle of a company of Uncle Sam's colored pets, commanded by an Anglo-Saxon Yankee, who immediately made him a prisoner. The Yankee captain inquired the position of our troops, and was informed by the musician, who gave the location in quite a different direction from where our troops were. The captain then replied, that he could easily get through to his lines. The musician remarked to him that he would pilot him past our lines. The captain allowed him the privilege, and, as a matter of course, the musician led him and his company into our lines, where they were all taken prisoners, without the firing of a gun.

About 7 o'clock, A. M., three of the enemy's gun-boats arrived at the scene of action, and commenced shelling our troops. These brilliant and substantial exploits of heroism of our troops were witnessed by the commander of the division, who, from the beginning of the battle, had occupied a position on an eminence in the rear of the line of battle. His cool sagacity comprehended every movement of the troops and its consequences, and, with infinite self-possession, amidst a continued shower of shot and shell, seeing that further sacrifice on the part of his troops was useless, about ten o'clock, A. M., he rode up in person to General McCulloch, and ordered him to withdraw his brigade from the scene of action, on account of his hearing that several transports, loaded with troops, had passed Lake Providence, on their way to reinforce Milliken's Bend. On the arrival of McCulloch's Brigade at the position taken by Randall's Brigade, they were heartily cheered by their comrades. The gun-boats continued shelling our troops until they were out of range of their shots.

Our loss in this engagement was 44 killed, 130 wounded, and and 10 missing. Total casualties, 184; including 2 officers killed, and 10 wounded.

The loss of the enemy numbered about 800, including the number of negroes that were drowned in the Mississippi River, in undertaking to swim to a transport that was lying at the opposite bank of the river.

General McCulloch's Brigade did not exceed 1,500 men when they went into action. The enemy had twice, if not three times that number, backed by three gunboats. In justice to General McCulloch, I will state that the battle was made in obedience to orders received from Major-General Taylor, commanding the District of Louisiana. His orders were imperative to General McCulloch to attack the enemy's works, and carry them at the point of the bayonet.

General Taylor was led to believe that the force of the enemy consisted only of one battalion of cavalry, and one brigade of negro troops, without artillery or gun-boats. From information received after the battle, we learned that the enemy were fully apprised of our intended attack, and had made full preparation to give us a warm reception, having received a reinforcement of several transports, loaded with troops, the night previous.

General McCulloch was entirely misinformed of the enemy's number and position, as his guide had deserted him when the enemy's skirmishers had opened fire upon him. Consequently, he had to rely on his own skill and ingenuity in ascertaining the nature of the ground over which his troops had to advance. Instead of finding, as was represented to him, an open field, without any obstruction, the ground we advanced over was exceedingly rough and broken, covered entirely with running briers and vines. It was also cut up with ditches, and obstructed with burdock hedges. In fact, so strong was the enemy's position, that General McCulloch acknowledged to several of his officers, after the battle was over, that nothing but the bravest and best of fighting, under the providence of God, could have given victory.

In General McCulloch's official report of the battle, he sincerely mourns the loss of his brave men, by remarking that it is truly deplorable, and his heart sickens at the contemplation of the battle, as well as at the scathing ordeal through which his brigade had to pass ; but, nevertheless, his confidence in and love for his brave men are by no means shaken. He hoped at some future time his brigade might meet the enemy in an open field, where they would have a fair chance, so as to gain a complete victory to compensate them for the gallant fighting they had done, and would do again, when called upon to meet the fire of the enemy.

McCulloch's Brigade, in company with Randall's, rested about half an hour after they were safe from the fire of the enemy. After refreshing somewhat, they took up the line of march back again to Richmond. About fifteen minutes' marching brought them to the hospital, located in some negro cabins designated as a hospital by having a yellow flag on top of the various cabins.

If one wishes to view the havoc of war, next to the battle-field this is the place to witness it; so fearful, so horrible are the scenes, that, long after you leave the place, perhaps haunting you to the verge of life, the screams of the wounded, the groans of the dying will ring in your ears, or some form, cold and stiff in death's icy embrace, be present to your mental vision.

But this is no time for these feelings; such is the fortune of war. It is consoling to see how some of the men bear up under their misfortunes, and endure the agony of dreadful wounds; many of them are smiling and happy, as if returning from a pleasure-party. "Well, they have popped me this time," exclaimed one poor fellow, with a ball through his face; "but I will be at them again." "Hallo, Bill," shouted, in a faint voice, a half-grown boy from an ambulance, to a friend on foot, who was holding up his shattered arm; "they have broken my thigh, but it is in a glorious cause." Many with slight wounds are hurrying up the surgeons to have them dressed, so that they may accompany the brigade on its march.

One more picture, and the tableau is complete—the burial of the dead. During the battle, trenches fifty feet long and three feet wide were dug, to receive the bodies of the brave men and officers. It was seldom a coffin could be procured, and the brave defender of his country had to be wrapped in his blanket, and, in his soiled and battle-stained garments, he was placed hastily in the trench, and left to rest in peace.

> "No useless coffin inclosed his breast,
> Nor in sheet nor in shroud we wound him;
> But he lay like a warrior taking his rest,
> With his tattered blanket around him."

After passing the hospital, we continued our march towards our old camp, near Richmond. We arrived in camp about sunset. As many of the troops were preparing to eat supper, we received orders to form in line of battle. Immediately orders are issued to take up the line of march back again the way we came. Various rumors are afloat that Haws' Brigade was surrounded by the enemy, with no possible chance of escape without assistance from the balance of the division. Hearing no more from Haws' Brigade since they parted with us at the forks of the road, the night previous, the rumor was generally believed that it was in a critical position. Continuing our march about two miles from camp, we heard the glad tidings that Haws' Brigade was all right, and was within a mile of us. The news proved true, and the balance of the division was ordered back again to their old camp-ground. Haws' Brigade arrived shortly afterwards, with quite a number of prisoners they had captured at Young's Point. How the report about their being surrounded originated I am unable to say. At dress-parade, in the evening, the following official report from General McCulloch was read to his brigade :

GENERAL ORDER No. 1.

On Saturday, we again met the enemy in force at Milliken's Bend, on the bank of the Mississippi River, under the protection of his gun-boats. Their pickets and skirmishers and outposts were steadily driven from ditch to ditch, and hedge to hedge, until they fell behind their breastworks, at which they made a stubborn and desperate stand, but which were carried by our troops with a charge not excelled since the war commenced. In this charge the regiments of Colonels Waterhouse, Allen, and Fitzhugh were the participants, until Colonel Flournoy's Regiment arrived, and assisted in driving the enemy from his barricade, in an angle of his works, on our left,—Colonel Waterhouse, with his regiment, gallantly charging over the levee, and entirely through the enemy's camp, to the water's edge.

Too much credit cannot be awarded to our gallant officers and men for the courage and gallantry displayed on this battle-field. Our loss of 184, in killed, wounded, and missing, shows but too plainly how firm was the resistance of the foe, while the hundreds which they left dead behind their breastworks and strewn over the field, attest, with equal clearness, how desperately and efficiently our troops fought. We met the enemy at fearful odds, and, with well-directed fire, bayonets, and clubbed guns, drove him from his stronghold, through his camp, and under the bank of the river and the protection of his gun-boats.

During this day's battle, all did their duty to such an extent, and so many commendable acts of gallantry were performed, that it is impossible to specify them here. The commanding general returns his grateful thanks to the officers and soldiers of his command for the gallantry with which they sustained our glorious cause upon this desperately-fought field, and he feels that a grateful country will award to them all he would ask. He assures them that, while his heart bleeds over the recollection of the dead and wounded of his command, the noble conduct of all increases his love for them, and confidence in those that are still left with him to defend our country and our cause.

(Signed,)   General HENRY E. McCULLOCH.

GENERAL WALKER'S REPORT OF HIS DIVISION AT MILLIKEN'S
BEND AND YOUNG'S POINT.

Major E. SURGET, *Asst. Adjt.-General:*

SIR,—I have the honor to forward herewith the report of Brigadier-Generals Henry E. McCulloch and J. M. Haws, of the operations of their brigades in this vicinity. In regard to the former, nothing could have been more admirable than the gallantry displayed by officers and men; and the failure of complete success was principally owing to the want of local knowledge and the incompetency of the guides, the great strength of the position, and the extreme difficulty of carrying it by a *coup de main.*

*   *   *   *   *   *   *   *   *   *

As soon as the enemy's pickets were encountered, it seems General McCulloch formed his brigade in line of battle, and advanced upon the enemy, who were posted behind the hedges, so as to fire through the openings. Upon reaching the hedges, it was found entirely impracticable to pass them, except through the few openings left for convenience by the planter. In advancing through the gaps, the line of battle was necessarily broken, and the frequency with which this became necessary before reaching the levee behind which the enemy, in superior force, was found posted, exposed the brigade to a galling fire, while broken into columns in order to pass through the openings in the hedges. Owing to these frequent interruptions the brigade was unable to advance in the order of battle. The brigade reached the open space between the last hedge and the first levee, about twenty-five paces in width, in some confusion, and the *ensemble* of the movement upon the enemy's position was thus necessarily lost, the different regiments of the brigade having reached the open space at different periods. Notwithstanding the galling and destructive fire of the enemy, the regiments of Allen, Fitzhugh, and Waterhouse, were formed and led against the enemy, driving them from their hiding-place. The enemy was securely posted behind the first levee, awaiting our advance. Notwithstanding the disadvantages our troops labored under, we drove them from its covers, and followed them across the open space between the two levees, using the bayonet freely. At the second levee, however, our men encountered the main force of the enemy, entirely covered from our fire, and, after a gallant effort to carry the position, were compelled to fall back behind the first levee. We continued to hold until the wounded were sent to the rear, and the men, exhausted by the excessive heat of the day and want of water, were withdrawn in good order by General McCulloch. Randall's Brigade, which by General Taylor's orders was held in reserve, six miles from the field, was hastened forward upon General McCulloch's request for reinforcements, but did not reach the scene of action until General McCulloch, having several times failed to carry the second levee, had drawn off his brigade. In the meantime, the enemy's gun-boats, four in number, had taken position so as to rake the open space between the second levee and the river with grape and canister ; and had our men succeeded in gaining the open space, the enemy, by retiring to the water's edge, would have given their gun-boats complete command of the position. Under such circumstances it would have been folly to have persisted in the attack, which could only have resulted in a fearful sacrifice of life ; and after making a personal reconnoissance as far as practicable, and otherwise gaining the best information possible, I determined not to order another assault ; but having sent off the wounded and rested the troops for several hours near the battle-field, in the cool of the evening, I determined to withdraw the two brigades, sending McCulloch's back to this place, and taking post with Randall's, four miles in advance, to cover the road along which General Haws' Brigade would return from Young's Point.

In regard to the operations of the brigade of the last-named officer, I have only to remark that my orders to him were peremptory, to attack the enemy at Young's Point. Our information of the strength and position of the enemy at that place was so recent, and was thought to be so entirely reliable, that I did not think it necessary to attach any conditions to this order. The failure to carry out my instructions can only be defended by the existence of circumstances entirely at variance with those supposed to exist, and upon which the order was based. The loss of several precious hours in finding a bridge, which would have brought on the attack in the heat of an excessively hot day; the exhausted condition of the men who would have gone into action under a burning sun, after an almost continuous march of nearly thirty miles ; the strong position of the enemy, defended by three gun-boats, are the reasons assigned by General Haws for assuming the responsibility of not attacking the enemy's position. From what I know of Brigadier-General Haws, I am satisfied that the conviction must have been overpowering that the attack would fail, after a useless sacrifice of life, or he would not have taken the responsibility he did.

In conclusion, it must be remembered that the enemy, behind a Mississippi levee, protected on the flanks by gun-boats, is as securely posted as it is possible to be, outside of a regular fortification.

(Signed,)   J. G. WALKER, Major-General.

THE FEDERAL REPORT OF THE BATTLE OF MILLIKEN'S BEND.

To Brigadier-Gen'l THOMAS, *Adjutant-General of the Army:*

GENERAL I have the honor to report that, in accordance with instructions received from me, Colonel Leib, commanding Ninth Louisiana A. D., made a reconnoissance in the direction of Richmond, on June 6th, starting from Milliken's Bend at 2 o'clock, A. M.

He was preceded by two companies of the Tenth Illinois Cavalry, commanded by Captain Anderson, whom he overtook three miles from the Bend.

It was agreed between them that the captain should take the left side of Walnut Bayou, and pursue it as far as Mrs. Ames' plantation, while Colonel Leib proceeded along the main Richmond road to the railroad depot, three miles from Richmond, where he encountered the enemy's pickets and advance, which he drove in with but little opposition, but, anticipating the enemy in strong force, retired slowly toward the Bend.

When about half-way back, a squad of our cavalry came dashing up in his rear, hotly pursued by the enemy. Colonel Leib immediately formed his regiment across an open field, and with one volley dispersed the approaching enemy. Expecting the enemy would contest the passage of the bridge over Walnut Bayou, Colonel Leib fell back over the bridge, and from thence to Milliken's Bend, from whence he sent a messenger, informing me of the success of the expedition, and reported the enemy to be advancing.

I immediately started the Twenty-third Iowa Volunteer Infantry to their assistance, and Admiral Porter ordered the gun-boat Choctaw to that point. At three o'clock, the following morning, the enemy made their appearance in strong force on the main Richmond road, driving the pickets before them. The enemy advanced on the left of our line, throwing out no skirmishers, marching in close column by division, with a strong cavalry force on his right flank.

Our forces, consisting of the Twenty-third Iowa Volunteer Infantry and the African Brigade—in all, 1,061 men—opened upon the enemy when within musket-shot range, which made them waver and recoil, a number running in confusion to the rear. The balance, pushing on with intrepidity, soon reached the levee, when they were ordered to charge, with the cries of "No quarter!"

The African regiments being inexperienced in the use of arms, some of them having been drilled but a few days, and the guns being very inferior, the enemy succeeded in getting upon our works before more than one or two volleys were fired at them. Here ensued a most terrible hand-to-hand conflict of several minutes' duration, our men using the bayonet freely, and clubbing their guns with fierce obstinacy, contesting every inch of ground, until the enemy succeeded in flanking them, and poured a murderous enfilading fire along our lines, directing their fire chiefly to the officers, who fell in great numbers.

Not till they were overpowered and forced by superior numbers, did our men fall back behind the bank of the river, at the same time pouring volley after volley into the ranks of the advancing enemy. The gun-boat now moved into position, and fired a broadside into the enemy, who immediately disappeared behind the levee, but all the time keeping up a fire upon our men. The enemy at this time appeared to be extending his line to the extreme right, but was held in check by two companies of the Eleventh Louisiana Infantry A. D., which had been posted behind cotton-bales, and part of the old levee. In this position the fight continued until near noon, when the enemy suddenly withdrew.

Our men, seeing this movement, advanced upon the retreating column, firing volley after volley at them while they remained within gun-shot. The gun-boat Lexington then paid her compliments to the flying foe, in several well-directed shots, scattering them in all directions. I here desire to express my thanks to the officers and men of the gun-boats Choctaw and Lexington, for their efficient services in time of need. Their services will be long remembered by the officers and men of the African Brigade, for their valuable assistance on that dark, and bloody field. The officers and men deserve the highest praise for their gallant conduct. The enemy consisted of one brigade, numbering about twenty-five hundred, in command of General McCulloch, and two hundred cavalry. The enemy's loss is estimated at 150 killed, and 300 wounded. It is impossible to get at anything near the loss of the enemy, as they carried killed and wounded off in ambulances. Among their killed is Colonel Allen of Texas.* Our loss in killed, wounded, and missing, amounts to 652.

Submitting the foregoing, I remain yours respectfully,

(Signed,)　　　ELLIS S. DENNIS,

Brigadier-General Commanding.

---

* Now teaching military school in Kentucky.

CHAPTER XV.

AFTER the battle of Milliken's Bend, we remained encamped near Richmond until the morning of the 15th (in the mean time our wounded and sick men were sent to Monroe). When our pickets were driven in by the enemy, General Walker immediately formed the division in line of battle; at the same time he ordered the 18th Infantry, under command of Colonel Culbertson, to take position at the upper crossing, about a mile north of Richmond, with instructions to hold the crossing at all hazards until he could get his wagon-train out of the way. Captain Edgar, having charged his guns with grape and canister, ordered six rounds of ammunition to be placed alongside of each gun. This having been accomplished, he ordered his men to conceal themselves as much as possible until he ordered them into action.

Presently, the enemy emerges out of the woods, and advances in martial array, their banners floating on the breeze, as if they were on parade. Colonel Culbertson passes along the line, speaking words of cheer to his men, telling them that the safety of the entire division was intrusted to them, and ordering their bayonets to be fixed. They stood like a stone wall, awaiting the approach of the enemy. On they came, like a huge avalanche pouring across the valley. It seemed to be a race with them, which of their regiments should be the most successful in capturing the rebel battery. Closer they came, until they got within about one hundred and fifty yards, when Captain Edgar ordered his men to be up and at them. Right manfully did his men go into action, handling their guns with alacrity and cheerfulness, throwing grape and canister amongst them, and slaying them by hundreds. The ground was covered with their dead and wounded. Captain Edgar's men were playing havoc amongst them. The 18th Texas Infantry, commanded by the brave and fearless Colonel Culbertson, crossed the bayou and charged the enemy at the point of the bayonet, driving them pell-mell into the timber. They were panic-stricken, as they never stopped to resist the charge of the brave 500. Although their numbers exceeded 18,000, under command of one of their ablest generals, General Davis, they anticipated that they were ambushed. Getting into the timber, they finally rallied. In the mean time Colonel Culbertson withdrew his regiment across the bayou again, and rejoined the balance of the division. This charge made by the 18th Infantry will compare favorably with any regimental charge that has ever been recorded. Too much praise cannot be awarded to Colonel Culbertson and Captain Edgar and their men for their gallantry and cool presence of mind on this occasion. The division fell back to Bayou Macon on the arrival of Colonel Culbertson's Regiment and Captain Edgar's Battery.

General Walker anticipated that the enemy would follow him up as soon as they got over their fright. Once across Bayou Macon, General Walker contemplated giving battle. As was expected, the enemy's cavalry followed us up to Bayou Macon. Our rear-guard skirmished with them from Round-away Bayou up to within a few hundred yards of the crossing of the bayou.

One of their officers, more persevering or braver than the balance of them, advanced ahead of their main column. He came in contact with one of our soldiers who was tired and unable to keep up with the main body of our troops. He was ordered by the officer to surrender, whereupon he ordered the officer to surrender to him. Neither would surrender to the other; consequently they commenced firing at each other. The private soldier proved to be the best shot, as he killed the officer. He took possession of the officer's horse and accouterments, and continued his march to camp. He arrived in camp in due time, and was highly complimented by his officers for his bravery. After crossing Bayou Macon we camped for the night, having marched ten miles.

During the greatest portion of the night we remained under arms and in line of battle. It was generally believed among the troops, that the enemy would attempt to cross the bayou during the night.

On the morning of the 16th we learned, much to our surprise, that the enemy had fallen back towards Milliken's Bend. We took up the line of march for the town of Delhi. While on the march we met General Tappan's Brigade of Arkansians, on a forced march, coming to our "rescue." They informed us that they heard a great many of "Walker's Greyhounds" had been captured by the enemy. After assuring them that the *greyhounds* were too quick for the enemy, they became reconciled. After marching twelve miles we camped for the night.

On the 17th the march was resumed. After marching seven miles we encamped near a spring of fine water, northeast of the town of Delhi, the terminus of the railroad built from the town of Monroe. We remained at this camp until the morning of the 22d.

CHAPTER XVI.

MARCH FROM DELHI IN THE DIRECTION OF GOODRICH'S LANDING.—TEXAS
CAVALRY.—CAPTURE OF FORT MOUND.—RETURN TO DELHI.—THE AP-
PEARANCE OF THE TROOPS.—FALL OF VICKSBURG.—SURMISES ABOUT
THE SURRENDER OF VICKSBURG.—ON THE CARS.—ARRIVAL AT MONROE.

N the morning of the 22d, the march was resumed in
the direction of Goodrich's Landing, on the Mississippi River, where the enemy was supposed to be
intrenched. After marching twelve miles, we camped near
the village of Monticello, on Bayou Macon.

May 23d. Marched ten miles. Our march to-day lay
through a pleasant valley, bordered on each side by the green
forest trees. We passed by once-pleasant homesteads, already
desolated by war; green fields, and orchards in full bloom,
despite the desolation and ruin around them. After crossing the Tensas River, we camped on its banks until the morning of the 26th, when we took up the line of march back the
way we came; marched fourteen miles and camped.

May 27th. Marched eight miles up Bayou Macon, and
camped.

May 28th. Early this morning we resumed our march;
left Bayou Macon and marched back again four miles in the
direction of Goodrich's Landing, between Milliken's Bend
and Lake Providence, on the Mississippi River. While on
the march, we met Colonel Parsons' Brigade of Cavalry, coming from the direction of Gains' Landing. As they passed
by us, I could not but admire their horsemanship; they all
appeared to be excellent horsemen, and at a distance their
general appearance was decidedly showy and gallant. Their
uniform contained as many colors as the rainbow; their arms
consisted mostly of Enfield rifles, slung to their saddles, while

around the waist of each was buckled a heavy cavalry sword, which clattered at every movement of their horses. A pair of holster pistols attached to the pommels of their saddles completed their equipment.

A short distance from Goodrich's Landing, the cavalry came across a fort, built on an Indian mound—one of the " high places," where aborigines worshiped or made mausoleums for their dead. It towers above the roofs of houses, and looks down upon the negro cabins like a mountain in the dead level of the surrounding marsh and swamp. Traditions claim that this section of the country has been the hunting-ground of the Choctaws, an old confederacy of red tribes, who once possessed the lower Mississippi lands, beginning with the "Houmas," near the coast, and numbering many clans, whose very names are now forgotten. These clans or tribes built their forts from Bayou Bœuf to the Arkansas River, ranging across the Teche and Atchafalaya Bayous, and through all the beautiful Attakapas country. They waged a fierce and determined war against the French for nearly a century, before their remnants, broken and disheartened, migrated to the wilderness far beyond the Mississippi, and were ultimately lost amidst the predatory hordes which roved around the bases of the Sierra Madre.

This fort or mound, near Goodrich's Landing, was garrisoned by negro troops for the purpose of raiding and destroying everything that could assist any of our troops. They devoted their time, headed by their officers (white men), in burning private residences, corn-cribs, cotton, etc.

On the arrival of the cavalry at the fort, they waited some time for General Randall's Brigade. As soon as they arrived, both forces surrounded the fort, and demanded the surrender of the same. The enemy at first refused to surrender, but seeing the position of our troops, ready to carry the place at the point of the bayonet, they finally surrendered to our forces, conditionally. The garrison consisted of 1,200 negro troops and twelve white officers. After the surrender, we remained encamped near the fort until the morning of the

30th, when we took up the line of march back again to our old camping-ground at Delhi. After marching twenty miles we camped on Bayou Macon for the night.

May 31st. Marched four miles, and arrived at our old camp-ground.

While we remained encamped in the Mississippi bottoms, Falstaff's ragged regiment was well uniformed in comparison with our troops. No two were costumed with any attempt at uniformity, and each individual stood forth a decided character. But few of the troops had shaved for weeks, and, as a consequence, there was a large and general assortment of unbrushed black, gray, red, and sandy beards, as well as ferocious mustaches and whiskers—enough to rig out an army of West India buccaneers. A more brigandish set of Anglo-Saxon forces has never been collected. Then as to costume, it is utterly impossible to paint the variety our division presented. Here would be a fellow dressed in homespun pants, with the knees out of them ; on his head might be stuck the remnant of a straw hat, while a faded Texas penitentiary cloth jacket would perhaps complete his outfit. His neighbor, very likely, was arrayed in breeches made out of some cast-off blanket, with a dyed shirt as black as the ace of spades, and no hat at all. Then would come a man with a woolen hat made like a pyramid, sitting jauntily upon his head, while, to introduce his style of hat, he had it covered over with assorted buttons ; and, to top the climax, had a red tassel sewed on top. Notwithstanding his gaudy hat, a part of a shirt, and occasional fragments only of what had once been a pair of military pantaloons, made up the rest of his attire. But, singular as it may seem, there could hardly be found a merrier, I might be going too far in saying a happier, set of men in Christendom. Our very looks bred good humor ; for there was something irresistibly ludicrous in the appearance of each man—a quaint solemnity and droll gravity of countenance, which would elicit some facetious and good-natured remark from his neighbor. The comic and eccentric were strangely mingled with the tragic and melodramatic ; but the former predominated to a degree that completely stifled any pathetic feelings which might otherwise have arisen, and induced us to laugh rather than cry at the forlorn but fantastic figure each one presented in the moving panorama.

So completely disguised were we all, that I doubt whether our anxious mothers would have recognized us; and even could they, by some well-remembered mark, have detected an errant son, methinks they would have been slow to acknowledge one who had wandered so far from their hearthstone as to have lost their very identity.

We remained at our camp at Delhi, awaiting the long-looked-for "Fourth of July," which, according to the enemy's report, was to decide the fate of Vicksburg. Bets of Confederate money were freely exchanged amongst the troops, regarding the fate of the doomed city. On the night of the 3d of July, pretty much all the members of our division, for curiosity's sake, remained awake all night to listen to the cannonading, which could be distinctly heard from our camp. As the hours flew by, the sentries on post would cry out, "11 o'clock, and Vicksburg all right!" and so on, during the hours of the night. Morning at last dawned, and still the cannonading continued, up till the hour of 7 o'clock, when we heard the report of about a dozen shots in rapid succession. A gloom of sadness appeared to have come over the troops. Some of the men accounted for the rapid firing by remarking, that the Yankees were celebrating the "Fourth of July" in the old style of by-gone days, but the general belief among the troops was, that Vicksburg was in possession of the enemy; which proved, alas! too true. It was not until the morning of the 7th that we knew, for certain, the fate of Vicksburg. Our first information (outside of the Yankee sources) was from a parolled officer that had just arrived at Delhi. Even then it was not credited by General Walker, as he immediately had the officer arrested and put under guard, until he was recognized by some of the leading citizens of Delhi, when he was released from custody.

As soon as it became known for certain, in camp, that Vicksburg had surrendered, a perfect storm of indignation burst forth among the troops. What! surrender, and that too on the 4th of July, above all other days? Impossible. The men broke forth in bitter denunciation of Lieutenant-General Pemberton, boldly proclaiming that he had sold it to the enemy. Surrender on the 4th of July! Why should that day, of all others, be chosen for our humiliation? The Southern soldier preferred dying—a thousand times preferable—to making the National anniversary a thrice memorable natal day, and give to the United States a new impulse for prosecuting the war. Would it not be received as a good omen, and infuse a new spirit into the efforts of the foe for our subjugation? Such were some of the fierce denunciations used, whether justly or not, the world has never discovered. Yet it seems scarcely possible, or probable, that General Pemberton could have been actuated by such perfidious motives.

But the question is asked by the author of this work, How did the prisoners that were captured at Milliken's Bend and Young's Point, nearly a month previous to the fall of Vicksburg, know about the circumstances? Kind reader, bear with me a little further, and I will endeavor to substantiate proof that the surrender of Vicksburg was a premeditated affair between the Federal and Confederate commanders.

The writer of this book had occasion to pay a visit to Colonel Gregg of the 16th Dismounted Cavalry, who was seriously wounded at Milliken's Bend, and then lying in hospital at Richmond. On the gallery of the hospital was seated Lieutenant-Colonel Baxter, of the 28th Dismounted Cavalry, and a Yankee officer (belonging, I believe, to the 2d Illinois Cavalry), in conversation about the war. I was cordially invited to take a seat. During the conversation, the Yankee officer (who was captured at Milliken's Bend) informed Colonel Baxter that General Pemberton would certainly surrender Vicksburg on the morning of the 4th of July. If it did not prove true, he, the Yankee officer, was willing to wear a ball and chain during the war. On the contrary, if his remarks proved true, he wanted Colonel Baxter to use his influence in setting him at liberty. Ponder, gentle reader, on those remarks, and what is your verdict? Then, again, take the surrender of Vicksburg in general, and the causes attached to it. Was not General Pemberton guilty of gross neglect of duty in two ways? 1st. In not fortifying Vicksburg so as to resist an attack from the rear with the least possible loss of life. 2d. In not procuring supplies for the garrison sufficient to make a protracted defense in case of a siege. This is the great and chief cause of complaint. Immense quantities of supplies could have been got in the Yazoo Valley; yet no efforts were made to obtain these supplies, or to transport them to Vicksburg, although it was known that General Grant was making strenuous exertions to cross the Mississippi River and attack Vicksburg from the rear, and might succeed at any moment. Again, the large quantities of supplies which accumulated at Snyder's Mills were allowed to remain there, and were eventually destroyed. These are indisputable facts, and are placed on record as necessary to the completeness of the history concerning the siege and fall of Vicksburg.

On the morning of the 7th, we took up the line of march, up Bayou Macon again, to Monticello, for what purpose I am unable to say, unless it was to quiet the excitement in camp about the fall of Vicksburg. Marched eleven miles and camped on Bayou Macon until the next morning, when we marched back again to our camp at Delhi, and remained there until the beginning of the 11th, when we bade adieu to our old camp, and went aboard the railroad cars bound for the town of Monroe, distant forty miles. We arrived at Monroe at 1 o'clock, P.M. On our arrival we marched through the principal streets of the town, to see and be seen by the ladies. After our promenading we encamped about half a mile south of the town, on the banks of the Washita River, until the following morning. The town of Monroe has one long, broad, handsome street, and many cross streets, shaded by trees and adorned with fine mansions. Before the war it was a great cotton mart, and the plantations around are very productive and well adapted to grow the raw material.

CHAPTER XVII.

GENERAL WALKER'S REPORT OF THE OPERATIONS OF HIS DIVISION IN MADISON AND CARROLL PARISHES.

Lieut.-Colonel S. S. ANDERSON, *A. A. General T. M. Department :*

BY direction of the Lieutenant-General commanding the Department, and for his information, I have the honor to lay before you the following report of the operations of my division in the parishes of Madison and Carroll, opposite Vicksburg, Mississippi. In order to a better understanding of the subject, I include in this review the operations of the division previous to the departure of Major-General Taylor to Alexandria, after the partial failure of the attack upon Milliken's Bend, on the 7th of June last, up to which time, he being present, I was acting under his immediate orders. Marching from Alexandria on the 27th, 28th, and 29th of May, the brigades of McCulloch, Randall, and Haws were embarked on board transports at Le Croix ferry, on Little River, on the 28th, 29th, and 30th, respectively, and proceeded down Little River to its junction with the Ouachita and Tensas ; ascended the latter to the mouth of De Rossel Bayou, where McCulloch's Brigade, which was accompanied by Major-General Taylor, debarked on the afternoon of the 30th, and immediately took up its line of march for Perkins' Landing, on the Mississippi, six miles below New Carthage. Early the next morning, I arrived with Randall's Brigade, and proceeded with it towards the same point, where it was known the enemy had a camp of instruction and insurrection for negroes, which it was hoped General McCulloch would be able to surprise and capture. The delay, however, in constructing

a bridge over De Rossel Bayou, and an entire want of cavalry
to cover our movements, enabled the enemy to escape upon
his transports. General McCulloch reached the Mississippi,
barely in time to enable his artillery to send a few shots into
the enemy's transports as they left the landing. Upon coming
up with Randall's Brigade, I found the point evacuated, and
two gun-boats anchored off the site of the abandoned camp.
Here, being entirely destitute of cavalry and guides, and being entirely ignorant of the topography of the country, it was
impracticable to proceed further.

General Taylor had, as he informed me, directed the cavalry of Colonel Harrison to meet us at the point of de-
barkation, but for some reason they did not reach us. As
Harrison's men were mostly residents of this very region, and
as we confidently expected its co-operation, no other guides
had been provided ; and. as the country was entirely deserted,
none could be procured. Haws' Brigade having arrived during
the night of the 31st, the whole division was crossed over to
the west bank of the Tensas, and proceeded across to Bayou
Macon, ascending its left bank to the intersection of the road
leading from Delhi to Richmond ; received their much-needed
subsistence from the former point, constructed a trestle bridge
across the Tensas, and crossed that river on the 6th of June,
and the same evening reached Richmond, which, two days before, had been taken possession of by a squadron of Harrison's
Cavalry, which had joined us on Bayou Macon. At Richmond,
we intersected the road by which Grant's army had passed
below Vicksburg, and by which, until recently, he had drawn
all his reinforcements and supplies, but which was now no
longer used, as the fall of the water and the drying up of the
swamps gave the enemy a much shorter line from Young's
Point to Bedford's, opposite Warrenton, Mississippi. A few
weeks previous to our coming, the enemy's operations could
have been seriously embarrassed by cutting his line of communication at Richmond, but the golden opportunity had
passed. The opening of the Yazoo River enabled the enemy's
army to draw their supplies from the Upper Mississippi, and

land them at Snyder's Bluff, to the rear of Vicksburg.   On the
6th of June, I was directed by General Taylor to attack, with
McCulloch's Brigade, the enemy's position at Milliken's Bend,
distant from Richmond about twelve miles; and, simultaneously, Brig.-General Haws was ordered to attack the enemy at
Young's Point, twenty miles distant, while I was directed by
General Taylor to remain at a point between the two places
with Randall's Brigade, in order to reinforce either the one or
the other, as circumstances might require.   Brig.-General
McCulloch gallantly attacked the enemy at Milliken's Bend,
about daylight, on the 7th; drove him from all his positions, as
far as the river-bank, where a second levee was encountered
(behind which the enemy rallied, supported by four gun-boats,
three of which arrived during the progress of the action), from
which the efforts of our brave men, led by their gallant commander, were unable to dislodge him; and, after suffering a loss
of nearly two hundred in killed and wounded, and our men
being no longer able to continue the contest, from sheer exhaustion, produced by extreme heat and want of water, General
McCulloch withdrew his brigade in perfect order, bringing off
his wounded.   At this moment, I arrived upon the field with
Randall's Brigade, and finding McCulloch's men no longer in
a condition to afford any assistance, should the attack be renewed by Randall's Brigade, and that the enemy was being
constantly reinforced by transports coming from below, and
that his position was an exceedingly strong one, which would
cost us a heavy loss to carry, for which in my judgment, success
would be an inadequate compensation, I determined, therefore, not to renew the assault.   I remained, however, in the
immediate vicinity of the enemy's position until night, destroyed
the gin-houses, and drove off the stock belonging to the cotton plantations that were being cultivated by lessees of the
Federal government.

   The enemy's loss in this engagement, I have reason to believe, amounts to at least eight hundred, in killed and wounded.
We captured about sixty negro soldiers, with two white officers
who commanded them, sixty or seventy stand of arms, and

two hundred head of horses and mules, and a number of cattle.

In the mean time, nothing was known of Brig.-General Haws' operations; but, during the night I received intelligence that he was on his return, without having attacked the enemy at Young's Point, as directed. Upon his rejoining me on the following morning, he reported that his march to Young's Point was delayed several hours by the incompetence of his guides, and that, in consequence, instead of reaching the point to be attacked at daylight, as intended, he did not reach it until half-past ten o'clock in the morning; and that the excessive heat of the day, the want of water, and a march of thirty miles, continued for twenty-eight hours without sleep and but little rest, had so exhausted his troops as to have rendered hopeless any attack upon the enemy's fortified position.

Major-General Taylor's instructions to me, delivered to Brig.-General Haws, were imperative to make the attack, but I am convinced from what I know of the state of exhaustion resulting from excessive heat and fatigue, that General Haws' men were incapable of the physical exertion necessary to carry a fortified position defended on the flanks by gun-boats. How far these considerations justify a failure to obey an unconditional and imperative order, I am not prepared to say.

In my frequent interviews and conferences with Major-General Taylor, on the subject of relieving Vicksburg, he always expressed the utmost anxiety, which was fully shared by myself and my command, to strike a blow that would bear directly upon the conduct of the siege, with the small force at his disposal, numbering less than five thousand effective men upon leaving Alexandria—reduced, on the 8th of June, by sickness, resulting from excessive heat, bad water, malarious climate, and the casualties of battle, to something less than four thousand. After that date, General Taylor considered that, with this small force, no material aid could be afforded the garrison at Vicksburg. The justice of these views, I think, will be better appreciated from an examination of the topography of the country opposite Vicksburg.

*　　*　　*　　*　　*　　*　　*　　*

It will be seen that, in marching into the peninsula at the extremity of which Vicksburg is situated, the route is parallel to the Mississippi, both above and below the point to be reached, and that a small force once east of Young's Point and Warrenton, would inevitably be cut off from returning. The forces of the enemy at Young's Point, which, since General Haws' demonstrations, have been considerable, could be increased to any extent in a few hours, and would have but two or three miles to march, by a good road leading along Walnut Bayou, and intersecting the road leading towards Vicksburg, and by which we would be compelled to march. Nearly the same is true in regard to Bedford, nearly opposite which the left of Grant's army rests. But, suppose we could have eluded the vigilance of the negro spies—and the country in that region is filled with them—and the watchfulness of the enemy's scouts and pickets, which, since our attack upon Milliken's Bend, have been doubly on the alert, we would still encounter an insuperable obstacle to our further progress, at the canal dug by the enemy across the peninsula. This canal, not more than a mile and quarter in length, effectually bars the approach of even a much larger force than ours to the river-bank opposite Vicksburg, and a delay of only a few hours at the canal would draw upon the rear of our small force such an attack as would result inevitably in our destruction or capture. These considerations seemed so just, that I was directed by General Taylor to withdraw my division to Alexandria, by way of Monroe, as soon as steamboat transportation could be procured at the latter place. Accordingly, Randall's Brigade left Richmond on the 3d, and, proceeding to Monroe, and embarking on transports, had reached Columbus, on the Ouachita River, when the order for my withdrawal from the swamp was countermanded, and Randall's ordered to rejoin me at Richmond, and I was instructed to proceed to Bedford, and to break up the plank-road from there to Young's Point, and to strike at the enemy wherever I could do so effectually. I was awaiting the arrival of Randall's and Tappan's Brigades before marching

towards Bedford, when, about eight o'clock on the morning of the
15th, I was attacked, at Richmond, by a division of the enemy's
forces, coming from Milliken's Bend, numbering between seven
and eight thousand, three light batteries, and eight hundred
cavalry, under the command, as I afterward understood, of
General Devin or Davis. My whole force, consisting of
McCulloch's and Haws' Brigades, terribly reduced by sickness, did not exceed fifteen hundred effective men, with a light
battery of four guns, and twenty cavalry. With such a force
I could not hope to more than hold the enemy in check until
my sick and wounded could be removed. With this view, I
continued to engage the enemy, until between twelve and one
o'clock, P. M., when, having effected my purpose, I retired
from Richmond towards the Tensas, which I crossed about
sundown. The enemy did not attempt to follow me in force,
and except some skirmishing between his advance and my
rear-guard, my march was unmolested.

So large a number of sick men has, perhaps, never belonged to so small a force; and no command was ever so
rapidly reduced in strength in the absence of an epidemic.
Excessive heat of the weather, the deadly malaria of the
swamps, the stagnant and unwholesome water, are the causes
to which are attributable these sad results. My division
looked like a vast moving hospital. We had sick men in
wagons and carts, wounded men on litters, borne by soldiers,
and a crowd of enfeebled and emaciated men for whom no transportation could be had, who were straggling along in front of
the marching column, which accommodated its movements to
their feebleness. I had the satisfaction, however, of bringing
off every sick and wounded man, and lost only about fifteen
killed, wounded, and missing, in the engagement in the morning. I had no means of knowing the loss of the enemy, but I
have reason to believe that it was considerable. On reaching
the Tensas River, I was joined by General Tappan's Brigade,
thirteen hundred strong, which raised my whole effective
force to twenty-eight or twenty-nine hundred men—a force
too small with which to resume the offensive, as the care of

my large number of sick and wounded men required my first attention.

Major E. Seuget, *A. A. Gen'l:*

Major,—Since the date of my last report, the forces under my command have broken up the plantations engaged in raising cotton under Federal leases, from Milliken's Bend to Lake Providence, capturing some 2,000 negroes, which have been restored to their masters, with the exception of those captured in arms, and a few, the property of disloyal citizens of Louisiana. I consider it an unfortunate circumstance that any armed negroes were captured; but, in the cavalry expedition which broke up the plantations below Lake Providence, Colonel Parsons, commanding two cavalry regiments, from the district of Arkansas, acting under my orders, encountered a force of 113 negroes, and three white officers, in a fortified position. The officers proposed to surrender upon the condition of being treated as prisoners of war, and the armed negroes unconditionally. Colonel Parsons accepted the terms. The position, a high mound, the side of which had been scarped and otherwise strengthened, was of great strength, and would have cost many lives and much precious time, if captured by assault. Under these circumstances, Brigadier-General Tappan, who came up before the capitulation was consummated, approved the convention. This was on the 30th ult., and I had made all my arrangements to push, the next day, towards Providence and Ashton, some miles above, where I intended to establish my batteries for the annoyance of the enemy's transports. That night I received General Taylor's instructions to march my division to Berwick Bay. I immediately returned to Delhi, and had embarked one of the brigades on the railroad train, when I received instructions from Lieut.-General Smith to remain in this vicinity. On the 5th inst., General Smith was here in person, and directed me to proceed to Ashton, on the Mississippi, and endeavor to blockade the river against the enemy's transports and supply-boats. In

accordance with these instructions, I marched from here on
the 7th inst. The same morning, Captain James, who had
been sent with a flag of truce to deliver a communication
from General Taylor to General Grant, returned and reported
the delivery of the dispatch to the enemy's pickets, at
Young's Point. He brought intelligence, derived from
sources that I did not credit, that the garrison at Vicksburg
had capitulated on the 4th inst. Not considering this entirely certain, I continued my movement, but the same day I
received the intelligence, unfortunately too well authenticated
to admit of a doubt. At the same time I received instructions from Lieutenant-General Smith to return to this point,
and, if forced to abandon the Washita Valley by superior
numbers, to fall back on Red River, towards Natchitoches.

I am now engaged in burning all the cotton I can reach,
from Lake Providence to the lower end of Concordia Parish,
and shall endeavor to leave no spoil for the enemy. I have
also instructed the cavalry to destroy all subsistence and forage on abandoned plantations, that, from its proximity to the
river, may give the enemy facilities for invasion. When this
destruction is effected, I shall withdraw the greater portion
of my force towards the Washita River, to some more
healthy locality. The ravages of disease have fearfully weakened my force, and I consider it essential to its future
usefulness that it should be removed from here as early as
practicable.

CHAPTER XVIII.

MARCH FROM MONROE TO ALEXANDRIA.—GENERAL McCULLOCH LEAVES
THE DIVISION.—AMUSING ANECDOTE OF AN ORDNANCE SERGEANT EN
ROUTE FOR BERWICK BAY.—OPERATIONS OF GENERAL DICK TAYLOR.—
THE "GREYHOUNDS" RESTING.—CAPTURE OF FORT BEAUREGARD.—THE
"GREYHOUNDS" ON THE ENEMY'S TRAIL.—PREPARING FOR BATTLE.—
ARRIVAL OF GENERAL SCURRY.

AGREEABLE to the orders of Lieutenant-General Kirby Smith, the division took up the line of march for Alexandria, on the 12th of July, after taking a parting adieu of the citizens of Monroe, but not before we gave them to understand that we would soon again pay them a visit. This kind of a promise we could safely give to the citizens of any town or village in Louisiana or Arkansas. It was a noted fact that our division always paid the second visit to the citizens of those towns, whether they were welcome or not. This seemed to be part of our programme.

After crossing the Washita River at Trenton Ferry, about a mile and a half north of the town of Monroe, we arrived at camp, situated about a mile west of the town of Trenton. We remained at this camp until the morning of the 19th, when we proceeded on our journey towards Alexandria, via Campti, on Red River. Our route of march was over the same section of country that we had previously traveled. After marching five miles, we arrived at camp early in the day.

July 20th. Marched five miles.

July 21st. Marched eight miles.

July 22d. Marched ten miles, and camped near the town of Vernon. At this place General H. E. McCulloch took farewell of his brigade. He had received orders from General Kirby Smith to report to General Magruder, in Texas. After his arrival in Texas, he was assigned to the command of the northeastern portion of the State, with his headquarters at Bonham, in Fannin County. He fulfilled this position with honor to himself and his adopted State, until the close of the war. His duties were very laborious and tedious on the frontier, he having to guard against the murderous Comanches, as well as to look after the enemy, who were continually making raids from Fort Smith, Arkansas, towards the Texas frontier. In addition to protecting the frontier people from raids by the Indians and Federals, he had to protect them from the pests of the country, known by the name of Jayhawkers. After he left the brigade, Colonel George Flournoy was assigned to the command.

July 23d. Passed through the village of Vernon, and marched twelve miles.

July 24th. Marched fourteen miles.

July 25th. Marched ten miles.

July 26th. Marched eleven miles.

July 27th. Marched thirteen miles, and arrived at Campti, on Red River, thus making the second trip to this place within the short period of a few months. We remained encamped close by a lake until the morning of August 3d, when we left camp and proceeded five miles down the river-bank. Arriving opposite Grand Ecore, a steamboat was in readiness to ferry us across to that place, where we camped on the sand-flats until the following morning, when transports arrived from Shreveport to carry us to Alexandria. On the morning of the 4th, we went aboard and proceeded down the river. On our trip down the river one of our doctors took a little too much "benzine." (Notwithstanding it was war-times, there was a bar-room on every boat that plied on Red River. As a matter of course, no privates need apply.) The doctor had for his companion an ordnance-sergeant, belonging to the ——— Regiment, whom he frequently treated. While emptying their glasses, the M. D.'s conversation was about medicine, and he commenced spouting Latin, which led the bar-keeper to believe that they were both doctors. After they had had several drinks together, the "doctor's" head became dizzy; so he concluded to go to his state-room, leaving the ordnance-sergeant the bar-keeper's guest. Several soldiers were lookers-on, putting one in mind of the fable of "The fox and the grapes." One of the soldiers, more witty than the rest, approached the ordnance-sergeant, addressing him as "doctor," and asked his permission to get some whisky. The sergeant being a jolly fellow, understood the joke, and at once ordered the bar-keeper to let his men have as much whisky as they wanted; at the same time notifying the men not to get drunk, as he would be held responsible for their behavior. The commander of the regiment, seeing his men merrier than common, soon ascertained the facts, and the bar-keeper was immediately placed under arrest; and he, to save himself from being court-martialed, went in pursuit of the would-be doctor, and had him arrested. The bar-keeper was soon set at liberty. A short time afterwards this same ordnance-sergeant appeared in the *rôle* of a conscript officer, on Black River, which he carried out to perfection. Getting tired of camp-life, he strayed away from camp, for the purpose of getting a good dinner. He came across a house, ten miles from camp, and seeing no soldiers about, he alighted and asked for dinner. As dinner was getting ready for him, he got into a conversation with the host of the house. He soon discovered that he was not in the service. He informed the host of the house that he was a conscript officer. On hearing this announcement, the host begged him not to conscript him, as he had to provide for fifty soldiers' wives and widows. After dinner, the ordnance-sergeant, *alias* the conscript officer, asked what his bill for dinner was. The host replied that he would make no charge, and gave him to understand that as long as he was in the neighborhood, he was welcome to make his headquarters at his house. Thanking him for his kindness, he informed him that, as a conscript officer, it would be necessary, before he could exempt him

9

from military duty, to have the fifty soldiers' wives and widows at his house the next day, as he wanted to witness them himself. The following day he came again to dinner, when, sure enough, he beheld fifty soldiers' wives or widows present. After eating dinner, he made a patriotic speech to the women. He told them, in case they failed to get a good support from the party that he had exempted from military service, they must write to his headquarters, at Shreveport.

Shortly after our arrival at Alexandria, General Walker received orders from General Taylor to hold his division in readiness to march for Berwick Bay. This order was afterwards countermanded, owing to the fall of Port Hudson. We remained encamped near Alexandria, until the 10th day of August. In the meantime we learned that General Dick Taylor was in possession of the La Fourche country, having defeated the Federal Generals Weitzel and Dwight. After capturing Berwick Bay, he moved his forces in the direction of New Orleans, which he was confident he could capture, provided the fall of Port Hudson had not taken place so suddenly, as there were but few troops in the vicinity of New Orleans.

On the morning of the 10th we took up our line of march for Camp Green, in the piny woods, situated about twenty-five miles southwest of Alexandria; marched ten miles, and camped on Bayou La Moore, opposite the residence of Governor Moore. Owing to the poor quality of the "blue beef" we had been getting for several weeks past, some of the troops concluded to "charge the commissary," and see if there was anything more substantial than blue beef. After having been assured by some of their officers that they would get better beef in a few days, they quietly withdrew, fully convinced that the "Commissary Department of the C. S. Army" was nothing more than a myth, and had no reality but in the name.

August 11th. Marched fifteen miles, and arrived at Camp Green. During our march to this camp we passed through —I might safely say—the richest valley on earth, then verdant with rustling canes, or yellow with broad acres of ripening corn—all giving promise of an abundant harvest. The health of the troops at this camp was very good, owing, I suppose, to the *morning exercise* we took before breakfast, in the way of marching five miles. Whether the medical department advised this exercise for the health of the troops, I am unable to say. This kind of exercise was considered rest for "Walker's Greyhounds." In our retired encampment, where the long-leafed pines bent their green and palmy tops together, almost shutting out the blue sky, we seemed to have found that

> " Boundless contiguity of shade,
> Where rumor of oppression and deceit,
> Of unsuccessful or sucessful war,
> May never reach us more."

We remained encamped at Camp Green until the morning of the 31st of August. Nothing unusual transpired in camp at this place, with the exception of the 16th Infantry being ordered on picket below Alexandria.

On the morning of the 31st, when about moving camp, we learned from some parties just arrived from Alexandria, that the enemy was in possession of the town of Monroe, on the Washita River, and that 7,000 more of the enemy had crossed Bayou Macon, from the direction of Lake Providence, and were advancing in the direction of Bayou Bartholomew, while another force of them was within a few miles of Little Rock, Arkansas. After marching five miles, we camped near a running stream of water, and remained there until the morning of Sept. 2d. Shortly after our arrival in camp, Randall's Brigade took up the line of march for Harrisonburg, on the Washita River. On the morning of the 2d, we took up our line of march again, for the purpose of finding a better camp-ground. Marched eighteen miles, through the piny woods, in a zigzag form, before we struck camp.

Sept. 3d. Marched twenty miles, and camped where wood and water was in abundance. This camp was known by the name of Camp Texas; the country here was rolling land, covered with open woods. We remained at this camp

until the morning of the 5th, when we took up the line of
march for Alexandria, owing to dispatches received from
Colonel Randall, informing General Walker that the enemy
had captured Fort Beauregard, and had burned the town of
Harrisonburg to ashes.   After marching six miles on the
Alexandria road, we filed off to the left, in the direction of
Bayou Rapides, and finally struck camp, after marching twelve
miles.   We remained at this camp until the morning of the 7th,
when we left camp again ; marched six miles and camped
within two miles of Alexandria, where we remained until the
26th inst.   Shortly after our arrival in camp, we learned that
the enemy had re-crossed the Washita River, and was on their
way to the Mississippi River.   In a few days afterwards,
Randall's Brigade rejoined the balance of the division.

While encamped here, application was made by company
commanders to division headquarters to grant them the privilege of furloughing two men from a company.   Their application was referred to district headquarters, and refused.
There was much excitement and dissatisfaction in camp
After long months of severe service, enduring untold hardships
and trials, fighting several battles with a courage and bravery
which had made their name distinguished everywhere, the
only boon asked, the only favor which could have been con-
ferred on them as a recompense for their deeds, was refused.
Now they could look forward only to a life in the army until
the termination of the struggle.   The disappointment was
most bitterly felt, and it is not surprising that it found
expression in still more bitter words.

On the morning of the 26th we received marching orders
to proceed to the town of Washington, Parish of St. Landry.
Marched fourteen miles, and camped on Bayou Bœuf.

Sept. 27th.   Marched fourteen miles, passed through the
village of Cherryville, and camped two miles beyond the
village on Bayou Bœuf.

Sept. 28th.   Marched fourteen miles, and camped within
four miles of Evergreen.

Sept. 29th.   Marched fifteen miles, passed through the

villages of Evergreen and Big-Cane, and camped within four miles of the town of Washington. From the time we left Alexandria until we arrived at this place, it rained incessantly, making the roads impassable to travel. The day after our arrival in camp, about 500 Yankee prisoners passed through our camp, escorted by some of Green's Cavalry, en route for Alexandria. They were captured at the battle of the Fordoche. We remained encamped at this place until the 3d of October, when we took up the line of march for Simmsport, on the Atchafalaya Bayou. Marched seven miles, and camped near Evergreen.

Oct. 4th. Marched twelve miles, and camped at an old plantation on the Simmsport road.

Oct. 5th. Marched eighteen miles; passed through the village of Moreauville. At this place we met Mouton's Division of Louisiana troops, who were nearly all dressed in Federal uniforms that they had captured at Brashear City. They were a fine body of troops, and did good service in the Attakapas country. We arrived at camp, within four miles of Simmsport.

Oct. 6th. Early this morning we marched back again, over the road we came, for Washington. Marched eighteen miles, and camped at the same camp we occupied on the night of the 4th.

Oct. 7th. Marched fifteen miles, and camped two miles from Evergreen.

Oct. 8th. Marched eight miles, passed through Big-Cane, and camped at our old camping-ground. Immediately after our arrival in camp, the 16th Dismounted Cavalry, under command of Colonel Gregg, was sent on picket, to Morgan's Ferry, on the Atchafalaya Bayou. They returned the following evening to camp. They reported that the enemy's gun-boats in the Atchafalaya had shelled them, but without doing any harm to them. On the morning of the 10th, apparently to keep the "Greyhounds" in marching trim, we left camp at daylight, and marched seventeen miles: passed through Evergreen again, and camped on Bayou Houghpower, where we remained until the morning of the

13th, when we were on the march again. Marched eleven miles, and camped on Bayou Bœuf.

Oct. 14th. Marched seventeen miles, towards Washington, on the Bayou Bœuf road.

Oct. 15th. Marched ten miles.

Oct. 16th. Marched ten miles.

Oct. 17th. Marched three miles, and encamped alongside of Mouton's Division, and a portion of Green's Cavalry, near a little village named Moundville. Shortly after our arrival in camp, the 13th Dismounted Cavalry, commanded by Colonel Burnett, was ordered on picket, below the town of Opelousas. While encamped near Moundville we learned that the enemy, numbering about 27,000, under command of General Franklin, was encamped within seven miles of Opelousas. General Tom Green's Cavalry were daily skirmishing with them.

On the evening of the 18th, General Dick Taylor and staff arrived in camp from Alexandria, to take command in person of the entire army that was concentrated at this place. He is a son of old "Rough and Ready." He has a good record of past services under Stonewall Jackson, in Virginia. In his masterly retreat before General Banks, when that Federal commander made his rapid march from Brashear City up the Teche, ascending to Alexandria, and thence diverging to Port Hudson, time after time his troops contested the enemy's progress with barely a force of 5,000 men against 50,000 of the enemy. He abandoned Franklin, on the Teche, after a hard-fought battle, evacuating New Iberia after destroying the enemy's flotilla and defense ; falling back from Alexandria only when Admiral Porter's guns and mortars had rendered it untenable. But the numerical damage which his troops sustained was slight, and their war spirit seemed to wax rather than wane before the enemy's advance. No sooner did General Banks wheel his army Mississippi-ward than his war-spirit blazed behind him.

Owing to his arrival in camp, the troops anticipated being brought into action every day. Preparations were made by him to give the enemy a warm reception if they should advance. Many were the rumors afloat in camp about the advance of the enemy: occasionally we would hear that they were within a few miles of our camp; then, again, we would hear of their retreat.

On the morning of the 21st, the 16th Infantry, cómmanded by Colonel Flournoy, was sent to the assistence of General Green's forces, and also to relieve the 13th Infantry, which was on picket below Opelousas.

Oct. 22d. Early this morning the enemy advanced on Opelousas, driving the 16th Infantry and Green's Cavalry before them. The 16th Infantry arrived at camp in the evening. They reported that the enemy took possession of Opelousas at about 10 o'clock, A.M., and was advancing on Washington.

Oct. 23d. To-day the enemy took possession of Washington. Green's Cavalry fell back towards Moundville. The 11th Infantry, commanded by Colonel Roberts, and the 18th Infantry, commanded by Colonel King, were ordered to Moundville, to reinforce the cavalry. General Taylor formed his line of battle, in a position to sweep the road that they would be most likely to advance on; parks of artillery were planted, ready to belch forth at a moment's notice; the infantry was sheltered by a ditch in their front. Every minute seemed like an hour to us, till the ball should be opened. The enemy advanced to Moundville, but, seeing our infantry pickets, fell back to Washington, followed by our two infantry regiments, who were continually skirmishing with them. They were ably assisted by all of Green's Calvary, except his old Arizona (or Sibley's) Brigade, which was left in position on the infantry's right flank—it was commanded by Colonel Bagby,—the brigade of Partisan Rangers under Colonel Meyers, and the 2d Louisiana Cavalry, commanded by Col. Vincent. All the cavalry was under the command of General Tom Green. There were several batteries of light artillery, including the Valverde, Semm's, Edgar's, Daniels', Mesh's, and Haldeman's. The number of our forces concentrated here was about 11,000, not half the number of the enemy.

Notwithstanding the smallness of our forces, compared with the enemy, General Taylor was determined to give battle if the enemy advanced.

The two infantry regiments, reinforced by Colonel Harrison's (formerly Speight's) Regiment, the 15th Infantry, belonging to Mouton's Division, formed themselves into a brigade commanded by Colonel O. M. Roberts, and advanced on the town of Washington, accompanied by Green's Cavalry. On their arrival at Washington, the enemy was rapidly retreating across the prairie to Opelousas ; in the mean time General Taylor established his headquarters at Moundville.

Leaving Colonel Roberts' Brigade at Washington for the present, we will return to the maneuvering of the balance of the troops. Hearing of the retreat of the enemy, the division fell back about two miles to a better camp-ground. Shortly after our arrival at the new camp-ground, General Scurry arrived in camp from Texas. He was assigned to the command of the 3d Brigade, thus relieving Colonel Flournoy from command of the brigade. General Scurry was generally known by all the troops in the division, owing to the prominent position he held in the Arizona expedition, and the bravery he displayed in the battles of Valverde and Glorietta, which he fought and won; and his masterly retreat from New Mexico, gave evidence of no little skill. We believe, to him is mainly due the credit of saving, after its capture, the celebrated Valverde battery, which has made itself heard and felt by the Yankee invaders on more than one occasion. At the retaking of Galveston by General Magruder, he commanded the land forces, and distinguished himself by his deliberate coolness and skill throughout the battle.

Through respect towards him, the bands of the brigade serenaded him. After the music had ceased playing, several of the officers, and the majority of the men, called upon him to make a speech. He informed them that he despised speech-making nowadays, but in a few days expected to meet the enemy, and then he would address a few remarks to them, and he expected the troops of the 3d Brigade to respond to them as brave soldiers should do.

General Scurry's staff consisted of the following-named officers, viz. :

Major T. J. SCURRY, *Quartermaster.*
" H. H. HAYNIE, *Commissary.*
Captain S. F. A. BRYAN, *Ordnance Officer.*
" J. F. WOOFORD, *Commissary of Subsistence.*
" JAMES CLARKE, *Aid-de-Camp.*
" A. N. MILLS, *Assist. Adjt.-General.*

While remaining at this camp, a regiment from each brigade went on picket every night. We remained at this camp until the 26th inst., when we fell back some twelve miles and camped near the village of Holmesville. At this camp we witnessed the shooting of a deserter, who was making his way towards the enemy ; he was captured by our cavalry scouts. We remained encamped near Holmesville until the 8th of November. On the morning of the 3d, news was received from Colonel O. M. Roberts that his regiment and King's Regiment, in conjunction with Harrison's Regiment of Infantry and Green's Cavalry, had met the enemy at Bayou Bourbeaux, and completely routed them.

On the 6th they arrived in camp, escorting the prisoners they had captured at the battle of Bayou Bourbeaux.

CHAPTER XIX.

> " A nation's flag, a nation's flag,
> If wickedly unrolled,
> May foes in adverse battles drag
> Its every fold from fold.
> But in the cause of liberty,
> Guard it till death or victory ;
> Look you, you guard it well !
> No saint or king has tomb so proud
> *As he whose flag becomes his shroud.*"

HE night of the 23d of October, 1863, found the brigade of infantry commanded by Colonel O. M. Roberts (consisting of the 11th, 15th, and 18th Regiments of Texas Infantry) bivouacked near the town of Washington, St. Landry Parish, Louisiana. It was a most uncomfortable night—cold, dark, and rainy. The troops, greatly wearied by the day's march, lay down to sleep, supperless. The following day they expected to meet the enemy in battle. But the ever-vigilant " Texas Cavalier," General Tom Green, notified them the following day " to abide their time " until he had made all the necessary arrangements for a decisive battle. They remained encamped near Washington, awaiting orders. General Green's cavalry were employed in skirmishing with the enemy, who were encamped some eight miles southeast of the town of Opelousas.

On the evening of the 2d November, Colonel Roberts received orders from General Green to report with his brigade at his headquarters, near Opelousas, on the following morning.

After a tiresome and laborious tramp, they marched through the town of Opelousas to the tune of "Dixie," as daylight was dawning, on the morning of the 3d. They halted near General Green's headquarters to cook breakfast. After breakfast, a general advance of the cavalry and infantry forces was ordered by General Green. On arriving within three miles of the enemy's camp they halted to rest. While the troops were resting, General Green held a consultation with his field-officers, after informing them that General Dick Taylor had ordered him to attack the enemy's rearguard, then encamped on the west bank of Bayou Bourbeaux (Boggy Creek), eight miles south of Opelousas. Close by the enemy's camp was a skirt of timber, about six hundred yards wide, running through the prairie. A large body of the enemy, consisting of part of the 13th Army Corps, under command of General Burbridge, were encamped: their forces consisted of about five or six thousand veteran troops of the Northwest. They were the rearguard of Franklin's army, who were encamped four miles further south, on Carrion-Crow Bayou. The road from Opelousas to the enemy's camp led southward, along the western side of the skirt of timber, for a mile or more, and then turned abruptly eastward through the skirt of timber and across the bayou, where there were several bridges, and then on southward, through the prairie, to Carrion-Crow Bayou. The Federal rearguard camps were situated about two or three hundred yards south from the point where the road turned eastward to cross the bayou.

The plan of the battle adopted by General Green and his officers was as follows: Colonel O. M. Roberts, with his infantry brigade, was to move southward upon the enemy, under shelter of the timber, between the bayou and the road, driving back the pickets and outposts. The brigade of Partisan Rangers, under command of Colonel Majors, were to exhibit themselves in line of battle on the prairie eastward, in sight of the enemy, so as to attract their attention in that direction. Colonel Bagby's brigade of cavalry, accompanied by the Valverde Battery (I believe) and General Green, was to advance from the northwest, towards the enemy's camp; dismount, give the signal, by firing cannon, for the fight to commence, and, as soon as practicable, form a line on the right of the infantry. Colonel Majors' rangers were to advance upon the enemy, so as to fall in on the right of Bagby's brigade, and to act in conjunction with or in support of the dismounted cavalry and infantry, in what was intended to be an almost simultaneous concentration and dash of all of Green's forces upon the enemy's camp. The plan was then and there formed *impromptu* by General Green, who, when asked by one of his field-officers, "How many of the enemy do we attack to-day?" replied, "I do not know the number, but I do know that there are not too many for us to attack." (We had no reserve force.) The officers having been informed of their respective duties, and having made the arrangements and preparations for a battle which was then certain to come off, each brigade moved off to assume the position and perform the part assigned to it. The infantry brigade was formed in line of battle, in the following manner: The 15th T. V. Infantry, commanded by Colonel James H. Harrison, took their position on the right of the brigade; the 18th T. V. Infantry, commanded by Colonel King, was assigned the center, and the 11th T. V. Infantry, commanded by Lieutenant-Colonel James H. Jones, took their position on the left of the brigade. Very soon our infantry skirmishers came upon our cavalry pickets, who were amusing themselves, as it were, in shooting down a wide lane, one and a half miles long, at the enemy's pickets, who were firing back in return. The infantry skirmishers continued to advance, followed by the brigade. Majors' cavalry had already gone on towards their position, and here Bagby's cavalry turned off obliquely to the right. General Green and staff followed after. General Green, beholding his cavalry pickets wasting their ammunition without any effect, at once ordered Colonel Roberts to clear the lane. That heroic and indefatigable officer, who was on his way home to recover his broken health, hearing that his regiment was ordered to the front, hurriedly returned to lead his gallant men to victory. Though very pale and feeble, his dark eye was lit up by martial music; his frail form appeared full of vigor and vitality. Imagine the old veteran colonel of Walker's Division at the head of his column, with his sword drawn, gallantly leading his men to victory! Soon the lane was cleared of the enemy, driving them before him. After getting through the lane, he formed his men in line of battle, in the edge of the timber, and moved steadily forward, driving the enemy's outposts into their camp. Seeing some trees cut down near the camp, he anticipated that probably the enemy might have some masked batteries behind the trees; he halted his brigade a few moments, until he could learn the facts. Hearing from his sharpshooters, who were some distance in advance of his brigade, that no artillery was placed behind the trees, he ordered his brigade to advance in the direction of the enemy's camp. Nearing the enemy's camp, he beheld them in line of battle, ready to give the Texans a warm reception on their arrival. Nearer his brigade advances, showing a bold and solid front to the enemy. His sharpshooters fire, and stop to reload again; then moving forward, nearing their camp, they meet with a large body of the enemy. Upon which they fall back gradually, and rejoin their command. Soon the war-worn old veteran gave the command, in his sonorous voice, "Charge them, boys!" which was quickly done, notwithstanding the enemy was formed in a ravine, anticipating a charge from the Texans. They placed their artillery so as to bear on our troops, from the edge of their camp. Fortunately, their shots passed over our men, doing no harm. In the meantime a large body of the enemy's cavalry had been forming to charge our infantry in their rear, by forcing the passage of the bridges, in opposition to a force under Major Carroway, of the 11th T. V. Infantry, who had been sent there by Colonel Roberts, aided by a cavalry company, under Captain Jack Waterhouse. Now the battle raged in all its fury. All of the field-officers, except Colonel Roberts, dismounted and led their commands with undaunted firmness. The voices of the brave officers, encouraging their men, could be heard, loud and distinct, amidst the crash and roar of a continued fire of small arms and artillery. Men fell thick and fast on both sides. Here it was that the gallant Captain Stillwell, of the 11th T. V. Infantry, fell mortally wounded, and Captain Richard Coke, the "nonpareil" officer of the 15th T. V. Infantry, while in the act of leading his men, was seriously wounded. The dashing Captain Christian, Adjutant of the 11th T. V. Infantry, was also seriously wounded; and the old veteran commander, Colonel Roberts, had his horse shot while cheering on his troops. The same misfortune happened to two of his acting aid-de-camps. Captain J. E. Hart, of General Green's Staff, and Major Carroway, who had just arrived from the bridge they were ordered to defend, informed Colonel Roberts, personally, that unless they got reinforcements immediately it would be doubtful whether they would be able to hold the bridge longer than fifteen minutes, as the enemy's cavalry was preparing to carry it by storm. Colonel Roberts informed them that, under the circumstances, he could not withdraw any of his forces then engaged with the enemy, to aid or assist them; he would communicate the facts to General Green as soon as possible ; in the meantime giving them to understand that the bridge must be held by them at all hazards, and that he was then fighting the enemy under great disadvantage. Colonel Roberts expected that all of General Green's troops would attack the enemy about the same time. From some cause the cavalry did not arrive until about fifteen minutes after the infantry was engaged. Those two heroic officers returned to their command, determined to hold the bridge at any sacrifice. It was certain that unless Colonel Roberts should be reinforced, his brigade would be lost; but, as the column of cavalry dashed madly forward, led by the heroic Majors and Bagby, and came in range of the enemy, their guns vomited among them a storm of bullets. The infantry firing ceases a few minutes. The command is given: "Fix bayonets! forward! double-quick ! " when the whole line, in perfect order, as if on parade, responded by a simultaneous shout, and rushed upon the enemy, driving them "pell-mell" over their camp-ground. With their lines broken, and they fleeing in disorder, the cavalry sweeps down upon their flanks, giving time for the infantry to breathe a few moments. But the ever-keen eye of the infantry brigade beheld part of the enemy's cavalry still in his rear, and still held in check by Major Carroway and Captain Hart. He gave the command, "Right-about face; forward march!" Few of the officers or men anticipating any further danger from the enemy, they kept talking at the top of their voices, as they advanced over the ground they had previously charged over. Soon they came upon the enemy's cavalry, who were killed or taken prisoners in a few minutes' time. So sanguine were the enemy of success that they formed a line covering the entire length of our rear, and were busily engaged in running off stragglers and wounded men that had fallen out of our lines, and were quietly awaiting our defeat, to capture our forces in their retreat. Just at that point of time General Green appeared on the field, much surprised in seeing the position of our infantry, until it was explained to him why the infantry brigade was turned in that direction. Our artillery did good service across the bayou, in firing upon the scattered troops of the enemy, as they were retreating southward across the prairie. All this time, however, the arms of Majors' and Bagby's brigades were resounding in the distance, as they pursued the retreating foe. Some of the enemy's artillery that escaped returned the fire, and an artillery duel ensued, which effected but little on either side, and ceased in an hour, when our forces were ordered back to camp, near Opelousas. The enemy came out in force, and their cavalry followed our forces several miles towards our camp.

This battle, from the first to the last firing, lasted fully three hours. It is impossible, in a short sketch of this kind, to do justice to the gallant conduct of the officers and men. It would afford the writer great pleasure to do so. Our forces lost, in the infantry brigade, twenty-one killed; wounded,

eighty-two; taken prisoners, thirty-eight. Our cavalry and
artillery lost in killed, three; wounded, twenty. We captured about six hundred prisoners, and killed and wounded
about two hundred. Most of the prisoners were captured by
the cavalry, and, doubtless, many feats of bravery were performed by them on that occasion, which would deserve a commendable notice if they could be detailed.

OFFICIAL REPORT OF THE BATTLE.

The Major-General commanding congratulates Brig.-Gen-
eral Green, and the troops under his command, upon the
brilliant feat of arms at the Bayou Bourbeaux, on the 3d inst.
A force greatly inferior to the enemy drove him from all his
positions, taking and destroying the camp of the 13th Army
Corps, of the United States army, and bringing off from the
field over 600 prisoners, including many commissioned officers,
seven regimental flags, and a considerable number of small
arms. The veterans of General Green's Division proved
themselves, on the occasion, worthy of the reputation won on
other fields. The little brigade of infantry, consisting of
Roberts' 11th, Speight's 15th (commanded by Lieut.-Colonel
Harrison), and King's 18th—the whole led by Colonel O. M.
Roberts, and not carrying over 950 muskets into action—
charged and broke the enemy's right wing, under a heavy fire
of musketry and cross-fire of artillery, and routed and dispersed a large cavalry force, which endeavored to pierce
their lines. The number of their killed and wounded attests
the spirit and gallantry with which this brigade performed
their share of the work of this memorable day. With equal
spirit and like success, Majors' and Bagby's Brigades, the
latter including Waller's Battalion, forced the enemy's left
and center, and compelled them to abandon the field.

For the blow thus vigorously dealt the enemy, the Major-
General commanding tenders his sincere thanks to Brig.-
General Green, to Colonels Majors, Bagby, and Roberts, and
to all the officers and men who participated in the action.

(Signed,)   Major-General TAYLOR.

GENERAL TAYLOR'S CONGRATULATORY ADDRESS TO THE
TROOPS OF "WALKER'S DIVISION."

Major-General WALKER :

GENERAL,—The Major-General commanding directs me to
say, in addition to what he has said in his " Official Report "
of the battle of Bourbeaux, that the conduct of the two regiments from your division, and at present under General
Green's command, has responded to his highest hopes and
expectations. They pressed the veterans of Vicksburg with
a coolness, resolution, and perseverance that was irresistible.
Their loss is, in Colonel Roberts' Regiment, four killed, and
in Colonel King's, ten, with a proportionate number of
wounded. The men are in cheerful spirits, and eagerly anticipate dealing a second blow.

The Major-General commanding presents his congratula-
tions on the conduct of your men.

(Signed,)   R. TAYLOR, Major-Gen. Commdg.
                    —— LEVY, A. A. General.

The day after the battle, the enemy having possession of
the battle-field, our men were buried in the prairie, near the
battle-field. About a week afterwards, Lieut. Airhuit, of the
11th Regiment of Infantry, with a detail of men, raised a
large mound of earth over them, which still stands, covered
with Bermuda grass,—an honored monument, humble though
it be, to the memory of the brave Texans who, on the bright
November day, nobly gave their lives to their country.

The court-house in Opelousas was made a hospital for our
wounded, and there occurred a scene that melted into tears
the most obdurate. It was the sympathy of the women.
The ladies of Opelousas and its vicinity, young and old,
Catholic and Protestant, came crowding in, and waited upon
our men just as if they had been their husbands and brothers.
Long will be remembered with heartfelt gratitude, by the
Texas soldiers, the appreciative kindness and sympathy of the
Louisiana ladies. About ten days after the battle, the enemy

10

embarked on board of their transports at Morganzia Landing, for New Orleans.

THE FEDERAL REPORT OF THE BATTLE OF BOURBEAUX.

Major WILLIAM HOFFMAN, *A. A. General of the* 13th *Army Corps :*

MAJOR,—I enclose herewith report of Brig.-General Burbridge, in regard to the battle of Bourbeaux, on the 3d inst. On the morning of the 1st inst., by order of Major-General Franklin, the troops of the 3d Division were ordered to march and encamp at Carrion-Crow Bayou, while General Burbridge, with the troops under his command, was ordered to march down the Teche, and cross it, and move by way of Grand Coteau, where the road from Vermilion to Opelousas crosses Muddy Bayou, about three miles from Carrion-Crow Bayou, in the direction of Opelousas, and go into camp there, on the north side of the bayou. Colonel Fonda, with about 500 mounted infantry, was also ordered to encamp near him. The troops all moved and went into camp, as ordered. The 19th Corps, on the same day, moved back to Carrion-Crow Bayou, and on the following day to Vermilionville, leaving the 3d and 1st Brigades of the 4th Division of the 13th Corps, to hold the positions before named. The position of the troops, on the morning of the 3d inst., was then as follows : Brig.-General Burbridge, with one brigade of the 4th Division, about 1,200 strong, with one 6-gun battery of 10-pounder Parrotts, and Colonel Fonda, with about 500 mounted infantry and a section of Nimm's Battery, on the north side of Muddy Bayou ; and the 3d Division, General McGinnis commanding, 3,000 strong, with one battery, at Carrion-Crow Bayou, three miles in the rear of General Burbridge. The two bayous before named run in an easterly direction, nearly parallel with each other, and along the stream there is a belt of timber, about 150 yards in width, while between the two is smooth, level prairie. To the right of General Burbridge's position was an extensive and dense tract of woods, while on his front and left, the country was high, open prairie. About 9 o'clock in the morning of the 3d, I received an order from General Burbridge, saying that the enemy had shown himself in some force. I immediately ordered out the 3d Division, and just as I had got them into line, I received another note from General Burbridge, saying that the enemy had entirely disappeared. Ordering the division to remain under arms, I rode rapidly to the front, and learning from General Burbridge and Colonel Fonda that all was quiet, and that such troops of the enemy as had shown themselves had all fallen back, I started to return to my headquarters, near the 3d Division. When I had arrived at about midway between the two camps, I heard a rapid cannonade. Sending two members of my staff to the rear, to bring up the 3d Division, I rode back to the front, and, crossing the bayou and passing through the timber to the open ground, I soon discovered that we were assailed with terrible energy, by an overwhelming force, in front and on both flanks. Many of the troops had broken, and were scattered over the field, and the utter destruction or capture of the whole force seemed imminent.

The attack on the right, through the woods, was made by infantry, and though our troops fought most gallantly on that wing, they were compelled to give way before overwhelming numbers. Here it was that we lost most of our men in killed and wounded. The 23d Wisconsin, Colonel Gubby commanding; 96th Ohio, Lieutenant-Colonel Brown commanding; and 60th Indiana, commanded by Captain Gatzler; and 17th Ohio Battery, Captain Rice commanding, fought with the greatest desperation, holding the enemy in check for a considerable space of time, but for which our entire train, with our artillery, would have been captured. As it was, General Burbridge was enabled to bring off every wagon, and all government property, with the exception of one 10-pounder Parrott gun, which was captured just as it was crossing the bayou, the horses having been shot. The bringing off of the section of Nimms' Battery commanded by Lieutenant Marland, after the regiment sent to its support had surrendered,

extorted the admiration of every beholder. While the fight
was proceeding, the 3d Division came up on a double-quick,
but by the time they had reached the middle of the prairie,
and one and a half miles from the scene of action, General
Burbridge's command had been driven entirely out of the
woods, while the rebel cavalry, in great force, charged through
the narrow belt of timber on the left, and were coming down
on his rear. By this time the 3d Division had come within
range, formed in line, and commenced shelling them, which
immediately checked their further advance, while General
Burbridge, who had again got his guns into position, opened
a cross-fire upon them, when the whole force of the enemy
retreated to the cover of the woods. Our whole force was
deployed in line of battle, and moved as rapidly as possible
through the woods, driving the enemy out of it, who retreated
rapidly. I moved the troops up on their line of retreat about
one and a half miles, while the cavalry pursued about three
miles. My men being brought up at a double-quick, were
very much exhausted, and it was not possible to pursue
further. Our losses are 26 killed, 120 wounded, and 566
missing. The loss of the enemy, in killed, was about 60;
number of wounded not known, as they carried all but 12 off
the ground; but wounded officers, who were taken prisoners,
represent the number of wounded as being very large. We
took 65 prisoners.

Brigadier-General McGinnis, being very ill, was not able to
be on the field. The troops of the division behaved admirably under the command of Brigadier-General Cameron, of
the 1st, and Colonel Slack, of the 2d Brigade. The action
of General Burbridge was gallant and judicious, from the
time I first saw him until the close of the engagement. The
conduct of the 67th Regiment, Indiana Infantry, was inex-
plicable, and their surrender can only be attributed to the
incompetency or cowardice of the commanding officer. They
had not a single man killed. Our mounted force, under
Colonels Fonda and Robinson, though very small, behaved
very handsomely. I left at Carrion-Crow Bayou, to hold

that position, three regiments of the 3d Division, namely, the 11th Indiana, 20th Wisconsin, and 24th Iowa, with one section of artillery. It was fortunate that I did so, for while the fight was proceeding with General Burbridge's command, Colonel Beylor, of the 1st Texas Mounted Rifles, swept around on our left, and attacked the camp at Carrion-Crow Bayou; but they were driven off with a loss of three killed; we lost none. I refer particularly to the report of General Burbridge for the names of those deserving honorable mention. On the 4th inst. the enemy sent in a flag of truce, proposing to give up such of our wounded as they had, not having the means to take care of them. I sent for and received forty-seven. They refused to give up our wounded officers— among them, Colonel Gubby, of the 23d Wisconsin, a most gallant and meritorious officer. Though wounded, I am pleased to learn that his wound is not severe, and that all our prisoners are well treated. As to the force of the enemy engaged, opinions are conflicting; but, from the best data I have, I judge them to have been from six to seven thousand, the whole under the command of Brigadier-General Green.

(Signed,)   C. C. WASHBURNE,

Major-General Commanding.

CHAPTER XX.

ON THE MARCH.—EXPEDITION ACROSS THE ATCHAFALAYA BAYOU.

BOUT noontime, on the 8th November, we took up our line of march for Simmsport. Marched ten miles, and camped near the town of Evergreen.

Nov. 9th. Passed through Evergreen, and marched fourteen miles.

Nov. 10th. Marched sixteen miles; passed by Moreauville and Simmsport, and camped on the banks of the Atchafalaya Bayou. The engineer corps, under command of Captain Boyd, were employed in constructing a pontoon bridge across the bayou. While awaiting the completion of the bridge, many of the troops employed their leisure time in fishing. On the morning of the 12th, the troops crossed the bayou on flat-boats, the bridge not having been completed. About sunset all the troops had crossed. We camped for the night near Colonel Simms' residence, opposite Simmsport.

Nov. 13th. Marched ten miles, in the direction of the Mississippi River; camped on Bayou Letsworth, within four miles of the river. We remained at this camp until the 20th inst. On the evening of the 14th, a detail of twenty-four men from each regiment in the division went on picket, at the mouth of Red River. The following day, the pioneer corps, accompanied by the 8th Infantry (Colonel Young's Regiment), and Daniels', Edgar's, Halderman's, Semms' and West's Batteries of Light Artillery followed after. During the night they took their positions on the banks of the river. The morning of the 16th dawned to behold the river-bank bristling with cannon, ready to open fire on any of the enemy's "craft" that should attempt to run the "gauntlet." In the afternoon a transport made her appearance, and was signaled from the gun-boats. She "about shipped," and returned up the river again. Shortly after the transport left, the gun-boat Cherokee hoisted anchor, and steamed down the river, on a reconnoitering tour. After passing our lowermost battery, she returned to her mooring again, satisfied, I suppose, that the banks of the river were clear of "rebels." Our artillery officers, having received orders not to waste any ammunition in firing at gun-boats, but to pay particular attention to transports, allowed the gun-boat to pass by unmolested. Nothing worthy of note transpired in camp, except the usual changes of the different regiments relieving each other on picket, until the morning of the 18th, when along came a transport loaded with troops. When opposite our batteries, she rounded to and tied up, on the opposite bank of the river, waiting, I suppose, until the heavy fog on the river should clear off. Morning at last dawned, and preparations were made to open fire on her. Three companies of the 16th Infantry were ordered to take position on the river-bank, with instructions to open fire on her as soon as the artillery fired. When about ready to leave her mooring, our batteries opened fire on her, tearing her from stem to stern. The infantry fired some thirty rounds before she floated down the river. One of her wheel-houses was torn away; the stove in the kitchen was upset by a cannon-ball; and, from the upsetting of the stove, the kitchen or cook-house caught fire, doing considerable damage. The gun-boat Cherokee soon came to her assistance, and escorted her down the river.

From New Orleans papers, received in camp shortly afterwards, we learned that the name of the transport was the Black Hawk. After the return of the gun-boat Cherokee, she commenced shelling our troops, but without doing any damage. While the cannonading was going on, a portion of Mouton's Louisiana Division arrived, in time to participate in the frolic. They seemed fully determined not to allow the Texas troops to have all the fun. As soon as they had taken their position, our troops returned to camp on Bayou Letsworth, excepting our artillery, who still remained to assist Mouton's troops. During the evening, five gun-boats made their appearance; black clouds of smoke came belching forth from their chimneys. When opposite our batteries, they rounded to and formed for action. The signal being given by the Cherokee, "Rats, to your holes!" was the cry among the troops. Broadside after broadside was given without dislodging our troops. Apparently to change their programme, they changed their position to cross-firing. During the cannonading, our troops did not return the fire, having no ammunition to waste at random. The cannonading continued for about three hours. Our loss was one man killed. He was killed while playing cards, near the top of the levee. A round shot ricochets, and strikes him, with a dull, heavy sound, and bounds over him. He is stone dead. The two men on each side of him, playing the game with him, drop their cards, rise up, lift the corpse, lay it down under a tree in the rear, cover his face with his blanket, come back to the old place, lie down on the same fated spot, and grasp their muskets to avenge his death, without saying a word! How brave, how cool, how dauntless these men are! One of the gun-boats, more daring, probably, than the rest, concluded to come close up to the river-bank, to see, I suppose, whether the rebels had skedaddled. One of our batteries opened fire on her, with grape and canister, tearing away her wheel-house, and otherwise damaging her, thus compelling her to withdraw in a hurry. Satisfied, I suppose, that she had experienced enough from the rebels, several of the other gun-boats came to her assistance, and towed her to her anchorage, at the mouth of Red River. On the morning of the 19th, the 19th Regiment of Infantry, commanded by Colonel Wash. Jones, in company with Daniels' Battery, proceeded down the river-bank to Morganzia Landing, about twenty miles distant, to watch a better opportunity for transports. On their arrival at Morganzia they placed their battery so as to sweep the river either way. The enemy seemed to be aware of their movements, as all of their transports were escorted by gun-boats. On the morning of the 20th, the division took up the line of march, in the direction of Morganzia Landing. After marching fifteen miles, we arrived at camp. We remained at this camp until the evening of the 30th, when we took up the line of march back again to our old camp-ground, on Bayou Letsworth. During the march, the 19th Infantry rejoined the command. We encamped at our old camping-ground over night. The following morning, December 1st, we took up the line of march for Plaquemine, a small town on the Mississippi River. Marched twenty miles down Bayou Letsworth, and camped.

Dec. 2d. Marched ten miles. Our march to-day was principally through a cane-brake.

Dec. 3d. Marched eighteen miles. Passed by the old battle-field of Bayou Fordoche. We beheld several corpses exposed to the rays of the sun, some of them apparently only half buried. A detail of our men was left, in charge of an officer, to put the graves in proper order. After passing the battle-field some two miles, we camped on Bayou Gross Tete, where we remained until the morning of the 8th. This section of country might have been termed the " Paradise " of Louisiana before the war ; but alas, what a change has befallen it now ! The houses are all deserted ; occasionally you meet with a few old, faithful negroes, left by their owners to take care of their place until their return. Here you can behold mansion after mansion, including costly sugar-houses, now going to decay. While we were encamped here we learned that the enemy was aware of our programme. The garrison at Plaquemine was heavily reinforced, and, in addition to the reinforcements of the garrison, there were thirteen gun-boats, at the mouth of Plaquemine Bayou. General Walker, believing it would be folly on his part to undertake to capture a place which, even if successful, it would be impossible for him to hold, declined making the attempt ; consequently, we about-faced and marched back in the direction of Morgan's Ferry, on the Atchafalaya Bayou. After marching eight miles, we arrived at camp. While on the march, the 16th Infantry, commanded by Colonel Flournoy, and Captain

Daniels' Battery, were sent on an expedition to the Mississippi River, to interrupt the passage of any transports plying on the river. The day after their arrival, the steamer Van Pool made her appearance. When opposite our battery, she was summoned to surrender. Not complying with the request, our troops opened fire on her, killing the pilot, and wounding the captain and several other parties on board. She finally made her escape, considerably the " worse for wear." After the transport got beyond the reach of our guns, our troops withdrew from the river to rejoin their command. Soon after they left, three gun-boats came down the river, and commenced shelling where they supposed the rebels were.

On the morning of the 9th we continued our march. Marched twenty-one miles. The weather commenced to be squally ; the rain fell in torrents ; many of the troops were unable to get to camp ; our train and artillery had to remain in the swamps, the roads through them being impassable in the black darkness of a cloudy night. Their situation was by no means an agreeable one.

Dec. 10th. Marched ten miles, and arrived at Morgan's Ferry ; the rain was pouring down in torrents. The troops quickly put up their blankets in tent form, on their arrival, for the purpose of making a shelter for the night. The roads were knee-deep in mud, oftentimes holding the men fast, who, in the struggle, left their shoes behind, or fell into some hole, out of which they were dragged coated over like a pie-crust. The artillery got stuck in the mud, and the men had to drag it out. Sometimes rider and horse would roll into deep ruts. They were soon up again, the men and horses looking like some strange animals covered with a coat of mud-mail.

CHAPTER XXI.

GENERAL WALKER'S REPORT, GIVING HIS REASONS FOR FAILING TO ATTACK PLAQUEMINE.

Major W. M. LEVY, *A. A. & I. General :*

MAJOR,—In order to carry out what I supposed to be the wishes of the Major-General commanding the district, that I should attack the enemy at the town of Plaquemine, I left the mouth of Red River on the morning of the 1st of December, and, after much difficulty in getting our artillery and train over the interior roads rendered necessary to take in order to avoid the banks of the Mississippi, my advance reached this point (Lavina) last night. Previous to my reaching here, my information in regard to the strength of the enemy's force at Plaquemine, and the nature of the defenses, natural and artificial, led me to hope it possible that, by rapid movements, we could carry the place by a *coup de main*, before the enemy could receive intelligence of our designs, or before he could receive reinforcements. At this point, however, I have received the most exact and entirely reliable information in regard to the strength of the garrison, and the nature of the defenses. In addition, I am well assured that a spy of the enemy yesterday afternoon carried him the information of our movement, which leaves no longer a hope that we will be able to effect a surprise. We are still forty miles from the point to be attacked. There is an absolute certainty that we will meet such resistance as will render the capture of Plaquemine, if not impracticable, only possible at an expense of life that we cannot afford. I am fortified in this opinion by the unanimous concurrence of Brigadier-General Mouton, commanding division, and his brigade commanders, and the brigade commanders of my own division. The circumstances of my position and the great necessity to preserve from useless sacrifice the only force left us for the defense of Western Louisiana, compelled me to abandon the attempt on Plaquemine, a position of no strategic importance, and to content myself for the present with opposing such obstacles as may be in my power to the navigation of the Mississippi River.

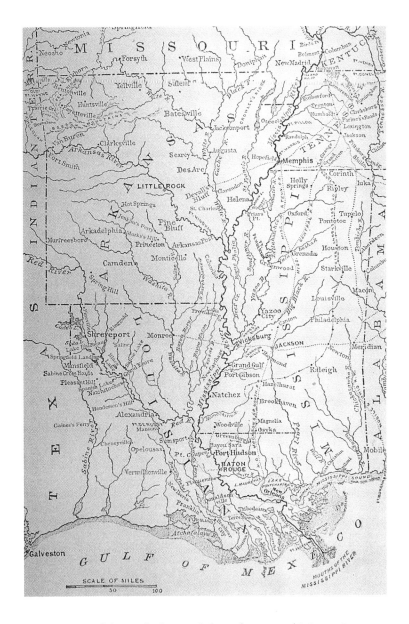

Map of the Red River and the Arkansas and Missouri
Campaigns of 1864
Plate 1

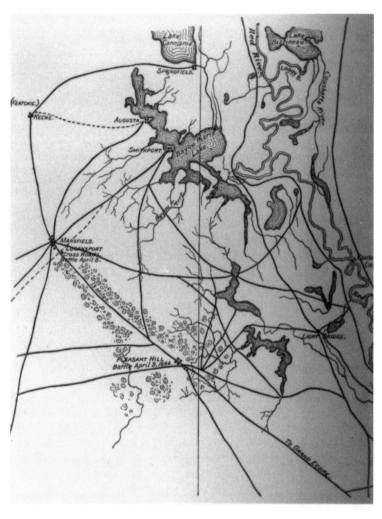

Map of Vicinity of Mansfield and Pleasant Hill
Plate 2

General Edwin Kirby Smith, C.S.A.
Commander of the Trans-Mississippi Department
Plate 3

Lieutenant General Richard H. Taylor, C.S.A.
Commander of the District of West Louisiana
Plate 4

Lieutenant-General
T.H. Holmes, C.S.A.
Predecessor to General
Smith as Commander of
the Trans-Mississippi
Department.
Plate 5

Brigadier General
Henry E. McCulloch,
C.S.A. First
commander of the Texas
Infantry Division, later
commanded a Brigade
under General Walker.
Plate 6

Major General John G. Walker, C.S.A.
Commander of the Texas Infantry Division
Plate 7

Major General Thomas J. Churchill, C.S.A.
Commander of the Arkansas Division
Plate 8

Brigadier General
Thomas N. Waul, C.S.A.
Brigade Commander of
Walker's Division
Plate 9

Brigadier General
C.J. Polignac, C.S.A.
Brigade Commander of
Walker's Texas Division
Plate 10

Brigadier General
William R. Scurry, C.S.A.
Brigade Commander
under General Walker,
killed at battle of
Jenkins' Ferry.
Plate 11

Brigadier General James
M. Howes, C.S.A.,
Brigade Commander
under General Walker.
Plate 12

Brigadier General Thomas Green, C.S.A. Cavalry Division Commander, killed at battle of Blair's Landing.
Plate 13

Major General John A. Wharton, C.S.A. Cavalry Division Commander, murdered in Houston, Texas, on April 6, 1865.
Plate 14

Major General John H. Forney, C.S.A. Succeeded Walker as Commander of the Texas Division in late 1864.
Plate 15

Major General Simon B. Buckner, C.S.A. Chief of Staff to General E. Kirby Smith.
Plate 16

Brigadier General
Hamilton P. Bee, C.S.A.
Cavalry Division
Brigade Commander
Plate 17

Brigadier General
Richard Waterhouse,
C.S.A.
Succeeded Scurry as
Brigade Commander
Plate 18

Plate 20

Plate 19

Plate 21

Top left: Colonel Edward Clark, Commander of the 14th Texas Infantry, Governor of Texas Mar.-Nov. 1861. Top right: Colonel Oran M. Roberts, commander of the 11th Texas Infantry, Governor of Texas 1879-1883. Bottom: Colonel Richard B. Hubbard, Commander of the 22d Texas Infantry, Governor of Texas 1876-1879.

Plate 22

Plate 23

Top left: Colonel George M. Flournoy, 16th Texas Infantry Commander. Top Right: Colonel Overton Young, 12th Texas Infantry Commander. Bottom: Captain William M. Edgar, Artillery Battery Commander.

Plate 24

Major General Nathaniel P. Banks, U.S.A.
Commander of the Union Army in the Red River Campaign
Plate 25

Major General Andrew J. Smith,
U.S.A. Commander of Elements
of XVI and XVII Corps.
Plate 26

Major General Cuvier Grover,
U.S.A. Division Commander.

Plate 27

Major General T.E.G. Ransom,
U.S.A. Commander of a
detachment of the XIII Corps.
Plate 28

Major General J.A. Mower
Division Commander in
XVI Corps.
Plate 29

Major General Frederick Steele,
U.S.A. Commander of
Department of Arkansas.
Plate 30

Major General Edward R.S.
Canby, U.S.A. Successor to
General Banks.
Plate 31

Major General W.B. Franklin,
U.S.A. Commander of the XIX
Army Corps.
Plate 32

Brigadier General Albert L. Lee,
U.S.A. Cavalry Division
Commander.
Plate 33

Rear Admiral David Dixon Porter U.S.N.
Commander of the Mississippi Flotilla
Plate 34

U.S. Fleet in Red River at Alexandria, Louisiana
Plate 35

Joseph Bailey
Plate 36

Bailey's Dam
Plate 37

Photo credits:

Battles & Leaders, ed. by R.U. Johnson and C.C. Buel: frontispiece, *plates* 1, 5, 10, 16, 26, 27, 28, 29, 30, 31, 32, 34, 36, 37

Encyclopedia of the New West, ed. by J. H. Brown: *plates* 8, 21

General Kirby Smith by A.H. Noll: *plate* 3

History of Southwest Texas: *plate* 24

Indian Wars and Pioneers of Texas by J.H. Brown: *plate* 6

Official Records of Union and Confederate Navies: *plates* 2, 35

Texas In the War 1861-1865, ed. by H.B. Simpson: plates 11, 13, 14, 18, 19, 20, 22, 23

Lawrence T. Jones, III: *plates* 7, 9, 12

Michael Parrish: *plates* 4, 17

Richard Whitmire: *plates* 15, 25, 33

CHAPTER XXII.

RECROSSING THE ATCHAFALAYA BAYOU.—MARCH TO BAYOU DE GLAIZE
AND MARKSVILLE.—FORTIFYING AT YELLOW BAYOU.—SPENDING
CHRISTMAS IN CAMP.—PREACHING IN CAMP.—OPENING OF THE NEW
YEAR.—MATCH DRILL.—GENERAL HAWS LEAVES THE DIVISION.—
ARRIVAL OF GENERAL WAUL.—COTTON SELLING.—OPERATIONS OF
SCURRY'S BRIGADE.—LANDING OF THE ENEMY AT SIMMSPORT.

N the morning of December 11, 1863, we commenced
re-crossing the Atchafalaya, at Morgan's Ferry.
After all the troops had crossed, including Mouton's
Division, we camped two miles from the ferry. The rain commenced pouring down in torrents. We built huge fires, and
remained standing by them all night. It was impossible to
lie down, as the camp-ground was entirely covered with water.

Dec. 12th. Left camp at sunrise, without any breakfast.
Marched ten miles, through the bottoms, and camped on the
bayou bank.

Dec. 13th. Marched seventeen miles. Passed through Simmsport, and camped on Bayou De Glaize, about two miles and a
half north of Simmsport. Soon after our arrival in camp, the
weather cleared off. We remained at this camp until the
morning of the 15th, when Haws' and Randall's Brigades
were ordered to Marksville, there to go into winter quarters.
Although late in the season, it was better late than never.
Scurry's Brigade remained behind for the protection of the
Atchafalaya country. After the arrival of Haws' and Randall's
Brigades at their camp, near Marksville, they commenced
preparations to protect themselves from the winter's blast, by
building huts and making their quarters comfortable.

Scurry's Brigade was more fortunate, in having better quar-

ters than Haws' and Randall's Brigades. The day after the
withdrawal of Haws' and Randall's Brigades, Scurry's Brigade moved from their camp on Bayou De Glaize, to the Norwood plantation, one mile north of Bayou De Glaize, where
they took possession of some negro cabins (then vacated),
making themselves perfectly at home. A company from each
regiment in the brigade was sent on picket at Simmsport, to
protect the pontoon bridge in the Atchafalaya Bayou,
and to be on the lookout for the enemy. Nothing worthy of
notice transpired in camp until the morning of the 23d, when
Scurry's Brigade crossed the Atchafalaya Bayou, and proceeded in the direction of the Mississippi River, in order to
capture a foraging party of the enemy that was playing general havoc along the bank of the Mississippi River. The 16th
Infantry, commanded by Colonel Flournoy, was sent in advance of the brigade to ascertain the strength of the enemy.
They advanced within a few miles of the enemy's camp.
Night overtaking them, they slept on their arms during the
night.

We will accompany a regiment going out on picket, in order
to give our readers an idea of how the men got on. Their
blankets are thrown over their shoulders; their guns are clean
and bright; they take up the line of march in the direction of
the enemy. Arriving within a few miles of the enemy, they
halt and establish their reserve posts, while, further on, they
place their pickets, with strict orders to keep a sharp lookout.
It was night; the men had to scramble through the brush and
trees, through ravines, to gain the different stations.

Thus, our pickets in front quietly and noiselessly keep their
posts. They are relieved every two hours, and go back to
join their commands, who are grouped around a blazing fire
in some ravine, sheltered from the enemy's observation. Here
they refresh themselves out of their haversacks, and, perhaps,
join in a game of cards, or listen to those wonderful tales that,
like those of the " Arabian Nights," are got up for the enter-
tainment of the company.

Only the experienced can know the real state of a man's mind when on picket duty, especially if in hourly expectation of the enemy's approach. They alone can understand the watchfulness and care necessary to protect the line, as well as the body of the sentinel. Eyes and ears must be ever ready to catch the faintest sound, and the musket must be in place for instant duty in the event of an alarm.

On the morning of the 24th, our pickets reported that the enemy had embarked on board of their transports during the night, owing, I suppose, to hearing of our approach. Scurry's Brigade soon returned to their old camping-ground, without the opportunity of having a " brush " with the enemy.

Leaving Scurry's Brigade at their old camp, we will proceed on our journey to Marksville, where Haws' and Randall's Brigades are encamped, and see how they are enjoying Christmas. For the most part, the men were actively engaged during the day, by the duties and routine of camp-life. It is only at night that this busy hum of martial life and bustle sinks into repose. Then five thousand camp-fires glow and sparkle from hill and dale, looking, through the darkness of night, like the gas-lights of a city. The imagination can easily picture the scene. The sentinel's challenge, the sound of music from the bands, ring clearly and musically on the night air ; and the camp-fires glow and flare, around which the men are grouped, singing, joking, and laughing, with a lighthearted ease, as if they never knew " dull care." Most of them are full of practical jokes, light and sparkling as champagne, and had a gay faculty of taking the sunny side of everything. Near one of the huge fires a kind of arbor was nicely constructed of the branches of trees, which were so interwoven as to form a kind of wall. Inside this were seated a couple of fiddlers, making elegant music on their fiddles. Around the fire, groups were dancing jigs, reels, and doubles. Even the officers' colored servants had collected in a group by themselves, and, while some timed the music by slapping their hands on their knees, others were capering and whirling around in the most grotesque manner, showing their white teeth as they grinned their delight, or " yah, yah"ed, at the boisterous fun.

It is no wonder that a great portion of the troops were gathered around there, for it was Christmas night, and home thoughts and home longings were crowding on them; and old scenes and fancies would arise, with sad and loving memories, until the heart grew weary, and even the truest and tenderest longed for home associations that blessed Christmas night. On the right of the camp-ground was another arbor, lately erected for prayer-meetings at night. It was beautifully lighted up with burning pine-knots. Gathered under the arbor were a number of soldiers, quietly and attentively listening to the words which fell from the lips of the preacher standing in their midst—the preacher with his gray locks and wrinkled brow showing the foot-prints of time. Amongst the groups of eager listeners were men just entering the threshold of life, yet whose vocations placed their feet upon the verge of the grave. The rows of tents, the black groupings of adjacent shelters, all made an impressive scene. Occasionally, mingling with the preacher's words, came laughter from some group assembled round a camp-fire near by, or a shout of some unthinking, free-hearted stroller about camp. Words rich with eloquent meaning rolled from that aged preacher's lips, like rippling waves of ocean, successively, rapidly, breaking upon a sandy shore; the light of hidden power burned in his eyes, as he pleaded —warned his hearers of the life to come, and the consequences of an unprepared condition for its hidden realities. The exhortation finished, a closing hymn was sung, rolling its waves of fine melody out upon the night's still air, over the adjacent prairies. The benediction pronounced, the audience dispersed to discuss—some in serious, others in jocular vein—the subject-matter of the discourse.

Such is one of the occasional, more impressive scenes from camp-life on a Christmas night.

No wonder if, amidst such scenes, the soldier's thoughts fled back to his home, to his loved wife, to the kisses of his darling child, to the fond Christmas greetings of his parents, brothers,

sisters, and friends, until his eyes were dimmed with the dews
of his heart. The soldier feels a longing desire, particularly
at Christmas-time, for the pleasant, genial firesides and loving hearts of home. How many of that group, ere another
Christmas comes around, will sleep in a bloody and nameless
grave? Generous and kind hands may smooth the dying soldier's couch, or he may linger for days, tortured by thirst and
pain, his festering wounds creeping with maggots, his tongue
swollen, and a fierce fever fastening upon his body, as he lies
out on that dreary battle-field; or, perhaps, he has dragged
himself beneath the shade of some pine-tree, to die by inches,
where no eye but God's and his pitying angels' shall see him,
where no human aid can succor him. Years afterwards, some
wayfarer may discover a skeleton, with the remains of a knapsack under the skull. This is too often the end of the soldier's dreams of glory, and all

"The pride, pomp, and circumstance of glorious war."

It is but a short transition from love, and hope, and life, to
sorrow and death. Another Christmas, and many a Texas
home will be steeped in affliction for the loving friends who
have laid their bones on the battle-fields of Arkansas and
Louisiana.

Dec. 26th. To-day, the troops received four months' pay, in
Confederate money, a species of money not very useful to the
soldier.

Dec. 27th. Last night we had a heavy thunder-storm and
bitter norther; but, after rain, look out for the rise in Red
River, and the Atchafalaya Bayou! Everything was very wet,
and the camp-fires had hardly begun to smoke, when there
was an alarm of gun-boats coming up Red River. "Fall in!"
was shouted on all sides. So soon as the different regiments
were formed in line, the alarm proved to be a hoax. The
troops returned to their quarters, and resumed cooking their
breakfast; the day was spent in growling about the parties that
gave the false alarm.

Dec. 28. To-day opened with cold, piercing weather; in the

afternoon, it commenced to snow. The men retired under their blankets, and into their huts. The wind howled above us, and the snow fell thick and fast.

Dec. 29th. During last night the weather cleared up, but notwithstanding that, the morning was dark, damp, and gloomy, enveloping the prairie near us in such an impenetrable fog that nothing was discernible in the direction of the river. At noon, however, the sun appeared and rapidly absorbed the veil in its majestic brightness. At dress-parade, orders were read to us, that no person was allowed to cross the Atchafalaya without a permit from district headquarters. If this caution had prevailed from the commencement, it would have kept out the Yankee spies, who were acting in the garb of cotton buyers, and at the same time gathering all the information necessary for the enemy to profit by. Many of the troops suspected there was foul play used in some manner or shape, and meetings were held among themselves, denouncing the cotton-buying scheme as an act of treason to the honest and patriotic people of the South. In this movement I consider they acted with prudence and forethought, as they had justifiable grounds for their action. Many of our men that were taken prisoners at Pleasant Hill, afterwards recognized some of the said cotton-buyers acting in the capacity of staff officers to General Banks, the Federal commander. After the troops had the assurance that no more cotton would be sold to the enemy, nothing unusual transpired in camp, except the general routine of camp-life, such as guard-duty, drills, details for cleaning camp, cutting wood, bringing water, and the various other daily duties upon which our boys throve and grew fat. The gay songs and amusing incidents, so common to a soldier's life, kept us all in fine spirits, and were sources of pleasure in helping to beguile time of its monotony, until the morning of the 30th, when it was generally reported in camp that five gun-boats and one transport loaded with troops had arrived at the mouth of the Atchafalaya Bayou. In the mean time, General Scurry had formed his brigade and Halderman's Battery at Simmsport, to give the enemy a warm recep-

tion in case they made their appearance. Late in the evening, we learned, much to our surprise, that the enemy was on
their way up Black River, to attack Fort Beauregard again, at
Harrisonburg. General Polignac's Division crossed Red River
to harass and annoy the enemy, which they accomplished,
compelling them to withdraw from Black River, without being
able to reach Fort Beauregard. Our loss was comparatively
small, while the enemy's must have been great. General
Polignac's troops fought them an entire day from behind the
levee, killing many of their pilots and gunners.

Thus closed the monotony of camp life for the year 1863.
The weather was unusually rainy and stormy; yet happy,
very many happy hours were spent in those rough huts, despite storms without.

The new year dawned clear and pleasant, with the thunder
of war echoing over the land. The year 1864 witnessed one
of the most fierce, desperate, and bloody struggles that the
world had ever seen. The holidays passed away without
anything of interest transpiring. Of course the towns of
Alexandria and Shreveport were the theater of many gay and
festive scenes among the post-officers. To the private soldier
they differed little from other days. He had the same round
of duties to perform, without relaxation or relief. Ah! how
he missed the joyous scenes and festivities of more peaceful
times, when he mingled in gay throngs, or participated in the
pleasant reunions around the home altar! Such memories
were of the past, while the present was full of clouded realities, and the future seemed to contain no olive-branch of
peace for the land.

The excitement about the gun-boats being pretty much
over, Scurry's Brigade commenced building fortifications at
the mouth of Yellow Bayou, a short distance from Simmsport.
Nothing of any importance transpired in camp until the morning of the 13th, when it was again reported that the enemy's
gun-boats had entered the mouth of Red River, and it was
generally supposed that they would ascend up as far as Alexandria, or perhaps attempt to enter the Atchafalaya Bayou,

and destroy the pontoon bridge. On the morning of the 14th our pickets reported that the gun-boats had withdrawn during the night. After the excitement about the gun-boats had died away, nothing of interest transpired in camp until the morning of the 20th, when a match-drill for an elegant banner took place between the 8th Regiment (Colonel Young's) of Haws' Brigade, and the 11th Regiment (Colonel Roberts') of Randall's Brigade. The banner was awarded to the 8th Regiment, by General Walker, in a neat and appropriate speech.

The ordinary routine of camp duties took place every day without disturbing the monotony of a soldier's life—without anything worthy of notice, until the first day of February, when a squad of 100 men, from Scurry's Brigade, crossed the Atchafalaya Bayou, for the purpose of capturing a company of the enemy that was encamped on the opposite bank of the Mississippi River. Our troops intended to cross the river during the night, on an old flat-boat they had secured. After arriving at the bank of the river, they waited until dark. After they embarked on board, they discovered that the boat was in a leaky condition and not safe; consequently they returned to their camp the following day. In the mean time Captain Clark, of General Scurry's staff, crossed the river in a skiff, and set fire to a large quantity of the enemy's cotton that was piled up opposite the mouth of Red River.

The balance of the month of February passed by without hearing any further news from the enemy's gun-boats. The troops were enjoying fine health. A liberal system of furloughing was granted by General Walker, which gave general satisfaction to the troops.

During the latter part of February, Brigadier-General Haws, commanding the 1st Brigade, was relieved from command, and was assigned to the command of Galveston Island, Texas. General Haws was an officer very much respected by his troops. Before his departure for Texas, a meeting of the officers and soldiers of his brigade was held, in order to express their feelings. The meeting was a large and enthusi-

astic one, and prominent speakers were on hand. A commit-
tee was appointed to draft resolutions in regard to the loss of
their commander. The resolutions were as follows, and were
fully indorsed by the entire troops of his brigade :

" Whereas, we are called upon to surrender our honored
commander, Brigadier-General J. M. Haws, to another field
of duty, in the holy cause of our struggling country, the wisdom of whose rulers has selected him to a sphere of action
more consonant with his acknowledged abilities,

" Therefore, *Resolved*, That we cannot permit him to depart without bearing with him an earnest expression of our
high regard. By his mild, but firm, discipline, his unflinching
pursuit of the dictates of duty, coupled with a paternal solici-
tude for the safety and comfort of his troops, he has now not
only the esteem, but the unfeigned affection of every officer
and soldier of his command. Happily combining the most
distinguished traits of a soldier and a gentleman, he required
not our cordial wishes, however eagerly tendered, to insure
the proudest success, wherever duty may call or his own fer-
vid patriotism lead him."

Shortly after General Haws' departure, Brigadier-General
T. N. Waul (late of Waul's Legion) arrived in camp from
Texas to take command of the 1st Brigade. The following
officers comprised his staff, viz. :

> Major H. B. ADAMS, *Quartermaster.*
> " M. S. MUNSON, *Commissary.*
> Capt. JOHN G. ASHE, *Asst. Insp.-General.*
> 1st Lieut. R. W. BRODUAX, *Aid-de-Camp.*
> Capt. ADOLPH KING, *Asst. Adjt.-General.*

On the first day of March, four gun-boats, loaded with
troops, ascended the Washita River to Fort Beauregard, at
Harrisonburg, for the purpose of again destroying the fort.
When this fort had been occupied previously by the Federal
troops, they destroyed it, as they believed, forever ; but as
soon as they adjourned, after their depredations, sufficient
force was employed to make the fort impregnable against
any force hereafter that the enemy might bring against it.

Heavy firing was heard in the direction of Fort Beauregard. After bombarding the fort for several hours they finally withdrew, without doing much harm to the fort or garrison.

On the evening of the 4th, the gun-boats that had been bombarding Fort Beauregard made their appearance off the Atchafalaya Bayou. Captain Halderman's Battery was placed in position at Simmsport, supported by Scurry's Brigade, where they awaited the approach of the enemy. Late in the evening a courier arrived from the mouth of the bayou, and informed General Scurry that the gun-boats had withdrawn. On the morning of the 5th, General Scurry's Brigade quit work on the fortification known as Fort Humbug, on Yellow Bayou, which proved afterwards a very appropriate name.

March 6th. All of the sick of the division were ordered to be sent to Alexandria, there to be transported on boats to Shreveport.

On the evening of the 7th, Scurry's Brigade was notified to hold itself in readiness to march at a moment's notice; news was received that Banks' army, numbering some 30,000, was encamped at Brashear City, and its destination supposed to be the Red River country. Having received no further news from the enemy until the 11th, no particular notice was taken of the alarm. We ascertained on that day that the enemy was encamped near the town of Franklin, on Bayou Teche. On the evening of the 12th, Scurry's Brigade took its position at "Fort Humbug." They learned that several of the enemy's gun-boats and transports, loaded with troops, had arrived at Simmsport, even before our infantry pickets were informed by our cavalry pickets of the approach of the enemy. Our infantry pickets were taken completely by surprise. They made a narrow escape from being captured.

General Scurry was not a commander to be daunted; neither he nor his troops feared to meet the enemy, whatever might be their numbers—however tried their bravery. From information received afterwards, it seems that General Scurry was aware of the approach of the enemy: he was informed a

few days previous, by a young lady living across the Atchafalaya Bayou. The heroism of this young lady, riding several
miles through the woods, showed what Southern women
would do for their country. It is to be regretted that her
name was not jotted down to adorn the pages of this history. Yet she is not forgotten in the minds of Scurry's
Brigade.

General Scurry, hearing of the landing of the enemy at
Simmsport, at once sent a courier to General Walker, informing him of the landing of the enemy. Scurry's Brigade, having remained in line of battle some time without seeing or
hearing anything about the enemy, had some doubts about
their landing. Many of the troops even doubted the landing
of the enemy; but they soon learned that the report was
too true, by the rapid advance of our infantry pickets, in a
"double-quick," coming towards us. On their arrival we
learned from them that the banks of the Atchafalaya were
literally crowded with live Yankees. They informed us,
furthermore, that they lost all their cooking utensils, and, if
they had not been better runners than the Yankees, they would
have had *them* with their cooking utensils. General Scurry's
line of battle was so arranged that, in case of an attack from
the front, the attacking battery would suffer severely before
they would be able to cross the bayou in front of our fortifications. The bridge across Yellow Bayou was destroyed by
our pioneer corps, after our infantry pickets had crossed.
General Scurry and staff appeared to be in the height of their
glory, as they rode along the line. General Scurry made a
brief remark to his troops, informing them that, although he
did not make a speech to them when he took command of the
brigade, when called upon to do so, he would now address
them a few words, and the sum and substance of his remarks
were, "that he expected every officer and soldier of his brigade to do his duty." Three hearty cheers were given for
General Scurry, three for General Walker, and three for
"Fort Humbug." After the cheering had terminated, the
troops waited anxiously behind their breastworks, until late

in the evening, expecting to see the blue-coated gentlemen ;
but it seems they took matters coolly, from the fact that they
remained behind the protection of their gun-boats until the
following morning, apparently not caring whether Scurry's
Brigade held possession of Fort Humbug or not.

CHAPTER XXIII.

THE RETREAT FROM YELLOW BAYOU TO MANSFIELD.—GENERAL SCURRY'S
REPORT OF HIS OPERATIONS.—LINE OF BATTLE.—CAPTURE OF FORT
DE RUSSY. —"BULL BATTERY." — A STAMPEDE. — ARRIVAL OF THE
ENEMY AT ALEXANDRIA.—FORCED MARCHES.—CAPTURE OF EDGAR'S
BATTERY AND THE 2D LOUISIANA CAVALRY.—PREPARING FOR BATTLE.
—DOUBLE-QUICKING.—ARRIVAL OF GREEN'S CAVALRY.

GENERAL WALKER, having been notified of the strength of the enemy at Simmsport, which consisted of some 15,000 infantry, 2,000 cavalry, and a like proportion of artillery, numbering in all about 18,000, part of the same forces that had been operating in the State of Mississippi, under General Sherman, and commanded by General A. J. Smith, immediately ordered General Scurry to fall back and join the main forces of the division, near Marksville. Scurry's Brigade, after taking a final adieu of Fort Humbug, left their camp about 10 o'clock at night, and fell back slowly. After marching twelve miles they camped near Moreauville. The following morning they marched five miles and formed a junction with the balance of the troops, at the Long Bridge, near Moreauville.

During the day, the enemy advanced in force as far as Moreauville, while their cavalry came a mile or two beyond, capturing three wagons belonging to Scurry's Brigade, which had been sent back to their old camp after baggage. After encountering our pickets they fell back.

GENERAL SCURRY'S REPORT OF HIS OPERATIONS.

Major R. P. McCLAY, *A. A. General:*

For the information of the General commanding, I have the honor to report, that on the 12th I was informed by the pickets stationed at Red River Landing, on the Mississippi River, that three transports, crowded with troops, accompanied by two gun-boats, had entered the mouth of Red River. Almost simultaneously a courier from the pickets on Old River arrived with information that these vessels had entered the Atchafalaya, and that fourteen gun-boats had entered the mouth of Red River. I immediately put the brigāde in motion for Simmsport, intending, if I arrived in time, to oppose, with all the means at my disposal, their landing; or, in case they had landed, to drive them aboard their vessels. My brigade numbered about 1,400 bayonets, with Halderman's Battery of Light Artillery, while the force of the enemy aboard of their transports was supposed to be, at least, 2,000. With no greater disparity than this, I felt perfectly confident of my ability to attack them with success. My command had passed the works at Yellow Bayou, when I received information that fifteen additional transports had entered the Atchafalaya, loaded with troops, escorted by three more gun-boats; that ten transports, with troops aboard, and ten gun-boats had gone up Red River. The movement down the Atchafalaya had, for the moment severed all communication with the small body of cavalry stationed east of the bayou, for the purpose of observing the enemy's proceedings on the Mississippi; thus depriving me of all means of watching a road leading from Red River, around the big bend of Bayou De Glaize, to Moreauville, immediately in my rear. This road was perfectly practicable for an army of all arms; and if the enemy chose to avail himself of it, he might interpose a superior force between me and other brigades of the division, and thus prevent my joining them with my command.

To preserve my communications with the forces under the immediate command of the Major-General, I resolved to fall back beyond the junction of the two roads, without engaging the enemy; for an engagement at that time could have had no other object than to ascertain the number of the enemy's forces. A conflict for such purpose would have resulted in a useless waste of life and blood, if not have hazarded the loss of the entire command, for an object that could be better attained by other means. A nearer approximation of their numbers could be had by ascertaining the number of vessels engaged in the transportation of the troops; and this, before leaving, I definitely ascertained to be twenty-seven transports, which landed their troops at Simmsport, and which, at a low estimate, would give them 18,000, including those on the ten transports that had gone up Red River. In addition to this there were equally urgent considerations impelling me to place myself immediately within easy distance of the other brigades of the division. The forces in front of me were a portion of Sherman's command; of this there could be no doubt. They came *down*, not up the Mississippi River. We had learned from various sources, the most reliable of which was proven—the Major-General commanding the district of Western Louisiana having expressed his belief in its truth— and which subsequent movements have proven to be true, that General Banks was organizing a very large force for an advance upon Alexandria, by way of Opelousas and the Bœuf, and that its appearance might be momentarily expected. It was evident that any delay in getting out of the trap thus laid for us would enable the foe to successfully accomplish the destruction of any of our forces that should be caught between them. Ordering the teams and other public property back to the bridge on Bayou De Glaize, I returned to my old position in the rear of the works on Yellow Bayou. These works were rendered almost useless for purposes of defense; the swamps, which, from being usually impassable at this season of the year, had been relied on to protect their flanks—otherwise without protection—having dried up, and being perfectly practicable for troops. I determined, however, to avail myself of whatever impediments they would oppose to the advance of the enemy, and remained in position until 10 o'clock, P.M., and then moved leisurely and without interruption back, and found the train encamped at the bridge on Bayou De Glaize. Up to this time the Major-General had been constantly notified, by courier, of my movements. At this point I received a communication from him, directing me to delay the enemy as much as possible, to enable him to make the necessary arrangements to secure the public property at Marksville, and that we would form a junction near Mansura. The position I occupied at the bridge on Bayou De Glaize being such that, in any conflict there, the enemy would be able to avail himself to the utmost of his great superiority of numbers, I determined to take position in the light works at the long bridge over Bayou De Bout. In the afternoon, after everything was crossed over, the bridge was burned, and the brigade moved about two miles to the last-mentioned place, and took position there for the purpose of making a stand. The position was naturally a strong one, and had been somewhat strengthened by the construction of the light works alluded to. I hoped to be able to hold the enemy in check here until the Major-General had completed his arrangements. His arrival in person relieved me from further doubts, and his assuming command put an end to all further independent action on my part.

(Signed,)   W. R. SCURRY,

Brig.-General Commanding.

On the arrival of General Walker, the division lay under arms all night (at the long bridge), behind some breastworks that were previously built by the Louisiana troops, for the better protection of the bridge. It became necessary to burn the bridge, to prevent the rapid advance of the enemy, on Fort De Russy, the key of Red River.

General Walker established his headquarters under a large tree, fronting the bridge. In the meantime a heavy picket force under command of Colonel Gregg, of the 16th Dismounted Cavalry, was ordered to watch the movements of the enemy till daylight, when General Walker would be able to make the best disposition of his troops. During the night our wagon-train was moved across Bayou De Lac. The following morning we marched to within half a mile of the village of Mansura, built in the middle of a prairie, and distant from the "Long Bridge" about two miles. Line of battle was at once formed. General Walker made every preparation to give battle at this place. He had selected level ground for his infantry to maneuver about on, while the site was solid enough for his artillery. He was so closely pursued that he was obliged to interrupt the enemy's march in order to be able to get his wagon-train out of the way. Besides, a retreating army must have some start, that they may be able to sleep and eat. It ought also not to have the enemy too close to it ; for to suffer an attack by the way, with their backs turned, is the most dangerous manner of receiving battle. There is then a moment, when the wisest thing that can be done is to choose one's ground, and there halt to fight. Such was the resolution adopted by General Walker. The generalship displayed on this occasion, considering the disadvantages under which he labored, has not been excelled during the war.

With a force of only about 6,000 men, and without a sufficient force of cavalry to watch the movements of the enemy, he kept at bay an army of 18,000, thereby showing his opponent, General A. J. Smith, that he had to deal with a foeman worthy of his steel.

The enemy had us apparently in a tight place (if they were not afraid), for, by throwing a force up Bayou De Glaize, they might have cut off our only road of retreat. As long as we remained in line of battle, they made no move to come out of the timber.

General Walker, seeing no possible chance of the enemy giving battle, and knowing that Banks' army was moving across the country to intercept him, fell slowly back to Bayou De Lac, marching twenty-eight miles closely pursued by the Federals. During the evening, our forces in the rear were much harassed by the enemy's cavalry, but a well-planned and executed ambush, at the end of a lane, resulted in wounding several of them, and putting the balance to flight ; this deterred them from pressing the pursuit, and by night it had ceased altogether. The bridge across Bayou De Lac was burned after all the troops had crossed over.

By this maneuver General Walker drew the whole force of the enemy upon the prairie, and, the bridge being burned, rendered pursuit impossible, except by Mansura or Bayou De Glaize, a distance of some twenty miles, to Bayou Hough-power; while for us it was but five miles.

After we crossed Bayou De Lac, the enemy advanced in the direction of Fort De Russy, on Red River, to co-operate with their gun-boats. They went forward some 10,000 strong, and were repulsed several times, with heavy loss. Finally they were reinforced by the whole of A. J. Smith's command. They came up in such numbers as to crowd entirely into the fort.

Fort De Russy is situated three miles from Marksville, on Red River. The garrison was composed of detached companies, one from each regiment in the division, numbering about 400 men, and was under the command of Lieutenant-Colonel Byrd. Nothing was saved from the fort but two large thirty-two pound Parrott guns. These pieces were removed before the arrival of the Federal forces, and accompanied our division on our retreat. These huge guns, transformed into field pieces, and each drawn by a dozen oxen, presented such a novel appearance that, when first seen by our troops, they created no little merriment. They were christened by the name of the "Bull Battery," by some of the troops, and were afterwards thus known during the entire campaign.

We remained encamped at Bayou De Lac until the evening of the 16th, when we made a night-march of twenty miles to Lloyd's bridge, on Bayou Bœuf, some twenty-five miles south of Alexandria. For several days after the capture of Fort De Russy, we were closely pressed by the enemy's cavalry. Sometimes they dashed upon the rear of our columns, and, as our command consisted of infantry alone, with the exception of one company of cavalry, commanded by Captain Faulkiner, our duties were necessarily much more arduous than they would otherwise have been. After our arrival in camp we learned that the enemy had taken possession of Alexandria.

March 17th. At 5 o'clock, P. M., we fell back some six miles further, to the piny woods, and camped.

March 18th. General Mouton's division formed a junction with our division to-day. It consisted of one brigade of Texans, commanded by the *French* General Polignac; and one brigade of Louisianians, commanded by Colonel Grey. Late in the day, we were joined by the 2d Louisiana Cavalry, commanded by Colonel Vincent. We marched thirty-one miles, traveling part of the night. While we were resting a few minutes on our night-march, we were thrown into excitement by the startling call, "Who goes there?" of one of our advance guard, followed by the heavy report of a musket. The hands of every man were instantly upon his gun, and every preparation was made to resist an attack from the enemy's cavalry; for, in the hurry and alarm, we could think of nothing else. Presently we heard a heavy tramp coming down the road, indicating a charge from cavalry. The troops all of a sudden stampeded, some of them running down the bank of a creek alongside of the road, while others jumped a fence on the left of the road. To add to the excitement of the moment, some wag yelled out, at the top of his voice, "Charge against cavalry!" Bayonets were fixed, and triggers were cocked; but we soon discovered the cause of alarm, in beholding two Texas beeves that had escaped from the drivers, and which were followed by some of them, in order to return them to the herd. This alarm having been satisfactorily witnessed by the troops, we again resumed the march, and arrived at camp, near Heuestone, in the piny woods, hungry and exhausted.

On the 19th the march was resumed. We marched twenty miles, and camped near Carroll Jones's, a wealthy free negro. At this point we were thirty-five miles from Alexandria, and out of all danger of being cut off from Shreveport. Sending all of our baggage ahead to facilitate our movements, we had no shelter to protect us from the elements, making the damp chilly ground our couch, and the azure sky our only covering. Add to this the tortures of hunger and want of sufficient apparel, which all endured with comparatively little murmuring or complaining, and it shows a spirit which nothing could break or conquer.

> " We are the sons of sires that baffled
> Crowned and *martyred* tyranny ;
> They defied the field and scaffold
> For their birthright—so have we."

It is a noted fact that, previous to our division going to battle, or anticipating one, the troops became, as it were, all at once, very religious. As a matter of course, we had a revival at these camps; preaching was a nightly occurrence. The scene at one of these gatherings was very impressive. A huge shelter protected the assembly from the night-dews. Rough seats, made of logs, covered the space beneath this shelter. Stands, on which were built fires from pine knots, shed a lurid light over the vast concourse. The hymns sung would rise in rich cadences, floating away on the evening breeze in solemn, harmonious strains, followed by an earnest prayer and an impassioned and eloquent discourse. It was a strange spectacle to witness—these rough, bronzed soldiers, inured to danger and hardships, making bloodshed the chief aim of their lives, exposed to the evil influences of a soldier's dissipated and reckless existence, thus striving to seek a " home not made with hands, eternal in the heavens."

March 20th. We learned to day, that Banks' army had formed a junction with Smith's army at Alexandria, thereby concentrating no less than 48,000 men, all as well armed and equipped as an army could be, with an abundance of ammunition and supplies, and transportation of the most costly kind, and almost unlimited in amount, for the purpose of crushing out or swallowing up our little army. It was the vain-glorious boast of the enemy at Alexandria, that before the end of April, all the " rebel troops " in Louisiana and Arkansas would be driven into Texas.

During the night of the 20th, all of our wagons were sent off in the direction of Shreveport. A squad of Louisiana cavalry brought in six prisoners that they had captured at McNutt's Hill. About midnight we were ordered to cook one day's rations, and to be ready to march at daylight. When about ready to proceed on our journey the following morning, the order of last night was countermanded. During the day we heard heavy firing in the direction of McNutt's Hill, distant from our camp about twelve miles. We learned afterwards that the 2d Louisiana Cavalry was falling back before the enemy. Edgar's Battery of Light Artillery, that was attached to Scurry's Brigade, was ordered to the front.

Notwithstanding the gloomy weather, a violent storm of rain and sleet having fallen while we were encamped here, everything betokened the greatest activity. General Dick Taylor had taken the field in person, and had immediate command of the army. The foe, encouraged by our continued retrograde movements, was becoming bolder, and even more daring every day.

On the night of the 22d an event occurred that cast a momentary gloom over our army. The splendid cavalry regiment commanded by Colonel Vincent, which had so recently joined us, was posted, under direction of General Taylor, as advance pickets on the Alexandria road. While our infantry was enjoying their quiet slumber, after laborious and tedious marches, a detachment of the enemy's cavalry, commanded by General Mower, made a circuitous march during the night, guided by some Jayhawkers, and attacked Colonel Vincent's command in the rear, capturing nearly 400 of the cavalry, besides the guns and men of Captain Edgar's Battery. This sad news fell like a thunderbolt on our division, as each brigade exhibited considerable jealousy towards the others concerning the Nonpareil Battery ; all three of the brigades claiming it as their battery. In consequence of this severe loss, and the non-arrival of the expected troops from Texas and Arkansas, General Dick Taylor declined making a stand at this point as he previously had contemplated. On the

12

morning of the 23d, our infantry pickets reported the rapid advance of the enemy. We formed in line of battle near Carroll Jones's house, awaiting the approach of the enemy. Some few of the 2d Louisiana Cavalry made their escape and arrived in camp. They reported that their capture was owing to the mistake of placing the pickets too far apart from each other, thereby allowing one of the Louisiana Jayhawkers an opportunity of creeping up to the line of pickets, and awaiting the approach of one of the couriers from the front. Challenging the courier, on his approach, for the counter-sign, and receiving it from him, he retired, and communicated it to the enemy. The enemy, on receiving the countersign, had no difficulty in surrounding their camp, and capturing them. After remaining in line of battle for about an hour, at Carroll Jones', and hearing no news from the enemy, we proceeded on our way towards Pleasant Hill; marched twelve miles, and camped for the night.

March 24th. Marched thirty miles, and camped at an old camp-meeting ground, situated in the midst of a pinery. Our commanders must have believed that we were made of cast-steel, the way they marched us. We remained at this camp for the purpose of practicing skirmish-drill, until the morning of the 29th. Whilst at this camp we heard the glad tidings that General Tom Green, with his cavalry, numbering about 13,000 men, had crossed the Sabine River, en route to reinforce us.

On the 29th, a pleasant but cloudy morning, the army was again on the move. Marched seventeen miles over a rough and hilly road, almost devoid of water.

March 30th. Marched thirteen miles. Caught up with our wagon train. We marched in rear of the train, and arrived in camp, near Fort Jessup, late in the evening.

March 31st. Marched twenty miles. Passed by Fort Jessup, an old United States fort before the annexation of Texas to the Union. The location of the old fort is one of exceeding loveliness—healthy, and combining every advantage for a flourishing settlement. There is a growth of heavy timber, some two miles in width, adjacent to the fort; while the rich bottom lands of the Sabine River afford great inducements to the industrious husbandman. Grain, of all kinds, grows in abundance. Cotton and sugar-cane yield well. There are still standing the remains of the fort, barracks, sutler's store, General Twiggs' dwelling, and some out-houses, but now crumbling away with decay. Reported that the enemy's cavalry was within seven miles of us.

On the morning of April 1st we marched ten miles, and camped near the town of Pleasant Hill. In the afternoon Green's Cavalry arrived from Texas. They met the enemy's cavalry on the Natchitoches Road. In accordance with Tom Green's style of fighting, he went right for them, chastising them wherever they made a stand. The whole country, far and wide, was aroused to the highest pitch of excitement by the retreat of our army. The inhabitants, all along the route of our retreat, were hurriedly quitting their homes, and flying before the approach of the invader, Consternation and alarm everywhere prevailed among the citizens. Old men shouldered their muskets and came to our assistance, to help drive back the invader. While on the march, we heard that the enemy had taken possession of Natchitoches about 2 o'clock, P. M.

On the morning of the 2d we marched five miles, in the direction of Bayou Pierre, southeast from Pleasant Hill. Heavy cannonading was heard by us in the direction of Natchitoches. About 6 o'clock in the evening, as we were preparing to cook supper, an officer of General Walker's staff arrived in camp to notify brigade commanders of the rapid advance of the enemy. He informed them that it now became a race between their men and those of the enemy, who should get to Pleasant Hill first. The division was formed in line rapidly; regimental commanders received orders to double-quick their regiments to Pleasant Hill, distant about five miles. On we sped, like lightning—every man for himself, and the "devil take the hindmost." To add to the excitement of the moment, courier after courier came galloping on their fast steeds, informing us that the enemy had surrounded our wagon-train, and that there was a possibility of our losing it, unless we hurried up. On we sped. Night overtook us in the race. We fell pell-mell over stumps and roots of trees, arriving at Pleasant Hill at 7 o'clock, making the distance of five miles in one hour, carrying our knapsacks and accouterments. On our arrival at Pleasant Hill, we formed in line of battle under the crest of the hill, and remained so all night, expecting every minute the approach of the enemy. Morning at last dawned, bright and glorious, but no enemy was in sight, much to the disappointment of the troops. They seemed to be perfectly worn out with the marching and counter-marching. They preferred meeting the enemy in a fair field, small as their number was, rather than to be harassed and annoyed by them. During the night the commissary department opened its coffers to the troops, allowing them to help themselves to provisions that they were unable to get transportation for.

April 3d. Marched ten miles in the direction of the town of Mansfield. We camped near a saw-mill, about half-way between Mansfield and Pleasant Hill.

April 4th. Marched twelve miles, leaving the Mansfield road to the left, and taking the Kingston road. On our march we passed twenty wagons loaded with flour, bound for Green's Cavalry. We encamped four miles from Mansfield, in a swampy bottom, and about thirty-seven miles from Shreveport. We remained at this camp until the morning of the 7th, in order to collect as much available force as possible, to meet the impending danger. Yet the great distance of the troops in Arkansas, and the absence of facilities for transportation, the advance of the Federal General Steele through Arkansas (he had already crossed the Washita River, driving before him the army of General Price, and intending to form a junction about the middle of April with Banks' army, at Shreveport), prevented the concentration of any of General Price's army at the battle of Mansfield.

In the meantime, General Taylor, with his apparently inadequate force, resolved to give battle, and to this end every preparation was made. On the night of the 7th, orders were received to cook one day's rations, and to be ready to leave at four o'clock the following morning. During the day, the enemy's advance reached Pleasant Hill, driving Green's Cavalry before them.

CHAPTER XXIV.

THE BATTLE OF MANSFIELD.—OFFICIAL REPORT OF THE BATTLE.

"Ours are no hirelings, trained to the fight,
  With cymbal and clarion, all glittering and bright ;
  No prancing of chargers, no martial display ;
  No war-trump is heard from our silent array.
  O'er the proud heads of freemen, the *lone star* doth wave—
  Men, firm as the mountain, and still as the grave.
  To day we shall pour out our life-blood like rain ;
  We come back in triumph, or come not again."

ON the morning of April 8th, 1864—a day set apart by
the President of the Confederate States for fasting,
humiliation, and prayer—" Walker's Division " moved
from their camp, situated four miles north of the town of Mansfield, to meet the enemy, who were advancing in heavy force
from the direction of Pleasant Hill, some twenty-four miles
distant. Arriving near the town of Mansfield, General Walker
formed his division in line of battle, and awaited the advance
of the enemy.

Orders were sent to General Tom Green, in command of
the Texas Cavalry, to fall back slowly, so as to decoy the
enemy towards our line of battle, where a well-planned ambuscade had been prepared for their reception.

In order that the situation of our army may be fully comprehended, I give the following explanation : The road from
our camp to Mansfield was over a remarkably high ridge,
flanked by ravines, where it would be impossible for one army
to attack another without suffering terribly from an ambuscade or masked batteries. The ravines, extending close to the
road, were covered with a dense, almost impenetrable growth of

black-jacks and hazel bushes. Many of the troops went to work with their knives, lopping off the branches of the trees and bushes which obstructed a good view of the road, in order to render their aim and fire more effective. The men waited and watched for the foe, with compressed lips and blanched faces, betokening the inward excitement, while every man kept his allotted place. We remained in this position until 11 o'clock, A. M., when General Taylor ordered General Walker to advance his division to meet the enemy, who were reported about half-way between Mansfield and Pleasant Hill; and, advancing cautiously, the head of the column soon moved off in the direction of Mansfield, the bands playing the favorite tune of "Dixie." The inhabitants of Mansfield appeared to be astonished when they beheld Walker's Division marching proudly back to meet the enemy, before whom they had so lately retreated. As the troops marched through the town, the sidewalks were thronged with ladies—misses and matrons—who threw their bright garlands at the feet of the brave Texas boys, beseeching them in God's name to drive back the enemy, and save their cherished homes; assuring us that they looked to us for protection. On hearing these patriotic words we felt that we were indeed "thrice armed," and, although greatly outnumbered, would in the end be victorious. Alas! how many a brave heart, which thrilled with patriotic emotion that morning, as we marched with flying banners through the town, was stilled in death before the last gleams of that day's sun rested upon the field of carnage! How many strong men, as they listened to the sweet voices of those maidens, and thought of their loved ones at home, ceased to think, or speak, or breathe, before that day had gone!

On our march to meet the enemy, we beheld Generals Taylor, Walker, Mouton, and Green, on the right of the road, apparently in deep consultation about the forthcoming battle. While they are engaged in council, I will sketch them in detail.

Major-General Dick Taylor is of middle stature, with a compact, well-knit frame. His face is regular, but almost bronze, showing unmistakable evidences of his Louisiana lineage. He has a glorious pair of dark eyes, that scintillate beneath his heavy brows and dark hair. A heavy, curved mustache covers his well-formed mouth. Such is his appearance, and his fighting qualities are in accordance. As a soldier, he has been wonderfully successful. Though some of his movements savored of rashness, when calmly weighed, they showed the good judgment and military genius that conceived them. When once he forms an opinion, he acts upon it with an unbending, uncompromising resolve.

Major-General John G. Walker is a man of slight frame, and apparently delicate constitution; of a grave, pleasing demeanor, and of most affable and courteous manner. He is kind and courteous to all, without compromising his dignity. He was beloved by his officers, almost adored by his men. As a general, Walker is calm and cautious; does everything by rule; leaves nothing to chance. He makes his arrangements for battle with caution and foresight, and is sure to have every brigade of his division move with clock-work regularity, and strike at the proper time and place. Nothing disturbs or unnerves him.

Major-General Mouton, commanding one brigade of Texans and one of Louisianians—forming a division—was a noble-looking man, of fine, dignified appearance. He was a courteous, refined gentleman, and a brave officer. He had fully the confidence of General Dick Taylor as a general. He took a distinguished part in protecting the people of Louisiana, his native State, from the ruthless invaders, until he fell, on that fatal day, the 8th of April, at Mansfield, in about the forty-fifth year of his age.

Major-General Tom Green is nearly six feet high, rather stoop-shouldered; his face is rather rounding, with a short, grizzly beard. His troops had unbounded confidence in him, and believed whatever he did was right, and that is everything. If sent on any expedition, no matter how hazardous or apparently useless, their only reply was, "Well, boys, if old Tom said so, it's all right." His career as a soldier has been a brilliant record of dashing exploits—of noble victories. General Tom Green and his cavalry have been through almost every battle-field west of the Mississippi River, and, wherever his banner floated, down went the enemy's. There are men who are soldiers by inspiration. Green is one. West Point may mould officers, and instruct them in the rudiments of war ; but it could not infuse into many the spirit and military genius of Tom Green.

After marching about four miles from Mansfield, on the Pleasant Hill road, we beheld Mouton's Division formed in line of battle on the left of the road. Immediately on the approach of Walker's Division, several batteries of light artillery took position on an eminence at the left of the road, and about three hundred yards in advance of Mouton's Division ; the position that the artillery occupied would enable them to " rake " the Pleasant Hill road from any direction. On the arrival of Walker's Division, they filed off to the right of the road through a skirt of timber, Waul's Brigade in front. A more gallant body of men, more spirited and resolved, never marched forth to battle. Next came Randall's Brigade, under that heroic and indefatigable officer. They marched forward at a quick step, in their usual rollicking and bold style, overflowing with impatient and long-restrained ardor for the fight, the promise of which had reconciled them to their long and laborious retreat before the enemy. Scurry's Brigade followed after Randall's Brigade, which brought up the rear of the division. The men in this brigade appeared to be in splendid condition. They were full of fun, led by their gallant chief, who looked every inch a soldier. A regiment of this brigade is ordered to advance, and take position in a ravine, some six hundred yards in advance of the main line, in order to ambuscade the enemy, provided they advanced before the general line of battle was formed. The balance of the troops of Walker's Division, after marching and countermarching and maneuvering, was formed in line of battle about 2 o'clock, P. M., behind a rail-fence, inclosing Moss's plantation ; the left of the division rested on the line of the Pleasant Hill road,

Scurry's Brigade on the right, Waul's in the center, and Randall's on the left.

The intervening space between Walker's and Mouton's Divisions was filled with several batteries of artillery, some of which were in position, as already mentioned. The cavalry, except that portion then skirmishing with the enemy, had been dismounted, and occupied the left of the line, with the exception of one regiment, who took their position on the right. After the line of battle was formed, the command was given to "stack arms." The fence in our front was pulled down. We remained inactive for about an hour, awaiting the approach of the enemy, who were reported to be in line of battle, about one mile in our front. The firing of our cavalry skirmishers became each minute more distinct. Presently, the regiment of Scurry's Brigade that had taken position in advance is seen double-quicking across the field, making towards their brigade. Guns are elevated in order to cover their retreat. All eyes are eagerly watching their approach, as they advanced to take their position in their brigade.

This calm before the storm—the period immediately preceding the conflict, when it is apparent that the deadly conflict is near at hand—is more trying even than the battle itself. Unsustained by the reckless excitement and wild furor of the actual strife, the strongest mind must shudder at the fearful thought that a few short moments more may usher the soul into eternity.

On the right of the division, and about fifty yards in advance, was our favorite leader, General Walker, surrounded by his staff officers, eating their lunch before they enter the conflict. Casting your eyes to the left of the division, you can behold General Dick Taylor, mounted on his black steed, followed by a lonely courier, advancing towards General Walker. On his arrival, the two generals converse together some twenty minutes. General Taylor then returns, going a little quicker than he advanced. This was owing, I suppose, to his hearing heavy firing on the left of the line, which plainly indicated that the work of destruction had commenced. Infantry skirmishers were at once pushed forward to feel the position of the enemy. News flashed along the line that the division of General Mouton had attacked a superior force of the enemy, in a strong position. For half an hour the echo of their guns swelled upon the evening breeze, and, during that period, an awful feeling of intense anxiety and suspense filled the minds of the troops not engaged in the conflict. The conflict ceases. Alas! we hear the melancholy tidings that the brave General Mouton was killed just as he had borne the banner of the " stars and bars " to victory.

When the gallant Louisianians learned the certainty of their idolized chieftain's death, many of these lion-hearted men threw themselves in wild grief on the ground, weeping scalding tears in their bitter sorrow. It is a fearful spectacle to see strong-hearted men thus give way to their feelings. It demonstrated the devotion felt for their gallant chieftain, and showed how deeply he was enshrined in these brave souls.

Shortly after the report of General Mouton's death, the cavalry mount, and move off to the right, in full gallop. Presently, General Walker and staff are in their saddles. He orders his brigade commanders to prepare for action. All being in readiness, he gives the command : " By the right of companies to the front, forward march ! " Every man moved off quickly, with a confident and determined step. The line of march was through a large field in our front, then through a skirt of timber, and into another field. Picture a nearly triangular space, broken by woods, fences, and fields,—its base a long ridge of underbrush running from southeast to northwest, its lower side traced by a line extending westerly to a line of woods that forms the left right-angle as you approach the area by a road, the Mansfield and Pleasant Hill highway, which intersects that area. As we approached a narrow skirt of timber, and about six hundred yards from the enemy's position, we beheld General Walker, mounted on his iron-gray horse, with his field-glass to his eye, taking observations of the enemy's position. His actions and features were a study for the closest scrutinizer of physiognomy. Not a quiver on his face—not the movement of a muscle, to betray anxiety or emotion, notwithstanding the shower of balls whizzing around him.

Resting a few minutes in the skirt of timber, the command was given, "By companies, into line!" After the line was formed, orders were given to "fix bayonets." In the mean time, the enemy continued firing upon us from their batteries. Soon the command was given to "double-quick." We immediately commenced advancing in the direction of the enemy, who were securely posted behind a rail-fence. They greeted our coming with a perfect shower of leaden hail. The men shouted, at the top of their voices, at each iron messenger as it approached, many indulging in jokes and witticisms, such as, "This kind of ball-music is fine for dancing." "Here comes another iron pill!" "Dodge, boys, but don't tremble!"

The fire of the enemy increases; it is terrible. He is gathering all his strength for one final struggle. Shells, canister, and bullets are falling around like a hail-storm. Our different brigade commanders ride along their lines, encouraging their men; still there is no faltering, but wild cheers, and on they press. When our army had arrived within about fifty paces, and before we had fired a shot, a general flash was seen along the enemy's line, and a storm of bullets went flying over our heads. They had aimed too high. Onward our troops advance, pale with excitement, compressed lips and blazing eyes betokening the spirit of their determination. Casting your eyes along the column, you behold the flags of the various regiments floating on the breeze, and each regiment trying to be the first to scale the fence. Nearer our troops advance; the color-sergeants flaunt their flags at the enemy, and fall; others grasp them and fall, and they are then borne by the corporals. In this fearful charge, there was no flinching nor murmuring—nothing but the subdued talk of soldiers, the gritting of teeth for revenge, as they saw their comrades falling around them. At last the fence is gained; over it our troops go, like an avalanche of fire! A loud and prolonged Texas yell deafens the ear; their cheers rise in one great range of sound over the noise of battle, and are heard far down the lines to the left, where the Louisiana boys are at it.

Nothing could withstand the impetuosity of our charge. After crossing the fence, we came abruptly upon the enemy's guns. With loud huzzas we rushed upon the enemy before they could reload. A murderous discharge of rifle-balls was poured into their very bosoms; afterwards, using our bayonets, we mercifully bayoneted them, ere they could recover from their astonishment. Their prostrate column was trampled in the mire. Ah! now comes the tug of war. The enemy is panic-stricken; they abandon their artillery; they cannot stand the bayonet charge; they retreat, and from their appearance, "every man is for himself." They sadly feel the loss of their artillery. Cheer after cheer bursts forth from our lines, as the enemy is seen fleeing, casting away their knapsacks and arms. Our cavalry now charges down on their flanks, making the very ground quake and the enemy tremble. Urged on by the excitement of victory, we pursue the flying foe, killing where they dare resist, and capturing them by hundreds. At last, their wagon-train, numbering over two hundred wagons, falls into our possession. Cheer after cheer again is loudly given by our troops, as they behold quartermaster stores of every description. The enemy, seeing the loss of their wagon-train, endeavored to rally their men for the retaking of the same; but, as often as they were formed, they were compelled to retire. The flight had become universal. The enemy had left on the ground, dying and dead, where the battle began, about one half of their forces; and, through the woods and along the road, our cavalry and artillery completely slaughtered them. Horses and men, by hundreds, rolled down together; the road was red with their blood. After pursuing them four miles, they finally made a stand at a peach and plum orchard, where they were reinforced by the 19th Army Corps. Entirely unconscious of the arrival of fresh troops to their assistance, we passed half-way through the field before we became aware of their reinforcements. Then came the terrible shock. Volley after volley, and shower after shower of bullets came whizzing down upon us. It was utterly impossible to advance, and to retreat beneath the range of their long guns seemed equally desperate. We lay down, arose again, and then involuntarily sought such shelter and protection as the ground afforded.

Encouraged by our brave leaders, our brave men attempted again and again to charge the enemy, who were behind their barricades of logs and fences, which they hastily constructed to cover their retreat; but human fortitude and human bravery were unequal to the task. The very air seemed dark and hot with balls; the thunders of the artillery-guns resounded through the heavens and seemed to shake the earth to its very center, and on every side was heard their crushing sound as they struck that swaying mass, tearing through flesh, bone, and sinew. The position of our line could have been traced by our fallen dead. Within a few short moments many a gallant spirit went to its long home.

The sun was now declining. General Walker, with his generals, was busily engaged in encouraging their troops, while sharing with them every peril. After General Walker had carefully reconnoitered the lines of the enemy, he ordered his brigade commanders to form their brigades for the final and successful charge. Some time elapsed before the troops were ready for the successful charge. Hark! there peals forth the signal-gun. A wild shout of enthusiasm burst forth from the Texas ranks as they rushed in full career upon the enemy's lines. The sun went down, and the struggle still continued. Twilight darkness is over the battle-field, but a blaze of intense light from our bayonets gleamed over the contending hosts. One by one the stars came out calmly in the sky, and the moon, in silent beauty, rose serenely in the east, and looked down with her mild reproof upon the hideous carnage; and still the struggling squadrons, with unintermitted fury dashed against each other. Beneath such blows men and horses rapidly fell. The clangor of the strife grew fainter and fainter. Still, in the gloom of the night, as the eye gazed upon the tumultuous mass swaying to and fro, it was impossible to judge who were gaining the victory.

The spectacle was so sublime, so awful, so sure to be followed by decisive results, that each army, as by common consent, suspended its fire to await the issue of this extraordinary duel. The roar of musketry and the heavy booming of artillery ceased. The soldiers rested upon their muskets, and the exhausted cannoniers leaned upon their guns, awaiting daylight to come to renew the battle.

Too much praise cannot be bestowed upon the doctors and chaplains of the division, for the care and kindness with which they looked after the dying and wounded. They spent the night with their lamps going over the battle-field, serving the dying, and attending those who might recover. Oh, what a boon is even a drink of cold water to a maimed soldier lying on the field of battle, tortured with pain and thirst!

The morning of the 9th had scarcely tinged the eastern horizon with the grayish dawn, when we discovered no enemy in sight, *much to our surprise.* The reason for the withdrawal of the enemy from the battle-field during the night, has been furnished me by an officer of the 16th Dismounted Cavalry. This officer was seriously wounded late in the evening, and fell into the enemy's hands. He was carried to a log cabin, in the rear of their lines, which was used as their hospital. In this cabin or hospital a council of war was held by the Federal generals. The attention of General Banks, the commander of the Federal forces, was attracted by the heavy moaning of the rebel officer. After questioning him about the nature of his wounds, he asked the officer the number of the Confederate forces engaged in to-day's battle. The officer replied that he was not aware of the strength of our forces; but he knew the main body of our forces were still behind, and that only the advance of our army were engaged in to-day's battle—but, on to-morrow, our entire army would be engaged. General Banks, believing the supposed dying officer's words, immediately ordered a retreat of his army to Pleasant Hill. Thus closed the memorable battle of Mansfield.

It is impossible for me to make individual mention of all those who on that day sacrificed their lives upon the altar of our country, but many a once happy home now mourns the loss of some brave soldier who on that night slept in death upon the sanguinary battle-field of Mansfield.

Our loss in the divisions amounted to 600 in killed, wounded, and missing. While the loss of the enemy amounted to 1,500 in killed and wounded, 2,000 prisoners, 20 pieces of artillery, including Nims's battery, the veteran battery of seventeen engagements, Chicago Mercantile battery, and the First Indiana battery, besides two hundred wagons and thousands of small-arms.

*　　*　　*　　*　　*　　*　　*　　*

OFFICIAL REPORT OF THE BATTLE.

GENERAL BOGGS, *Assistant Adjutant-General.*

GENERAL,—I have the honor to report to you that a battle occurred yesterday afternoon a little below Mansfield. The fighting continued until night, the enemy having been at times reinforced by the 19th Army Corps. We fought the 13th Army Corps all day, and late in the evening met the 19th Army Corps, and drove them back. We have captured about 2,000 prisoners, 20 pieces of artillery, 200 wagons, and thousands of small-arms. Our loss in officers has been severe, and we have many wounded.

(Signed,)　　R. TAYLOR, General Commanding.

CHAPTER XXV.

THE BATTLE OF PLEASANT HILL.

" Bide your time, the morn is breaking,
   Bright with freedom's blessed ray ;
Thousands from their trance awaking,
   Soon shall stand in martial array.
Man shall fetter man no longer,
   Liberty shall march sublime ;
Every moment makes us stronger,
   Firm, unshrinking, Texans, bide your time ! "

T daylight on the morning of the 9th of April we were reinforced by General Churchill's Division of Arkansians, and Parson's Division of Missourians. Shortly after their arrival, we took up the line of march in pursuit of the enemy, who was reported to be in the neighborhood of Pleasant Hill, some twelve miles distant. The road that the enemy retreated over was literally strewn with knapsacks, cooking utensils, etc., etc. They obstructed the road by felling trees, to retard our pursuit as far as possible. On our arrival within about six miles of Pleasant Hill, we met a squad of Green's cavalry, escorting some three or four hundred " Zouave " prisoners, dressed in their peculiar style of uniform, en route for Mansfield. Some of the soldiers noticing their eccentric uniform, remarked that the war must soon be over, supposing that the " rebels " had whipped all the men in the Northern States, and Lincoln was filling up his ranks with women. The Zouave prisoners were rather amused when they were informed by some of the Texans that the Texas troops had too much honor to fight women (alluding to the Zouave dress). On their arrival at Mansfield they

12

would all be paroled, on account of the Confederacy having scarcely provisions to feed their own troops, without providing for women prisoners. After the Zouave prisoners passed us by, we continued our march towards Pleasant Hill. On our arrival near the town, we learned, much to our surprise, that the enemy, having been reinforced by General A. J. Smith's Army Corps, were in line of battle at Pleasant Hill, awaiting our approach. Our Division was shortly afterward formed in line of battle, as on the day before. After moving through an old field covered with underbrush, we came into another field. On the opposite side of the field was posted the enemy to our left and front, and in the immediate vicinity of the town of Pleasant Hill. We discovered that the enemy had burned several houses in the town, in order to be able to work their artillery to advantage.

Pleasant Hill is a small village of about two hundred inhabitants, situated on a slight eminence thirty-five miles from Grand-Ecore: the town boasts of a hotel, three storehouses. and an Academy. During the night, General Kirby Smith, accompanied by Governor Allen, had arrived from Shreveport. General Kirby Smith having taken command in person, formed his general line of battle in the following order. General Green's Division of cavalry took position on the extreme left; Mouton's Division of infantry, commanded by Polignac, on the right of the cavalry; Walker's Division next, and Churchill's and Parson's Divisions on the extreme right. The Louisiana militia, under command of Governor Allen, was held in reserve, in case of an emergency. In justice to the Louisiana militia, I will state, that notwithstanding they were past the years of enduring the toils and hardships of a soldier's life, no braver or nobler body of men ever went into action; wherever their patriotic Governor led, they followed.

After the line of battle was formed, skirmishers were thrown forward to feel the position of the enemy. They had to advance in open and exposed order, while the enemy's skirmishers availed themselves of the trees, and every convenient cover.

The enemy kept up a constant galling fire upon our troops for about half an hour. Presently General Smith pushed forward his entire line, driving the cloud of skirmishers of the enemy before them. After advancing a short distance, we beheld the enemy drawn up in line of battle, in excellent order, with batteries strongly posted and in great force.

About four o'clock, P. M., the battle opened furiously by an attack on the enemy's left, by the Arkansas and Missouri troops. They passed down the hill obliquely to the right to support a battery, which was about to be placed within a few hundred yards, of the artillery of the foe. Though silent as they passed down the hill, a shout arose a few seconds after, which, from the direction they had taken, every listener could distinguish as theirs. The incessant roar of artillery came from the batteries at close range. Shells and round-shots, ploughed through their ranks, and shattered the trees. Thick volumes of smoke arose from the woods, and floated along the valley. Still the Arkansas and Missouri troops advanced, reserving their fire until they got into close quarters with the enemy. The latter came resolutely to meet them, like a sweeping avalanche. Our troops greet them by firing a volley along the entire line, mowing them down by hundreds. All the effort on the part of our troops to check or turn this human avalanche, proved unavailing, and for the first time our brave and determined men staggered and gave ground, and commenced to fall back. Our officers in vain tried to detain them, but our troops suddenly fall back, grouping around their officers. Our situation soon became most critical, and a few moments longer might have been disastrous; but General Walker seeing those two divisions falling back in disorder, immediately ordered General Scurry's brigade to reinforce them. The brigade stripped themselves of their blankets and knapsacks, in order that nothing might impede their work, and then swept down the hill, across the field, and on towards the enemy, delivering fire after fire on the enemy's forces. Batteries open on them right and left, hailing grape and canister into their very faces, while from the woods, a stream of lead was poured afore them. As their line swept along, the heroic General Scurry galloped towards the head of his column, hallooing, "Come on, boys, you have got your chance at last.". The order was quickly responded to, and with a desperate onset the whole line rushed forward upon the enemy. It was a fine sight, that charge of Scurry's Brigade to the death-struggle. General Scurry expected to be assisted by the troops he went to re-inforce, but the panic-striken troops were too slow in rallying to do any good. Those gallant fellows followed quickly their general, and soon cleared the way. The enemy poured into them a cruel, crushing fire ; but in vain, their onset could not be checked. But the field was not cleared ; the enemy seeing the comparatively small body of their assailants, fell upon our gallant troops in massed columns, driving back our for-ces. General Walker perceiving the critical position of Scur-ry's brigade, almost surrounded by four times their number, immediately ordered the brigades of Waul and Randall to charge the enemy at the point of the bayonet, as the only possible means of saving Scurry's brigade from destruction. In the very thickest of the fight rode the gallant warrior General Scurry, urging his men forward, exclaiming aloud, in his stentorian voice, "Scurry's brigade may be annihilated, but must never retreat." Hat in hand, cheering on his men, a rifle ball glances his cheek, slightly wounding him ; but without paying any attention to his wound, he continued cheering on his men. All of his brave troops seemed inspired with the same courage. Ah, yonder advances the gallant brigades of Waul and Randall, led by their gallant chiefs, coming to their relief. "Thank God," exclaims the heroic Scurry, "my brigade is saved." The dashing charge of Waul's and Randall's brigades compelled the enemy to withdraw their forces from their left, and concentrate them in their center to meet the charge. Right gallantly our troops charge across the open field in their front, as steadily and as coolly as if on parade. On their arrival within about one hundred yards of the enemy, they are ordered to lie down. The keen eyes of their commander saw the enemy in the act of firing, and he pursued this course in order to save the men from the enemy's first fire.

General Walker seeing this unexpected movement of his troops, galloped towards his men, to cheer them on : a nobly appearing chief, and full of vigor and life, as he dashed along the line inspiring his brave men with enthusiasm. Wherever he rode, cheer after cheer greeted him, for there is an irresistible spell around this officer, who has exhibited the real Napoleonic energy. He well knew that if his line faltered the least, and was not successful in driving the enemy from their position, Scurry's brigade would be sacrificed. While in the act of waving his hat, in cheering his men onward, he was pierced by a minie-ball, but paying no attention to his wound, he issued his orders to his brigade commanders amid a continual shower of shot and minie-balls. It was not until his chief of staff, Major McClay, saw him in the act of fainting from his severe, but not dangerous wound, that he was persuaded to dismount. Even after he was placed on a litter, he would not allow himself to be removed from the battle-field until he heard that Scurry's brigade was out of all danger. Never were troops better handled, and orders more quickly executed than by the troops of Waul's and Randall's brigades. They had already driven the enemy from the top of the hill. The piles of the enemy's dead attest the correctness of our aim, and the obstinacy of the conflict; most gallantly did those two brigades sustain their well-earned reputation, stimulated and encouraged by the conduct of their officers, and wakened to a perfect enthusiasm by the presence of their brigade commanders, Generals Waul and Randall, who, utterly regardless of all danger, rushed into the thickest of the fight, rallying their troops, where they showed any signs of wavering, disposing their forces so as to protect their weakest point. Our division artillery kept up a continual fire on the enemy's line, making sad havoc among them. The enemy form their second line of battle in a skirt of timber, about half a mile from their original line, for the purpose of mak-

ing another effort to regain the hill they were driven from ;
Mouton's Division, now commanded by the gallant and
chivalric French General Polignac, among the first to
abandon the ease and comfort of a luxurious home to engage
in the perilous conflict for Southern independence, is ordered
to reinforce Walker's Division. Standing erect in his saddle,
he hallooed aloud : " My boys, follow your Polignac." This
fine division of Texans and Louisianians need no appeal or in-
centive. It overflows with ardor and impatience for the conflict.
The Louisianians, burning to avenge the wrongs and insults
of their beloved State, shouted as they advanced, " Mouton !"
as their battle-cry; while the brigade of gallant Texans with
the cool and intrepid veteran Harrison to lead them, as he
led his regiment to victory at the battle of Borbeaux, responded with a shout.

The last division was Green's cavalry, forming close on
Polignac's, and ready to leap into the first opening where
fighting was to be done. The fight now became general. Each
line moved forward, encountering every few hundred yards or
so a battery strongly supported by the enemy's infantry, with
the same unvarying result. Often our men recoiled and faltered under the iron tempest from these terrible batteries, but
our indomitable chiefs would re-collect and re-form their men
and return to the charge. The enemy maintained his position
with unusual firmness ; three several times did our brave boys
charge them, when at times it became a hand conflict ; but
as often as we charged them, we were hurled back as if by a
resistless and superhuman power. Officers galloped along our
lines calling loudly for another charge. The lines halted. The
troops seemed transfixed with horror or stunned with dismay,
they neither advanced nor receded, but gazing at the frightful
line of the enemy, and then at the ground before them, covered with their killed and wounded comrades, they paused,
faltered, and seemed to be fast verging towards a panic.
It was a critical point in the bloody drama; the enemy's lines
must be broken. Generals Kirby Smith and Dick Taylor perceived this, and determined to throw themselves into the

breach, not in the spirit of bravado or a mere vain-glorious desire of parading their heroism ; least of all, from any such petty or ignoble weakness as that imagined by small minds— a feeling of chagrin and conscious injustice on account of the criticisms and censure that had been so heedlessly indulged in towards them by the thoughtless and misinformed (in judging them as selling the Trans-Mississippi Department to General Banks)—but from a high and lofty spirit of patriotism and self-sacrifice that looked only at the danger to their country and the cause, which confronted them. Seeing the inability of the other commanders to make their men charge the enemy's lines, both Generals Kirby Smith and Dick Taylor seized a musket, and called upon the troops to follow them. The grand figures of their commanders-in-chief mounted upon their large black stallions, looming up from the foreground, so conspicuous as target for the enemy's sharpshooters, seemed to expand to gigantic proportions, as they beckoned their men to the charge. The gallant troops of Walker's Division were the first to follow. - Polignac's Division and Green's Cavalry caught the heroic contagion, and now our line moved forward at double-quick, and then, with a wild rush, receiving the deadly iron blast as it swept down the slopes, and rushing over their batteries, they scattered the heavy masses of the enemy's infantry in the wildest confusion. This was the might-iest effort of physical force and courage of the day ; and when it was performed, the tall figure of the patriotic Governor of Louisiana, W. H. Allen, could be seen on the crest of the hill, waving his hat in triumph, while the shouts of our troops echoed far off, like the roar of many waters. The news is re-ceived that Scurry's Brigade, while in the act of crossing a ravine, about two hundred yards from the enemy, are attacked by a large force, and part of our forces are captured, numbering about two hundred and fifty officers and soldiers. The cause assigned for their capture was the fact that many of our troops, on their arrival at the ravine, deemed it a safe place to fight in ; every shot from the troops in the ravine made a vacancy in the enemy's ranks. Singular to relate, the men in the ravine found themselves in squads, without any of those squads seeing each other, really not knowing the strength of the forces until after they were taken prisoners, owing to the zig-zag shape of the ravine. The enemy had crossed the ravine above them, and marched diagonally between them, thus cutting off their retreat and compelling our men to surrender. Our cavalry, on the left, under the bold and fearless Green, pressed down upon the enemy's flanks, compelling them to retreat, leaving their dead and wounded on the battle-field, and leaving us in possession of their camps that they had occupied in the morning, we pursuing them as long as we could see any of them.

Night was over all, and the stars began to shine: our wounded and those of the enemy's were removed and cared for.

Our troops were now utterly worn out. The men fell down in the ranks from exhaustion. They had fought for two days, in incessant and unparalleled battles, routing and pursuing the enemy, which, if fully related, would fill a volume larger than this book. The shades of the evening began to gather over the scene. The curtain of night was about to fall on the bloodiest tragedy ever enacted in the Trans-Mississippi Department. As long as there was a streak of light by which a gun could be aimed, our indefatigable cavalry made use of it. Thus closed the battle of Pleasant Hill, in which less than 20,000 Southern volunteers proved the equals of a splendidly appointed army of 40,000 of the best soldiers in the United States army.

Our loss and that of the enemy was about in proportion to the battle of Mansfield. Banks' army returned to Grand-Ecore, on Red River, where they would be under the protection of their gun-boats. During their retreat they destroyed the balance of their train, lest we should draw on their Commissary again.

CHAPTER XXVI.

SCENES AFTER THE BATTLE.

F any of my readers have ever been in a battle, and many of them I know have, they will recall all the horrors of that sad scene—the blood and carnage of the fight, the wild shouts of victory and vengeance, the ghastly forms of the dead piled in all shapes, the groans of the wounded, who call on you in mercy to shoot them in order to put them out of pain. Some bodies are disfigured; they have either been torn to pieces by shells, or scattered about by horses and wheels of artillery. Their clothes alone keep the shattered remains together.

Dead and maimed horses lie about, some still plunging and endeavoring to drag their broken limbs after them. The poor animals look at you most reproachfully, as much as to say, I had nothing to do with all this carnage. I was brought here against my will, and why should I suffer? A visit to the first field-hospital is the most painful thing of all. It resembles a butcher's shamble, with maimed and bloody men lying on all sides;—some with their arms off; some with their legs off; some awaiting their time, while the doctors, with upturned cuffs and bloody hands, are flourishing their knives and saws, and piles of bloody-looking limbs are strewn around them, while some who have died on the dissecting table, add to the ghastly picture. After all, the physical sufferings here are not greater than the moral sufferings of dear ones at home, whose friends have been engaged in battle. They hear that a great battle has been fought—a great victory won. This is joyful news, indeed; but the heart yearns to learn the fate of friends. Many a parent, wife, sweetheart, tremblingly opens the newspaper and casts the eye along the list of killed and wounded. Alas! that cry and stifled groan tells the dreadful news. There is mourning in that house—mourning in many a house, North and South, for the soldiers that will never return. There are broken hearts, gray hairs, desolate homes, widows and orphans, as the price of victory.

There are some whose names appear missing in the newspaper, and yet they have not been heard from. Friends hope they have been taken prisoners. Comrades return from the war, but can tell nothing about them. Hope grows into suspense, the heart is sick of this uncertainty. The green leaves become brown and fall, the winter passes away, the beautiful spring smiles again, yet nothing is heard from the long absent, but not forgotten soldier. No, they will never hear from him till that great accounting-day, when all mankind shall be summoned together; for he dragged himself to die beneath the shade of a tree, where his flesh was picked by the birds of the air, and his bones have long since moldered into dust.

CHAPTER XXVII.

GENERAL TAYLOR AND GOVERNOR ALLEN'S ADDRESS TO THE ARMY OF WESTERN LOUISIANA.

GENERAL TAYLOR'S ADDRESS.

OLDIERS OF THE ARMY OF WESTERN LOUISIANA :—At last have your patience and devotion been rewarded. Condemned for many days to retreat before an overwhelming force, as soon as your reinforcements reached you, you turned upon the foe. No language but that of simple narrative should record your deeds.

On the 8th day of April you fought the battle of Mansfield. Never in war was a more complete victory won. Attacking the enemy with the utmost alacrity when the order was given, the result was not for a moment doubtful. The enemy was driven from every position ; his artillery captured, his men routed. In vain were fresh troops brought up. Your magnificent line, like a resistless wave, swept everything before it. Night alone stopped your advance. Twenty-one pieces of artillery, 2,500 prisoners, many stands of colors, 250 wagons, attest your success over the 13th and 19th Army Corps. On the 9th you took up the pursuit and pressed it with vigor. For twelve miles, prisoners, scattered arms, burning wagons, proved how well the previous day's work had been done by the soldiers of Texas and Louisiana.

The gallant divisions from Missouri and Arkansas, unfortunately absent on the 8th, marched forty-five miles in two days to share the glories of Pleasant Hill. This was emphatically the soldiers' victory.

In spite of the strength of the enemy's position, held by

fresh troops of the 16th Corps, your valor and devotion triumphed over all. Darkness closed one of the hottest fights of the war. The morning of the 10th dawned upon a flying foe, with our cavalry in pursuit, capturing prisoners at every step. These glorious victories were most deadly won. A list of the heroic dead would sadden the sternest heart. A visit to the hospital would move the sympathy of the most unfeeling. The memory of our dead will live as long as noble deeds are cherished on earth. The consciousness of duty well performed will alleviate the sufferings of the wounded.

Soldiers! from a thousand homes thanks will ascend to the God of battles for your victories. Tender wives and fond mothers will repose in safety behind the breastworks of your valor. No fears will be felt that the hated foe will desecrate their homes by his presence. This is your reward, but much remains to be done. Strict discipline, prompt obedience to orders, cheerful endurance of privations, will alone insure our independence.

*   *   *   *   *   *   *   *   *

GOVERNOR ALLEN'S ADDRESS TO THE SOLDIERS OF MISSOURI, ARKANSAS, TEXAS, AND LOUISIANA.

In the name of the people of Louisiana, I congratulate and thank you for our late brilliant victories. Your insolent foe, after months of preparation, advanced his vast columns, supported by an enormous fleet of gun-boats, marking his pathway with pillage, desecration, and wanton destruction. When he thought the fruits of victory within his grasp, and when his mercenary hirelings were gloating over their plunder, you fell on them with a blow so sudden and so crushing, that they were hurled back in terror and dismay on the path made desolate by their villainy. You have slain, wounded or captured one-third of their grand army, and every day brings some new token of your valor, some new trophy of your victory. You have stript the Federals of their well-appointed artillery and their rich-laden trains. You have met the Yankee chief in the day of his pride, and torn from him his laurels, and from his followers their stolen wealth. You have destroyed a portion of his boats, and more will doubtless fall into your hands. Louisiana will never forget her gratitude to the noble soldiers who have punished and rebuked the remorseless invader of their soil. Brave, gallant soldiers! you fight neither for pay nor for fame, but for independence and your sacred rights. Yet fame will be yours. It will be a proud boast of the children of another age, that their fathers fought at Mansfield and Pleasant Hill. In the midst of the turmoil and din of war the individual names of soldiers are unheard, but time hallows their memory and emblazons their deeds. A great, free, and noble race, dwelling in the land you are now making glorious with your chivalry and your blood, will gladly do honor to those who fought to make them free.

Soldiers! the God of battles has been with you. By his help and your own stout hearts and strong arms, you have gained the most complete victory ever won in this department. The veterans of Missouri vied with those of Arkansas, while the Texan and Louisianian rushed side by side into the shock of battle. We have to mourn the loss of many a gallant son. Let us drop a tear over their hallowed graves, then seize our weapons with a firmer grasp, and push the bayonet with a more deadly thrust.

Soldiers! the eternal God of justice will give us victory in the end. Our bleeding country will be redeemed and saved, and in due time you shall see your homes again.

From Western Louisiana you send your brothers in arms, now fighting under Lee, Johnston and Beauregard, the glorious tidings of your recent great victories. We have more work to do. This campaign, however, will be short. Our armies have thus far triumphed on every field. We have vanquished the enemy everywhere. Within the last forty days we have gained ten victories. Rest assured, that before the autumn sun shall shine upon your brave and manly forms, you will hear the welcome order :

> " Soldier, rest, thy warfare's o'er ;
>   Sleep the sleep that knows no breaking ;
> Dreams of battle-fields no more,
>   Days of danger, nights of waking."

CHAPTER XXVIII.

THE FEDERAL REPORT OF THE BATTLES OF MANSFIELD AND PLEASANT
HILL, AND THE RETREAT OF THE FEDERAL ARMY.

N the 13th of March, 1864, one division of the 13th
Corps, under Brigadier-General Mower, and one
division of the 17th Corps, under Brigadier-General
T. Kilby Smith—the whole under command of Brigadier-
General A. J. Smith—landed at Simmsport, on the Atchafalaya, and proceeded at once toward Fort De Russy, carrying it
by assault, at 4 30 P. M., on the afternoon of the 14th. Two
hundred and sixty prisoners and ten heavy guns were captured. Our loss was slight. The troops and transports under
General A. J. Smith, and the Marine Brigade under General
Ellet, with the gun-boats, moved to Alexandria, which was occupied without opposition on the 16th of the same month.

General Lee, of my command, arrived at Alexandria on the
morning of the 19th.

The enemy, in the mean time, continued his retreat through
Cheneyville, in the direction of Shreveport. Officers of my
staff were at Alexandria on the 19th, and I made my headquarters there on the 24th, the forces of General Franklin
arriving on the 25th and 26th of March; but, as the stage of
the water in Red River was too low to allow the passage of
the gun-boats or transports over the falls, the troops encamped near Alexandria, General Smith and his command
moving forward twenty-one miles to Bayou Rapids, above
Alexandria. There were but six feet of water in the channel,
while seven and one-half feet were necessary for second-class
boats, and ten feet for first-class boats. The river is narrow,
the channel tortuous. changing with every rise, making its

navigation more difficult and dangerous, probably, than any of the Western rivers, while pilots for the transports were reluctant to enter government service for this campaign.

The first gun-boat was unable to cross until the 26th; others crossed on the 28th, with some transports, and others still on the 2d and 3d of April—the passage being made with difficulty and danger, occupying several days.

Several gun-boats and transports, being unable then to ascend the river, remained at Alexandria, or returned to the Mississippi. While at Alexandria, Major-General McPherson, commanding at Vicksburg, called for the immediate return of the Marine Brigade—a part of General Smith's command—to protect the Mississippi, for which purpose it had been specially organized. The transports of the brigade were unable to pass above Alexandria. The hospital boat "Woodford" had been wrecked on the rapids in attempting to make the passage up. The troops were suffering from small-pox, which pervaded all of the transports, and they were reported in a condition of partial mutiny. It was not supposed, at that time, that a depot or garrison would be required in Alexandria, and this command, being without available land or water transportation, were permitted to return to the Mississippi, in compliance with the demand of General McPherson. This reduced the strength of the advancing column about three thousand men.

The condition of the river, and the inability of the transports to pass the falls, made it necessary to establish a depot of supplies at Alexandria, and a line of wagon-transportation from the steamers below to those above the falls. This was a departure from the plan of the campaign, which did not contemplate a post or depot at any point on the Red River, and involved the necessity of leaving a division at Alexandria for the purpose of protecting the depot, transports, and supplies. Brigadier-General C. Grover was placed in command of the post, and his division left for its defense. This reduced the force of the advancing column about three thousand men.

While at Alexandria, on the 21st instant, a movement was organized against the enemy posted at Henderson's Hill, twenty-five miles in advance. The expedition consisted of three brigades of General A. J. Smith's command, and a brigade of cavalry of the 19th Corps, under command of Colonel Lucas, of the 16th Indiana Volunteers; the whole under command of Brigadier-General Mower, of the 16th Corps. The enemy was surprised, losing two hundred and fifty prisoners, two hundred horses, and four guns with their caissons. Colonel H. B. Sargent, of my staff, was severely wounded in this action, and disabled from service during the campaign. This affair reflected the highest credit upon the officers and men engaged.

Anticipating by a few days the passage of the gun-boats, the army marched from Alexandria for Natchitoches, eighty miles distant by land, reaching that point on the 2d and 3d of April. The enemy continued his retreat, skirmishing sharply with the advanced guard, but offering no serious resistance to our advance.

The only practicable road from Natchitoches to Shreveport was the stage-road through Pleasant Hill and Mansfield, distant one hundred miles, through a barren, sandy country, with little water, and less forage, the greatest portion an unbroken pine forest.

A reconnoissance from Natchitoches on the 2d of April, under command of General Lee, discovered the enemy in force at Pleasant Hill, thirty-six miles distant, and established the fact that a portion of Green's command had arrived from Texas, and were then confronting us. Prisoners captured from Price's command indicated what had been feared from a loss of time at Alexandria—a concentration of all the available force of the enemy, numbering, according to the statement of prisoners and intercepted letters, about twenty-five thousand men and seventy-six guns.

The river was perceptibly falling, and the larger gun-boats were unable to pass Grand-Ecore. The troops under command of General A. J. Smith, who had hitherto moved in

13

transports by the river, now marched by land from Natchitoches, with the exception of one division of the 17th Corps—two thousand five hundred men—under Brigadier-General Smith, which, by order of General A. J. Smith, continued its movement by the river, in company with the fleet, for the protection of the transports. The arrangement of land transportation for this portion of the column, the replenishing of the transports from the supply-trains, and the distribution of rations to the troops, were made at this point; but the fleet was unable to ascend the river until the 7th of April. The condition of the river would have justified the suspension of the movement altogether, at either point, but for the anticipation of such change as to make it navigable. Upon this point the counsel of the naval officers was implicitly followed.

On the 4th of April, Colonel O. P. Gooding, commanding a brigade of cavalry, engaged upon a reconnoissance north of Red River, encountered Harrison's command—one thousand five hundred strong—in which the enemy was defeated, with considerable loss. Our loss was about forty in killed, missing, and wounded. The enemy's repulse was decisive.

The army was put in motion for Shreveport, via Pleasant Hill and Mansfield, April 6th. General Lee, with the cavalry division, led the advance, followed by two divisions of the 13th Corps, under command of General Ransom; first division, 19th Corps, under General Emory; and a brigade of colored troops under General Dickie—the whole under the immediate command of General Franklin. The detachments of the 16th Corps, under command of Brigadier-General A. J. Smith, followed on the 7th, and a division of the 17th Army Corps, under command of Brigadier-General T. Kilby Smith, accompanying Admiral Porter, on the river, as a guard for the transports.

The fleet was directed to Loggy Bayou, opposite Springfield, where it was expected communication would be established with the land forces at Sabine Cross-roads, a distance of fifty miles by land from Grand-Ecore, and one hundred miles by water.

I remained with my staff to superintend the departure of the land and water forces from Grand-Ecore, until the morning of the 7th, and then rode rapidly forward, reaching the head of the column the same evening, where the main body encamped. General Smith's command was at the rear of the column, on the march, but passed the negro brigade on the road to Pleasant Hill. A very heavy rain fell on the evening of the 7th, which greatly impeded the movement of the rear of the column, making the roads almost impassable for troops, trains, or artillery. The storm did not reach the head of the column. In passing the troops from Natchitoches to Pleasant Hill, I endeavored as much as possible to accelerate their movements.

The enemy offered no opposition to the march on the 6th. On the 7th the advance drove a small force to Pleasant Hill, and from thence to Wilson's farm, three miles beyond, where a sharp fight occurred, with the enemy posted in a very strong position, from which they were driven with serious loss, and pursued to St. Patrick's Bayou, near Carroll's mill, about nine miles from Pleasant Hill, where our troops bivouacked for the night. We sustained in this action a loss of fourteen men killed, thirty-six wounded, and nine missing. We captured many prisoners, and the enemy sustained great losses in killed and wounded. During the engagement, General Lee sent to General Franklin for reinforcements, and a brigade of infantry was sent forward ; but the firing having ceased, it was withdrawn. The officers and men fought with great spirit in this affair.

At daybreak on the 8th, General Lee, to whose support a brigade of the 13th Corps, under Colonel Landrum, had been sent by my orders, advanced upon the enemy, drove him back from his position on the opposite slde of St. Patrick's Bayou, and pursued him to Sabine Cross-roads, about three miles from Mansfield. The advance was steady, but slow, and the resistance of the enemy stubborn. He was only driven from his position on the cross-roads by artillery. At noon on the 8th, another brigade of the 13th Corps arrived at the cross-roads, under Brig.-General Ransom, to relieve the 1st Brigade.

The infantry moved from Pleasant Hill at daybreak on the 8th, the head of the column halting at St. Patrick's Bayou in order that the rear might come up. I passed General Franklin's headquarters at 10 A.M., giving directions to close up the column as speedily as possible, and rode forward as rapidly as possible to ascertain the condition of affairs in front, where I arrived between one and two o'clock. General Ransom arrived nearly at the same time, with the 2d Brigade, 13th Corps, which was under his command in the action at the cross-roads.

I found the army in line of battle, the skirmishers sharply engaged, the main body of the enemy posted on the crest of of a long hill in thick woods on both sides of a road leading over the hill to Mansfield on our line of march.

It was apparent that the enemy was in much stronger force than at any previous point of the march, and being confirmed in this opinion by General Lee, I sent General Franklin, immediately on my arrival, a statement of the facts, and orders to hurry the infantry with all possible dispatch, directing General Lee at the same time to hold his ground steadily, but not advance until reinforcements should arrive. Our forces were for a long time stationary, with some skirmishing on the flanks. It soon became apparent that the entire force of the enemy were in our front. Several officers were sent forward to General Franklin to hurry up the column. Skirmishing was incessant during the afternoon. At 4.30, P.M., the enemy made a general attack all along the lines, but with great vigor on our right flank. It was resisted with resolute determination by our forces; but overwhelming numbers compelled them, after resisting the successive attacks of the enemy in front and on the flanks, to fall back from their position to the woods in rear of the open field, which they occupied, retreating in good order. The enemy pressed with

great vigor upon the flanks, as well as in front, for the purpose of getting to the rear, but were repulsed in this attempt
by our cavalry.

At the line of woods a new position was assumed, supported by the 3d Division of the 13th Army Corps, under
General Cameron, which reached this point about 5 P.M.,
and formed in line of battle under direction of Major-General
Franklin, who accompanied its advance. The enemy attacked
this second line with great impetuosity and overpowering
numbers, turning both flanks and advancing heavily upon the
center. The assault was resisted with gallantry; but the troops
were compelled to yield the ground, and fall steadily back.
The road was badly obstructed by the supply-train of the
cavalry division, which prevented the retreat of both men and
artillery. We lost ten guns of Ransom's Division in consequence of the position of the train, which prevented their
withdrawal. Repeated efforts were made to re-form and
resist the advance of the enemy; but though their progress
was checked, it was without permanent success.

Brig.-General W. H. Emory, commanding 1st Division,
19th Corps, had been early notified of the condition of affairs,
and instructed to advance as quickly as possible, and form a
line of battle in the strongest position he could select to support the troops in retreat, and check the advance of the
enemy. The order to advance found him seven miles in the
rear of first battle-ground. He assumed a position at Pleasant Grove, about three miles from the cross-roads, on the
edge of a wood commanding an open field sloping to the
front. The 161st New York Volunteers, Colonel Kinsay commanding, were deployed as skirmishers and ordered to the
front of the hill, upon the edge of which the line was formed,
to cover the rear of the retreating forces, to check the pursuit of the enemy, and give time for the formation of the troops.

General Dwight, commanding 1st Division, formed his
troops across the road upon which the enemy was moving,
commanding the open field in front; the 3d Brigade, Colonel
Benedict commanding, formed to the left, and the 2d Bri-

gade, General McMillan, in reserve. The line was scarcely formed when the 161st New York were attacked and driven in. The right being threatened, a part of General McMillan's Brigade formed on the right of General Dwight. The fire of our troops was reserved until the enemy were at close quarters, when the whole line opened upon them with the most destructive volley of musketry. The action lasted an hour and a half. The enemy was repulsed with very great slaughter. During our fight a very determined attempt was made to turn our flank, but was defeated. Prisoners reported the loss of the enemy in officers and men to be very great. General Mouton was killed in the onset. Their attack was made with great desperation, apparently with the idea that the dispersion of our forces at this point would end the campaign, and with the aid of the falling river, leave the fleet of transports and gun-boats in their hands, or cause their destruction. Nothing could surpass the impetuosity of the enemy but the inflexible steadiness and valor of our troops. The 1st Division of the 19th Corps, by its great valor in this action, saved the army and navy. But for this successful resistance to the attack of the enemy at Pleasant Grove, the renewed attack of the enemy with increased force could not have been successfully resisted at Pleasant Hill on the 9th of April. We occupied both battle-grounds at night.

From Pleasant Grove to Pleasant Hill, where this action occurred, was fifteen miles. It was certain that the enemy, who were in reach of reinforcements, would renew the attack in the morning, and it was uncertain whether the command of General Smith could reach the position we held, in time for another engagement. For this reason the army toward morning fell back to Pleasant Hill, General Emory covering the rear, burying the dead, bringing off the wounded and all the material of the army.

It arrived there on the morning of the 9th, at half-past eight, effecting a junction with the forces of General Smith and the colored troops, under Colonel Dickey, which had reached that point the evening previous.

Early on the 9th, the troops were ready for action, the movements of the enemy indicating that he was on our rear. A line of battle was formed in the following order : 1st Brigade, 19th Corps, resting on a ravine, from the right ; 2d Brigade in the center, and 3d Brigade on the left. The center was strengthened by General Smith's forces, whose main force was held in reserve. The enemy moved toward our right flank. The 2d Brigade withdrew from the center to help the 1st Brigade. The brigade in support of the center moved into position ; and another, General Smith's Brigade, was posted on the extreme left position on the hill, in *echelon*, to the rear of the left main line. Slight skirmishing occurred during the afternoon. Between 4 and 5 o'clock it increased in vigor, and about 5 P. M., when it appeared to have nearly ceased, the enemy drove in our skirmishers, and attacked in force, his first onset being against the left. He advanced in two oblique lines, extending well over to the right of the 3d Brigade, 19th Corps. After a determined resistance, this part of the line gave way, and went slowly back to the reserves. The 1st and 2d Brigades were soon enveloped in front, right and rear. By skillful movements of General Emory, the flanks of the two brigades now bearing the brunt of battle were covered. The enemy pursued the brigades, passing the left and center, until he approached the reserves, under General Smith, when he was met by a charge led by General Mower, and checked. The whole of the reserves were now ordered up, and in turn we drove the enemy, continuing the pursuit until night compelled us to halt. The battle of the 9th was desperate and sanguinary. The defeat of the enemy was complete, and his loss in officers and men more than double that sustained by our forces. There was nothing in the immediate position or condition of the two armies to prevent a forward movement the next morning, and orders were given to prepare for an advance. The train, which had been turned to rear on the day of battle, was ordered to re-form and advance at daybreak. I communicated this purpose at the close of the day to General A. J. Smith, who expressed his concurrence therein.

But representations subsequently received from General Frank-lin, and all the general officers of the 19th Corps, as to the condition of their respective commands for immediate active operations against the enemy, caused a suspension of this order, and a conference of the general officers was held, in which it was determined, upon the urgent recommendation of all the general officers above-named, and with the acquiescence of General Smith, to retire upon Grand-Ecore the following day. The reasons urged for this course by the officers of the 13th and 19th Corps were: First, that the absence of water made it necessary to advance or retire without delay. General Emory's command had been without rations two days, and the train, which had been turned to the rear during the battle, could not be put in condition to move forward upon the single road, through dense woods, in which it stood, with-out difficulty and loss of time. It was for the purpose of com-municating with the fleet at Springfield Landing, from the Sabine Cross-roads to the river, as well as to prevent the con-centration of Texan troops with the enemy at Mansfield, that we had pushed for the early occupation of that point. Con-sidering the difficulty with which the gun-boats passed Alexan-dria and Grand-Ecore, there was every reason to believe that the navigation of the river would be found impracticable. A squadron of cavalry, under Mr. Young, who had formerly been employed in the surveys of this country, and was now connected with the engineer department, which had been sent on a reconnoissance to the river, returned to Pleasant Hill on the day of the battle, with the report that they had not been able to discover the fleet, nor learn from the people its pas-sage up the river. The report of General T. Kilby Smith, commanding the river forces, states that the fleet did not arrive at Loggy Bayou until 2 o'clock, P. M., on the 10th of April, two days after the battle at Sabine Cross-roads. This led to be-lieve that the low water had prevented the advance of the fleet. The condition of the river, which had been steadily falling since our march from Alexandria, rendered it doubtful, if the fleet ascended the river, whether it could return from any intermediate point; and probable, if not certain, that if it reached Shreveport, it would never escape without a rise of the river, of which all hopes began to fail.

The forces designated for this campaign numbered forty-two thousand men. Less than half this number were actually available for service against the enemy during its progress. The distance which separated General Steele's command from our field of operations (nearly two hundred miles) rendered his movement of little moment to us or the enemy, and reduced the strength of the fighting column to the extent of his force, which was expected to be from 10,000 to 15,000 men. The depot at Alexandria, made necessary by the impracticable navigation, withdrew from our forces 3,000 men, under General Grower. The return of the Marine Brigade to the defense of the Mississippi upon the demand of Major-General McPherson, and which could not pass Alexandria without its steamers, nor move by land for want of land transportation, made a further reduction of 3,000 men. The protection of the fleet of transports on both sides of the river made it necessary for General A. J. Smith to send General T. Kilby Smith's Division of 2,500 men from the main body for that duty. The army-train required a guard of 500 men.

These several detachments, which it was impossible to avoid, and the distance of General Steele's command, which it was not in my power to correct, reduced the number of troops from 42,000 to 20,000 men. The losses in the three battles of the 8th, 9th, and 10th of April amounted to about 3,969 men, and reduced our active force that amount. The enemy, superior to us in the outset, by falling back, was able to cover his great losses by reinforcements, which were within his reach as he reached his base of operations, while we were growing weaker as we departed from ours. We had fought the fight at Pleasant Hill with 15,000 against 22,000 men, and won a victory, which, for this reason, we were unable to follow up.

Other considerations connected with the actual military

condition of affairs afforded additional reasons for the course recommended.

Between the commencement of the expedition and the battle of Pleasant Hill, a change had occurred in the general command of the army, which caused a modification in my instructions in regard to this expedition.

Lieutenant-General Grant, in a dispatch which I received on the 27th of March, at Alexandria, which was dated March 15, gave me the following instructions : " If you find that the taking of Shreveport will occupy ten or fifteen days more than General Sherman gave his troops to be absent from their command, you will send them back at the time specified in his note (blank date) March, even if it should lead to the abandonment of the main object of the expedition. Should it prove successful, hold Shreveport and Red River with such force as you deem necessary, and return the balance of your troops to the neighborhood of New Orleans." These instructions, I was informed, were given for the purpose of having " all parts of the army, or rather all arms, act as much in concert as possible," and with a view to a movement in the spring campaign against Mobile, which was certainly to be made, if troops enough could be obtained without embarrassing other movements, in which event New Orleans would be the point of departure for such an expedition.

A subsequent dispatch, though it did not control, fully justified my action, repeated these general views, and stated that the commanding general would much rather the Red River expedition had never been begun, than that you should be detained one day after the 1st of May in commencing the movement east of the Mississippi.

The limitation of time referred to in these dispatches was based upon the opinion which I verbally expressed to General Sherman, at New Orleans, that General Smith could be spared in thirty days after we reached Alexandria ; but it was predicated upon the expectation that the navigation of the river would be unobstructed ; that we should advance at once upon Alexandria, Grand-Ecore, or elsewhere, on account of low water, and that the forces of General Steele were to co-operate at some point on the Red River, near Natchitoches or Monroe. It was never understood that an expedition that involved on the part of my command a land march of nearly four hundred miles in the enemy's country, and which terminated at a point which we might not be able to hold, either on account of the strength of the enemy or the difficulty of obtaining supplies, was limited to thirty days. The condition of our forces and the distance and difficulty attending a farther advance into the enemy's country, after the battles of the 8th and 9th against superior numbers, rendered it probable that we could not occupy Shreveport in the time specified, and certain that, without a rise, the troops necessary to hold it against the enemy would have to evacuate it for want of supplies, and impossible that the army should return to New Orleans in time to co-operate with the general movements of the army contemplated for the spring campaign. It was known at this time that the fleet could not repass the rapids at Alexandria, and it was doubtful, if the fleet reached any point above Grand-Ecore, whether it would be able to return. By falling back to Grand-Ecore we could determine the condition of the fleet, the practicability of continuing the movement by the river, reorganize the troops that had been shattered in the battles of the 7th, 8th, and 9th ; possibly ascertain the position of General Steele, and obtain from him the assistance needed for a new advance up the river or upon its southern bank, and perhaps obtain definite instructions from the government as to the course to be pursued. Upon these general considerations, and without reference to the actual condition of the respective armies, at 12 o'clock on the 9th, I countermanded the order for the return of the train, and directed preparations for the return of the army to Grand-Ecore. The dead were buried, and the wounded were brought in from fields of battle and placed in the most comfortable hospitals that could be provided, and surgeons and supplies furnished for them. A second squadron of cavalry, under command of Mr. Young of the engineer department, was sent to inform the

fleet of our retrograde movement, and to direct its return if
it had ascended the river; and on the morning of the 10th
the army leisurely returned to Grand-Ecore. The wounded
were immediately visited by Dr. Sanger, who took with him
clothes, rations, medicines, and other supplies, and pronounced them in comfortable condition.

The fleet sailed from Grand-Ecore on the 7th, and arrived at Loggy Bayou on the evening of the 10th, one day
after the battle at Pleasant Hill, and two days after the one
at Sabine Cross-roads. General T. Kilby Smith received a
verbal message on the evening of the 10th, and on the morning of the 11th written orders to return.

The transports were in a crippled condition, rudders un-
shipped and wheels broken. The enemy attacked the fleet,
on its return, near Pleasant Hill Landing, on the 12th, with
a force of about 2,500 cavalry, a strong reserve of infantry,
and ten guns, under General Green. But the troops, protected by cotton bales and bales of hay, with the gun-boats,
kept up a deadly fire and drove the enemy from the river.
For two miles the bank was strewn with the wounded and
dead. Among the rebel officers who were killed was General
Green, who was left dead upon the field. The troops of the
transports saw him fall, and claim it was the work of their
artillery—the gun-boats and transports firing at the same
time. The enemy, under Liddell, who had occupied the north
bank with 2,500 men, attacked the fleet on the 13th, but was
driven back with loss. The navigation up and down the river
was intricate and dangerous, and the steamers were frequently aground. Several of the boats were laden with ammunition and ordnance stores, but the energy of the officers
and men brought off every boat. The only loss in stores was
one hundred sacks of oats, thrown overboard to relieve a boat
aground. They reached Compte on the 18th with a loss of
one man killed and eighteen wounded, where they met a force
sent from the army for their assistance, and reached Grand-
Ecore on the 15th without furthur obstruction. General T.
Kilby Smith, to whom I am indebted for much of my infor-

mation on this subject, mentions with commendation Major D. C. Houston, who had the ammunition and ordnance stores in command, and Lieutenant-Colonel W. S. Albert, of my staff, who accompanied him; also officers and men of his own command, and masters of transport steamers. General Smith, who commanded the land forces and transports, is entitled to the highest commendation, for the energy, skill, and success with which he managed this most difficult affair.

Lines of defense were established at Grand-Ecore on the 12th of April, and orders given to attack the enemy if he approached. A pontoon bridge was thrown across the river during the night. Our pickets were driven in on the 13th. But the enemy appeared, upon a reconnoissance made in front, to have gone below, either for the purpose of attacking our troops at Alexandria or occupying Monet's Bluff, on Cane River. On the same day General Smith crossed the river with two brigades, two batteries, and a strong cavalry force, to aid the fleet still above Grand-Ecore. Dispatches were sent to General Steele informing him of the condition of affairs, and requesting him to join us at some point on the river. Orders were sent to New Orleans for reinforcements, and the lieutenant-general was informed of the state of affairs by telegraph, and of my intention to advance upon Shreveport if General Steele would come to my assistance, and of my intention not to withdraw without orders.

The fleet returned on the 15th in safety, without the loss of vessel or material of war. Admiral Porter, with whom I had a conference on his arrival at Grand-Ecore, advised against any further attempt to ascend the river without a rise, and his counsel was followed. The river had been steadily falling. Supplies were brought up to Ecore with great difficulty.

It was found that two of the gun-boats would not go below Grand-Ecore, and it was now certain that the fleet would not pass the falls at Alexandria.

Lieutenant-commander Selfridge, left in command of the fleet by the admiral, who had gone to Alexandria, sent me a dispatch dated 17th April, stating that he was informed the army was to withdraw immediately, and that it would be impossible in that case to get the boats down the river. I informed him at once that the army had no intention of withdrawing from that, position ; that I had sent to New Orleans for troops, and, by special messenger, to General Steele to cooperate ; and that till it was definitely ascertained that his assistance would fail us, and that my force would be insufficient to advance further upon the line against the enemy, who appeared to be in full force, I should entertain no thought of a retrograde movement, and never, if it left the navy in any danger. No such purpose was entertained, and till I received information in reply to my dispatches, it was my purpose to maintain my position. A copy of this letter is appended to this report. The next day I received instructions from Lieutenant-General Grant (to which I have referred), that if my return was delayed one day beyond the first of May, when it would be necessary for my command to co-operate with other armies in the spring campaign, it would have been better the campaign had never been attempted. These instructions, with the fact that the river was not likely to rise, the report received by Captain R. T. Dunham, that General Steele could not co-operate with us, and that the difficulty of passing the falls of Alexandria was hourly increasing, if the passage were not even then impossible, led me to change my determination.

It was not, however, until the entire fleet was free, transports and gun-boats, and that Admiral Porter, in charge of the "Eastport," which had been aground for some days several miles below Grand-Ecore, sent me word by Colonel W. S. Albert, whose statement is here appended, that she was clear, and further protection unnecessary, that orders were given, the 21st of April, to turn the supply-trains in the direction of Alexandria. The army moved on the morning of the 22d of April, every vessel having preceded both the marching orders and movement of the army. Any statement that the army contemplated moving from Grand-Ecore toward Alexandria, against the advice or without the approval of the naval officers in command, or until the departure of every vessel in the river, is without the slightest color of truth.

In my interview with Admiral Porter, on the 15th of April, he expressed the utmost confidence that the river would rise, and gave me no intimation of his withdrawal from Grand-Ecore, or of the proposed withdrawal of his vessels, nor of the apprehension of the retreat of the army. I gave him at that time distinct information of my plans, which were to advance. This fact was communicated to Lieutenant-Commander Selfridge, in my letter of the 17th of April.

The admiral expressed the same confidence to officers of the army who from long experience in the Red River country were equally confident that it would not rise. The difficulties attending the voyage of the "Eastport" were incident to the condition of the river, for which the army was in no wise responsible. I had offered every assistance possible, and did not leave this position while any aid was suggested or required.

Colonel Baily, after consultation with the general officers of the army, offered to float the "Eastport" over the bars by the construction of wing-dams, similar to those afterward built at Alexandria; but the assistance was declined. No counsel from army officers was regarded in nautical affairs.

The army marched from Grand-Ecore on the 22d of April, having been detained there ten days by the condition of the navy. To prevent the occupation of Monet's Bluff, on Cane River, a strong position commanding the only road across the river to Alexandria, or to prevent the concentration of the enemy's forces at that point, it became necessary to commence the evacuation without his knowledge, and to prevent his strengthening the natural defenses, by the rapidity of our march. The conflagration of a part of the town at the time appointed for our movement, partially frustrated our first object, but the second was fully accomplished.

The army marched from Grand-Ecore to Cane River, a distance of forty miles, on the 22d of April, and moved on the position held by the enemy, at daybreak, on the 23d. About 8,000 men and sixteen guns, under command of General Bel, were found in possession of the bluff, on the opposite side of the river, who were surprised to see the presence of our army, but ready to dispute our only passage to Alexandria. At daybreak one division of the 19th and 20th, the cavalry commanded by General Arnold and the artillery by Captain Classon, the whole under the command of General W. H. Emory, were ordered forward to the river for the purpose of forcing this position. The pickets were encountered on the west side of the river and quickly driven across; but the main division was found to be too strong to be carried by direct attack. A reconnoitering party, under Colonel Baily, of the 4th Wisconsin Volunteers, sent to ascertain the practicability of crossing the river below the ferry toward Red River, on the morning of the 23d, reported that the river was not fordable below the ferry; and that, owing to the impassable swamps on one side and the high bluffs on the other, it would be impossible to cross Cane River below the ferry. If we failed to dislodge the enemy, the only alternative was to attempt a crossing on the north side of the Red River, a very dangerous movement.

At the same time, a force under command of General H. W. Birge, consisting of his own division, the 3d Brigade of the 1st Division, 19th Army Corps, Colonel Fessending commanding, and General Cauwren's Division, were ordered to cross the river three miles above, turn the left flank upon the enemy, and carry the heights in reverse, if possible. Upon the success of this movement depended the passage of the river by the army. The route traversed by General Birge's command lay through bayous, swamps, and almost impenetrable woods. This force reached its position late in the afternoon. To accomplish their purpose it was necessary to carry two strong positions held by skirmishers and pickets, before the enemy was encountered in force on the crest of a hill commanding an open field, over which our troops were forced to cross in making the attack. The 3d Brigade, 19th

Corps, Colonel Fessending commanding, carried this position, which was defended with vigor, by assault. Its occupation compelled the retreat of the enemy from the bluffs commanding the ferry and ford.

Our loss in this brilliant and most successful affair, was about two hundred killed and wounded.

Colonel Fessending, who led his command with gallantry, was severely wounded. General Birge, as in all actions in which he was engaged, deserved and received the highest commendation. Lieutenant William Beebe, of the ordnance department, and Mr. Young, of the engineer department, both volunteers, were conspicuous in the fight. Mr. Young was twice wounded, and died in July, at New Orleans, of wounds received in this battle. The attack on the rear of the enemy's retreat failed in consequence of the difficulty encountered on the march, and the late hour at which our troops gained their position.

The enemy was thus enabled to escape with his artillery, by the St. Jessup Road, to Texas.

The main body of the army had moved from Clouterville, at 4 30, P.M., on the 23d, to the river.

They drove in the enemy's pickets three miles in advance of the river, and formed a line of battle in front of the enemy's position, while General Birge was moving on the enemy's left flank. The enemy opened with a heavy cannonade from his batteries, which was returned by our artillery with spirit and effect. The fire was continued at intervals during the morning, but the troops were held in reserve for the purpose of effecting the passage of the river the moment General Birge commenced his attack on the right. The attack lasted till dark, when the enemy retreated, leaving our forces in possession of the heights. General A. J. Smith's command had sharp skirmishing with the advance of the enemy on our rear on the 23d.

At two o'clock on the morning of the 24th, six guns were fired from the camp of the enemy in our rear. It was interpreted as a signal that they were ready for a combined

15

attack; but the enemy in front had then been driven from the river, and the contemplated movement upon our front and rear failed.

During the morning of the 23d, an effort was made by a portion of the cavalry under Colonel E. J. Davis, to turn the right flank of the enemy's position, by crossing the river below the ferry in the direction of Red River, which proved impracticable on account of the swamps. A sharp engagement took place on the morning of the 24th, between the troops of General T. Kilby Smith and the enemy in the rear, which resulted in the repulse of the latter. Our loss was about fifty in this affair.

Had the enemy concentrated his forces and fortified his position on Monet's Bluff, we could not have forced him from it, and should have been compelled to run the chances of crossing Red River above Cane River, in the presence of the enemy on both sides of the river. Orders had been sent to General Grover to move on Monet's Bluff with his forces, should it be occupied by the enemy, or our march be seriously obstructed; and his troops were in readiness for this movement. The army marched from Monet's Bluff on the 24th of April, and established lines of defense at Alexandria on the 25th and 26th of April.

In the intervening twenty-four days between the departure of the army from Alexandria and its return, the battles of Wilson's Farm, Sabine Cross-roads, Pleasant Grove, Pleasant Hill, Compte, Monet's Bluff, and several combats in the neighborhood of Grand-Ecore, while we were in occupation of that point, had been fought. In every one of these battles we were successful, except the one at Sabine Cross-roads. The failure to accomplish the object in view was due to other considerations than the superiority in numbers of the enemy in the field. In these operations, in which my command had marched 400 miles, the total loss sustained was about 3,980 men, of whom 289 were killed, 1,541 wounded, and 2,150 missing: a large portion of the latter have since been returned, but a considerable number returned at Red River.

None of the artillery or stores were lost, except the loss sustained at Sabine Cross-roads. We lost there Nims's Battery and a portion of the St. Louis Howitzer Battery, 150 wagons and 800 mules, captured by the enemy on account of the position of the train near the field of battle. Up to this time no other loss has been sustained by our army.

As soon as the lines of defense were completed, preparations were made for the return of the fleet, then above the falls.

From the difficulty encountered by the supply transports in passing the falls, it was known at Grand-Ecore as early as the 15th of April, that the fleet could not pass the falls, and the means of its release freely discussed by army officers. During the campaign at Port Hudson, the steamers "Starlight" and "Red Chief," were captured by the Illinois cavalry under Colonel Prince, at Thompson's Creek. The bed of the creek was dry and the boats were sunk several feet in the sand after the capture of Port Hudson. Colonel Baily constructed wing-dams, and floated them into the Mississippi. This incident naturally suggested the same works at Alexandria for the relief of the fleet. A survey was ordered to determine what means could be best undertaken. The engineers had completed the survey of the falls, captured from the enemy during the campaign. It was found, upon examining them and surveying the river, that the river channel was narrow and crooked, and formed in solid rock, and it would be impracticable to deepen its bed.

It was therefore determined to construct a dam and float the vessels over the falls. Capt. Palfrey, who made the survey, said he thought it feasible, and the only question was how long a time would be necessary for so great a work.

The management was intrusted to Lieutenant-Colonel Baily, of the Fourth Wisconsin Volunteers, who was used to such work, and had successfully freed the boats on Thompson's Creek. Colonel Baily had suggested building a dam while at Grand-Ecore, and had offered to relieve the "Eastport" when aground below Ecore by the same means, which offer was declined.

Material was collected and work commenced on Sunday, May 1st. The dam was completed Sunday, May 8th, and the "Osage," "Hindman," and two others came over the rapids at 4 P.M. The water had been raised by the dam seven feet, with a fall below the dam of six feet, making a fall of thirteen feet above and below the dam. The pressure of water at its completion was terrific. I went over the work at eleven o'clock on the morning of the 8th, and felt that the pressure was so great it could not stand. I rode immediately to the point where the fleet was anchored, to see if they were ready. I reached the fleet about midnight; scarcely a light or a man was to be seen. It was apparent the boats were not ready to take advantage of the completion of the dam, and feeling it could not stand another day, I wrote a note to Admiral Porter at one o'clock on the morning of the ninth, which was delivered in person at 2 A.M., by Col. J. G. Wilson, stating my belief as to the condition of the dam and the fleet, and asking that measures be taken to put the boats in condition to float over the dam at the earliest moment possible in the morning.

A little after five on the morning of the ninth I saw part of the dam swept away. The four boats that had passed the rapids the day before were able to pass below through the opening the water had made. Only one of the vessels above the falls, the "Lexington," was ready to move when the dam gave way, and came down and passed the dam safely, with all the vessels that were below the rapids. Had the others been ready to move, all would have passed the rapids and dam safely on Monday. Until after the dam had been carried away, no effort had been made to lessen the draught of the imprisoned vessels by lightening them of cargo, armament, or plating. Before the second series of dams were completed a portion of the armament and the plating, materially lessening the draught and depth of water, were removed. Lieutenant W. S. Beebe of the ordnance department, U. S. A., superintended the removal of the heavy naval guns from above the rapids by land, assisted by officers and men of the army. The army immediately commenced the reconstruction of the dam. This new dam was completed on the 12th of May, and on that afternoon all the boats passed below the rapids to the dam. At six o'clock in the evening the "Mound City" and "Carondelet" passed the dam in safety. The other boats remained above until the morning of the 13th. The water above the dam was falling, but at nine o'clock all the boats had passed safely.

Preparations had been made for a movement of the army the evening after the passage of the boats below the dam on the twelfth, and after all were below, on the 13th, orders were given to march.

The construction of the dam was the work of the army; but little aid or encouragement was received from officers of the navy, except Lieutenant A. R. Santhorne, commanding the "Mound City," who assisted in setting the cribs, and was always ready to assist the officers in charge of the work.

The soldiers labored zealously, night and day, from the 1st to the 13th of May inclusive, when the passage of the boats was completed.

Upon my arrival at Alexandria, on the 25th of April, I found Major-Gen. Hunter with dispatches from the Lieutenant-General, reaffirming instructions which I had received at Ecore, relating to operations of the army elsewhere and the necessity of bringing the Shreveport campaign to an end right away. The only possible means of executing the orders had already been taken. Gen. Hunter left on the 18th with dispatches to the Lieutenant-General, informing him of the condition of affairs;—that the fleet could not pass the rapids, that there was no course for the army but to remain for its protection; that it would be necessary to concentrate all our forces to protect both army and navy and destroy the enemy.

Major-Gen. McClernand, with the largest part of the forces necessary, recently, at Matagorda Bay, which had been evacuated by order of Gen. Grant, dated March 31st, arrived at Alexandria on the evening of the 29th April. Brigadier-Gen. Fitz Henry Warren, left in command of Matagorda Bay, followed with the rest of the forces in Texas, except on the

Rio Grande, where the batteries of the enemy at Marksville obstructed the passage of the fleet and army. While engaged in the construction of the dam, a dispatch was received from Major-Gen. Halleck, dated April 30th, as follows:

"General Grant directs that orders heretofore given be so modified as not to withdraw any troops from the operations against Shreveport and on Red River, and that operations be continued there until further orders."

This dispatch was not received until it was too late to move either up or down the river from Alexandria. It was of course then impracticable to execute these orders.

Lieutenant Simpson, of my staff, left by the gun-boat "Signal" with dispatches for Lieutenant-General Grant, Admiral Farragut, General Sherman, and General Rosecrans. The gun-boat Covington, having in convoy the transport Warner, accompanied the Signal. We received news on the 6th, of the destruction of the gun-boats and transport. The enemy had established a battery near Marksville, supported by a large infantry force. Communication with the Mississippi was closed from this date.

Lieutenant Simpson was captured, but destroyed his dispatches. The "City Belle," on her way to Alexandria with four hundred and twenty-five men of the 120th Ohio Volunteers, was captured by the enemy. Two hundred of the troops escaped.

The fleet passed below Alexandria on the 13th of May. The army, on its march, did not encounter the enemy in force until near Mansura; he was driven through the town in the evening of the 14th. At daybreak next morning our advance encountered his cavalry on the prairie, east of the town; he fell back, with steady and sharp skirmishing, to a belt of woods, which he occupied. The enemy's position covered three roads diverging from Mansura to the Atchafalaya. He manifested here a determination to obstinately resist our passage. The engagement, which lasted several hours, was confined to the artillery, until our troops got possession of the edge of the woods—first upon our left by General Emory, and subsequently on our right, by General Smith, when he was driven from the field after a sharp and decisive fight, with great loss.

The 16th of May we reached Simmsport, on the Atchafalaya. Being entirely destitute of any material for building a bridge to pass this river, about six hundred yards wide, a bridge was constructed of the steamers, by Colonel Baily. This work was not of the same magnitude, but was of as much importance to the army as the dam at Alexandria was to the navy. It had the merit of being an entirely novel construction, as no bridge of such magnitude was constructed of the same material. The bridge was completed at 1 o'clock, on the 19th of May. The wagon-train passed over that afternoon ; the troops next morning, in better spirit and condition to meet the enemy than at any time during the campaign. The command of General A. J. Smith, which covered the rear during the construction of the bridge and passage of the army, had a severe engagement under Polignac, on the afternoon of the 19th, at Yellow Bayou, which lasted several hours. Our loss was one hundred and fifty in killed and wounded ; that of the enemy greater, besides many prisoners taken by our army.

Major-General E. R. S. Canby arrived at Simmsport on the 19th May, and assumed command of the troops, as a portion of the forces of the division west of the Mississippi, to which he had been assigned.

Rumors were freely circulated about the camp at Alexandria, that the town would be burned upon its evacuation. To prevent this destruction of property, part of which belonged to loyal citizens, General Grover, commanding the post, was instructed to form a thorough police, and to provide for its occupation by an armed force, until the army had marched for Simmsport. The measures taken were sufficient to prevent a conflagration in the manner it had been anticipated. But on the morning of the evacuation, while the army were in full possession of the town, a fire broke out in a building on the levee, occupied by refugees or soldiers, in such a manner as to make it impossible to prevent a conflagration.

I saw the fire when it was first discovered. The ammunition and ordnance transports, and the depot of ammunition on the levee, were within a few yards of the fire. The boats were floated out in the river, and the ammunition moved from the levee with all possible dispatch. The troops labored with vigor to suppress the flames, but owing to the high wind and combustible matter of the building, it was found impossible to limit its progress, and a considerable portion of the town was destroyed. On the 1st of April, two or three days before the army moved from Alexandria to Natchitoches, an election of delegates to the constitutional convention was held at Alexandria, by request of the citizens of the parish of Rapides. No officer or soldier interfered with or took any part in it. It was left exclusively to the loyal citizens of the place.

Three hundred votes were cast,—a large majority of the voting population of the parish. Fifteen hundred votes were a full representation before the war.

Nearly five hundred men from this and adjacent parishes enlisted and gave efficient service during the campaign.

Under the general prize-law the naval authorities, upon their arrival at Alexandria, commenced the capture of cotton on both sides of the river, extending eight or ten miles in the interior. Wagon-trains were organized, gins set running, and the business carried on with great success, while the fleet lay at Alexandria. Some difficulty occurred with the marines, who insisted upon their right to pass the lines of the army, which was terminated by the advance of the army and navy to Grand-Ecore.

I was informed by parties claiming property which had been taken by the naval authorities, to whom I referred them, that upon application the property had been restored to them by the commander of the fleet. The army did not enter into competition with the navy in the capture of this property. In order to remove all the products from the country, that might aid in the rebellion against the government, General

Grover, in command of the post at Alexandria, and the quartermaster at Alexandria, after the departure of the army, were directed to gather all property that might remain there after its departure, and transmit it to the quartermaster at New Orleans, who was instructed to turn it over to the officers of the treasury, to be disposed of according to the laws of Congress.

Notice was also given to the supervising agent of the treasury, at New Orleans, that no trade was to be carried on with that portion until after its occupation by the army. No person was allowed to accompany this expedition as reporter, or for any other purpose, except on a written declaration that no trade by private parties would be permitted under any circumstances, and that no property on private account would be transported on public or private vessels to New Orleans; but that all property sent to New Orleans would be consigned to the chief-quartermaster, and by him turned over to the treasury agent, and held subject to such claims as would be approved at Washington.

Previous to my departure from New Orleans, the chief quartermaster, Col. S. B. Holabird, had been instructed that no privileges would be given to any party whatever, under any circumstances whatever, to trade in, dispose of, or sell private property; that property coming down from that country, so far as the army was concerned, would be turned over to him, and by him to the proper treasury officer.

The same information was given to the treasury agent. No person was given permission to accompany the army except on these express conditions, and then only to persons whose public position seemed a full guarantee against the abuse of the privilege, and when requests could not properly be refused. They were given to reporters of the public press, and to prominent officers of States whose troops were in the field.

Upon representation made by officers of the treasury department at Alexandria, that there would be some trouble in receiving such property, except upon the treasury regulations of the 26th of January, 1864, these regulations were officially promulgated for that purpose at Alexandria and New Orleans.

These orders were enforced by all officers connected with or representing the army. There was no privilege given to any person to trade in, dispose of, or transport private property; no privilege of this kind was recognized under any circumstances.

Every dollar's-worth of property that came into the army's hands, during this campaign, was either appropriated to its use, in kind, by the officers of the commissary or treasury department, receipts being given therefor, or transmitted to the chief quartermaster at New Orleans, and by him turned over to the Treasury Department, to be disposed of according to laws of Congress.

Where cotton interfered with the transportation of army material, refugees or niggers, or troops, upon the evacuation of the country, it was thrown from the boats to the levee. I intend this statement to be as comprehensive as language can make it, and to cover all possible methods, direct or indirect, by which officers or citizens could evade or violate these laws on the river, or at New Orleans, or appropriate public or private property to personal advantage, or deprive the government or individuals of any property which, by any interpretation of military orders or public laws, could be considered as justly belonging to them.

General Grover, commanding the post, Colonel S. B. Holabird, chief quartermaster at New Orleans, and Hon. B. F. Flanders, supervising special agent of the Treasury Department, will be able to account for public or private property coming into their hands during this campaign.

I was engaged upon the Gulf, hoping, by the capture of Galveston and Mobile, to put my command in readiness to co-operate effectively, by Mobile and Arkansas River, with General Sherman, in accordance with the campaign suggested by the Lieutenant-General commanding the armies, in his dispatches of the 15th and 31st of March, when I received instructions to communicate with the admiral and officers commanding the fleet and forces of the Upper Mississippi, upon the subject of the campaign against Shreveport.

I immediately complied with these orders. They had received similar instructions, and, upon communication, expressed their readiness to enter upon the campaign. With the forces contemplated, and the co-operation of the fleet, its success was reasonably certain. Under such circumstances I could not decline co-operating with them. I at once abandoned all other enterprises and gave my whole attention to this enterprise.

The first difficulty encountered was encountered in the navigation of the river. Sixteen days' delay in passing the rapids at Alexandria, and three days' delay at Grand-Ecore in awaiting the rise of the river, enabled him (the enemy) to concentrate his forces, and rendered impossible that celerity of movement on which the enterprise rested. Eight days of the delay at Alexandria may be attributed to the delay of organizing Franklin's command ; but the fleet was unable to pass the rapids until eight days after his arrival at Alexandria. This delay was owing to the impracticable navigation of the river; but it is not improper to say, that the forecast and diligence which are forced upon men in the daily routine of life would have forbidden an attempt to force a fleet of so much importance to the free navigation of the Mississippi, to a point from which it could never hope to escape, unless on the theory that the river ought to or would rise. The movement of the navy, in a dispatch of Rear-Admiral D. D. Porter, to which the Secretary of the Navy has given official publication and sanction, is attributed to the request of General Banks, who deemed the co-operation of the gun-boats so essential for success that he (Porter) had to run some risks, and get them over the falls. This implies that the responsibility of his action rests upon the army ; but it is not consistent with the facts.

The co-operation of the navy was an indispensable basis of the expedition. Major-General Halleck informed me, January 11th, that he had been informed that Admiral Porter would be prepared to co-operate with the army in its movements ; and the admiral himself informed me, February 26th, that he was prepared to ascend Red River with a large fleet of gun-boats, and to co-operate with the army at any time when the water was high enough. The fleet was as necessary to the campaign as the army. Had it been left to my direction, I should have preferred undertaking a campaign requiring but eight or ten light-draft gun-boats, to forwarding twenty heavy iron-clads 490 miles, on a river proverbially as treacherous as the rebels who defended it, and which had given notice of its character by falling when the other rivers were rising.

There is a better reason for disregard of the palpable difficulties of navigation, than the over-zealous counsels of the army officers in nautical affairs. Admiral Porter afterwards dispatched to me : " I have reached Grand-Ecore with my vessels with ease, and with some of them I reached Springfield Landing, the place designated for the boats to meet the army. My part was completed. The failure of the army to advance, and the retreat to Grand-Ecore, left me entirely at the mercy of the enemy." The records of the campaign do not all support the fiery ardor of this statement.

The fleet did not reach the designated point until two days after the first decisive battle with the enemy. The admiral occupied four days in moving 104 miles, on what he called a rising river, with good water, to the place appointed. General T. Kilby Smith reports, that the fleet made twenty-seven miles on the 7th, fifty-seven on the 8th, sixteen on the 9th, and nine on the 10th of April ; total, 104 miles. The failure of the fleet, with usual expedition, together with the fact that the gun-boats were unable to pass Grand-Ecore until the 7th, justifies the conclusion that its advance was hindered by low water, and governed the army in its retrograde movement to Grand-Ecore, as it did on every important occasion during the campaign. The admiral's dispatch does not state that, besides the mercy of the enemy, he had left to him General T. Kilby Smith's command of 2,500 men, whose most gallant act is not mentioned at all in what the admiral calls "this curious affair" between the enemy's infantry and the gun-boats. In view of the published dispatches of Admiral Porter, it is my duty to say, that every position of difficulty in which the army was placed was the immediate result of the delay of the navy. This may have been inevitable and entirely justifiable, from the condition of the river—it is not my province to pass judgment; but the fact remains, nevertheless.

During my term of service it has been my rule of conduct not to pass judgment on the conduct of other officers, but I feel it my bounden duty to say, in this official and formal answer, that the published statement of Admiral Porter, in reference to the Red River campaign, is at variance with the truth, of which there are many thousand living witnesses, and does foul injustice to the officers and men of the army ,to whom the navy department owes exclusively the preservation and honor of the fleet.

The partial disintegration of several commands assigned to this expedition was a cause of embarrassment, but not of failure.

The command of Major-General Steele, whose command, I was informed by Major-General Sherman, would be 15,000 strong, numbered, in fact, but 7,000 men; these operating over a line 700 miles in extent, whose purpose or results were entirely unknown to me.

I was informed by General Steele, that if any advance was to be made at all, it would have to be made by the Washita and Red Rivers, and that he might be able to move his command to Monroe for that purpose. This would have united our forces on Red River, and insured the success of the campaign. On the 28th of February, he informed me he could not move by the way of Monroe; and on March 1st, one day before I was ordered to move, I was informed by General Sherman that he had ordered General Steele to move direct to Shreveport. March 5th, I was informed by General Halleck that he had no knowledge of Steele's movement, except that he had been ordered to facilitate my movements toward

Shreveport. March 10th, General Steele informed me that his objections against the road I wished him to take were stronger, and that he would move to Washington, and thence to Shreveport. I received information on the 26th, dated March 6th, from Major-General Halleck, that he had instructed General Steele to make a real movement, as suggested by you (Banks), instead of a demonstration that he (Steele) thought advisable. In April, General Halleck informed me that he had ordered General Steele to coöperate with me with all available forces. April 16th, I was informed by General Sherman that he had ordered Steele to concentrate all his available forces with my army and navy. In May I received information of April 28th, from Steele, saying he could not leave Camden unless supplies were sent him, as those of the country were exhausted; that we could not help each other, our lines operating so far from each other; that he could not say, definitely, he would join me at any given time or place on Red River; and that from the distance between us I could render him no assistance—an opinion in which I concurred. I never received authority to give orders to General Steele; my orders were to communicate with him on the subject of the expedition. His orders he received from other sources. I have no doubt that General Steele did all in his power to insure success; but, as communication with him was necessary by special messenger, and occupied from fifteen to twenty days, for each communication, it was impossible for either of us to fully comprehend the relative position of the two armies, or to assist or support each other.

The command of General A. J. Smith was a partially independent command. General Sherman, in his dispatch of the 16th, dated the 10th, informed me that the thirty days for which he lent me General Smith's command would expire on the 10th of April—the day after the battle of Pleasant Hill. General Smith's instructions compelled him to correspond with Admiral Porter. His orders were dated "Headquarters, Red River Expedition, Steamer Clara Bell." He never received orders from me. He was in no wise accountable for the failure of the expedition, and may be said to have gained as much by its failure as by its success. After his thirty days had run out, he claimed the right to go to Vicksburg, notwithstanding the condition of the army or fleet, and did not hold himself responsible for any damage done them by his departure, nor for the lack of that attention which their preservation demanded ; that responsibility I was called upon to assume in written orders. I entertain no doubt that his official course was in consistency with his orders. I cheerfully acknowledge the generous efforts made by General Mower, of the 16th, and General T. Kilby Smith, of the 17th Corps, to infuse into the different corps that unity which was necessary for the success of the campaign.

I gladly accord to the men the honor of having fought a desperate enemy, superior in number, with as much gallantry and success as that which signalized my immediate command. No higher praise than this can be accorded any soldiers. Alexander's troops never fought better.

The result of the position of the cavalry-train, and the loose order of march of Major-General Franklin's command, on the 8th of April, before the battle of Pleasant Hill, has been stated. A commanding officer is responsible for what happens to his troops, no matter what the cause. I do not shrink from this responsibility. But while it was both proper and necessary for me to give personal attention to the movement from Grand-Ecore, on the morning of the 7th, it was supposed that the moving of a column of 15,000 men, moving in a single road for not less than fifty miles, in such a manner as to be able to encounter the enemy, if he offered resistance, might safely be intrusted to an officer of the reputation and experience of General Franklin, whose rank, except in one instance, was superior to that of any one of the officers in the Gulf Department.

I make no complaint of the navy, except in view of the prolific dispatches long since published on this campaign. I may properly repeat a few facts already stated. The success of the expedition depended on celerity of movement.

The navy delayed the army sixteen days at Alexandria, and three days at Grand-Ecore; it occupied four days in going 104 miles upon what the dispatches call a rising river and good water; where it arrived two days after the first, and one day after the decisive battle of the campaign, at Pleasant Hill. These are not opinions, they are facts; to the army they are bloody and pregnant events. The difficult navigation, the failure to concentrate the forces, and the limited time were the cause of its failure. We owe nothing to the enemy—not even our defeat.

Could any one of these difficulties have been avoided, the success would have been accomplished. But the occupation of Shreveport could not be maintained. The presence of the enemy would have required such a powerful force for its defense as could not have been obtained by the river, and for which no other preparation had been made, as suggested in my dispatches of March 30th. The only way of keeping this place would be by concentrating a force superior to that of the enemy, with time to pursue wherever he might go, even if it took us to Galveston and the Gulf Coast. This was suggested as a possible means of the results of the campaign, but was not embraced in the original plan, and it was specially precluded by the Lieutenant-General commanding the army.

I remain

Your obedient servant,

N. P. BANKS, M. G. V.

CHAPTER XXIX.

MARCHING ORDERS.—EN ROUTE FOR CAMDEN.—DEATH OF GENERAL TOM
GREEN.—ARRIVAL OF THE 3D TEXAS INFANTRY.—NAMES OF THE OFFI-
CERS.—MARCH THROUGH SHREVEPORT AND MINDEN.—GENERAL KIRBY
SMITH'S ADDRESS.—OPERATIONS OF THE ARKANSAS AND MISSOURI CAV-
ALRY.—EVACUATION OF CAMDEN.—IN PURSUIT OF THE ENEMY.—DESO-
LATION OF THE COUNTRY.—BREAKERS AHEAD.

THE morning of the 10th of April dawned, and beholding no enemy in sight, we learned, much to our surprise, that they had retreated during the night, as
they had done after the battle of Mansfield. Our division
received orders to fall back towards Mansfield. The Arkansians and Missourians were likewise ordered to fall back,
leaving the cavalry and Polignac's Division of Infantry to pursue the enemy.

After falling back from the battle-field, we continued our
march some ten miles, when we arrived in camp. Shortly
after our arrival in camp, we received orders to be ready, at a
moment's notice, to take up the line of march for Camden,
Arkansas, for the purpose of giving battle to the enemy, who
had possession of the town. The force of the enemy at Camden was variously estimated at 18,000 men, under the command of General Steele, who had previously preconcerted the
plan with General Banks to meet him at Shreveport. How
far the two armies got towards Shreveport the sequel will
show.

On the morning of the 11th we continued the march.
After marching about ten miles, we arrived at camp, north of
the town of Mansfield. Shortly after our arrival in camp, we
heard the melancholy news of the death of General Tom
Green. He was killed at Blair's Landing, on Red River,

16

while he was in the act of placing his artillery, in order to destroy the enemy's fleet.

April 14th. Marched twenty-one miles.

April 15th. Marched twenty miles. Shortly after our departure from camp, we passed by the camp of the 3d Texas Infantry, commanded by Colonel Sackett; they had just arrived from Texas, and were ordered to report for duty to General Scurry; they were assigned to his brigade. On our march through the city of Shreveport, you could behold thousands of officers gossiping over the late victories. We crossed Red River at Shreveport, on a pontoon bridge, and camped about two miles from the city.

April 16th. Marched ten miles, and camped on Bayou Red Chute.

NAMES OF THE OFFICERS OF THE 3D T. V. INFANTRY.

Colonel—P. N. SACKETT.
Lieut.-Col.—E. F. GRAY.
Major—S. G. NEWTON.
Surgeon—E. W. BRITTON.
Assistant Surgeon—R. L. HARRIS.
Quartermaster—F. SEIBERT.
Commissary— —— ——
Adjutant—HENRY MCCORMICK.

COMPANY A.

Captain, F. Frickie.
1st Lieut., E. Merreim.
2d Lieut., L. D. Brewster.
2d Lieut., F. Dreyzehner.

COMPANY B.

Captain, P. J. Biesenbuck.
1st Lieut., F. C. Radcliff.
2d Lieut., A. Koeing.
2d Lieut., Gusteve Uhl.

COMPANY C.

Captain, D. Lively.
1st Lieut., B. H. Luckett.
2d Lieut., W. C. Anderson.
2d Lieut., R. C. Daily.

COMPANY D.

Captain, J. B. Hicks.
1st Lieut., O. Newman.
2d Lieut., P. Scott.

COMPANY E.

Captain, Miles Elkins.
1st Lieut., Sam Fleming.
2d Lieut., G. W. Bird.
2d Lieut., Leonard Moss.

COMPANY F.

Captain, Jno. Rosenheimer.
1st Lieut., Manuel Ztuni.
2d Lieut., Jules Hafner.

COMPANY G.	COMPANY I.
Captain, F. H. Sherhagen	Captain, J. M. Trainer.
1st Lieut., P. Shardin.	1st Lieut., John Watson.
2d Lieut., Allison Ryman.	2d Lieut., L. H. Brown.
	2d Lieut., L. H. Brown.
COMPANY H.	COMPANY K.
Captain, T. H. Hulig.	Captain, Jules Bosi.
1st Lieut., Wm. Byrd.	1st Lieut., L. Sarasin.
	2d Lieut., H. Schlenning.

April 17th. Crossed Bayou Red Chute, on a pontoon bridge. Marched through the village of Fillmore, and camped near the town of Minden, after marching twenty miles.

April 18th. Passed through the town of Minden, with banners flying, and keeping step to the tune of "Dixie." The streets were crowded with young ladies, waving their handkerchiefs, and cheering us most lustily. Their enthusiasm seemed to know no bounds, and at every gate they stood with bouquets to present to the troops as they passed. May patriotic Minden long prosper, and never may her streets be trod by any hated foe! We arrived at camp early in the day, after marching twelve miles. We rested at this camp until the morning of the 20th. The men and animals were thoroughly fagged out. While remaining at this camp, the following patriotic address from General Kirby Smith was read on dress parade to us.

* * * * * *

God has blessed our arms with signal victories at Mansfield and Pleasant Hill. The general commanding finds it an appropriate occasion to pay a well-merited tribute to the endurance and valor of the troops engaged in these battles.

Collected from remote points—from Missouri, Arkansas, Louisiana, and Texas—after long and tedious marches, their combined courage has gained, on the soil of Louisiana, the patriot-soldier's highest reward, victory. They have driven in confused flight from the battle-field the boastful minions of despotism.

In the name of a grateful people I thank them for this splendid result. While we mourn for the glorious dead, and sympathize with the heroic wounded, let us take courage for the future.

By prompt obedience to orders and patient endurance, we will be enabled to repeat this great achievement whenever the enemy shall advance in force against any part of the Trans-Mississippi Department.

When the soldiers of Missouri, Arkansas, Louisiana, and Texas stand together in battle, with the blessing of God, we confidently expect victory.

The names of Mansfield and Pleasant Hill will be inscribed on the colors of the regiments engaged in these battles.

(Signed,)   General E. KIRBY SMITH.

On the morning of the 20th we marched six miles, to Walnut Creek, and camped, by order of General E. Kirby Smith, who had taken the field in person. He announced taking command in person as follows :

"Major-General E. Kirby Smith assumes command of the army of Arkansas. His headquarters will be at the junction of the Wire and Buena Vista roads.

Major-General Price is hereby assigned to the immediate command of the Missouri and Arkansas divisions of infantry."

After taking command, he wrote to General Taylor, describing the situation of the enemy at Camden. He estimated the enemy's force at about 18,000. He established his headquarters at Woodlawn, within seventeen miles of Camden. He immediately ordered a cavalry force of 3,000, under command of General Fagan, across the Ouachita River, to cut off the enemy's supplies, between Pine Bluff and Camden. He also instructed General Fagan to attack Pine Bluff and Little Rock, as those two towns had but a very small garrison for their defense. If successful in capturing those two towns, to cross the Arkansas River and destroy the enemy's depot at Duval's

Bluff, on White River, and unite his forces, if possible, with General McRae, who was engaged in collecting all the available forces inside the enemy's lines.

While encamped at Walnut Creek, our camps were completely beset by the female inhabitants of the surrounding country, many coming from a distance of fifteen and twenty miles, to see the soldiers, and hear the bands play. While remaining here, we learned that the Federal general, Steele, was strongly fortified at Camden, but that he was closely invested by General Price's army, with no possible chance of his escape.

Many amusing incidents occurred between the ladies and soldiers of this camp. The soldiers used to visit the farmers' dwellings, especially where there were some bright-eyed lassies; thus exhibiting that fondness for feminine society and companionship which characterized them when at home. A worthy private soldier, with his "chums," comprising an entire mess, had been frequent visitors at a farmer's house near the encampment, where two really handsome and accomplished ladies resided. Rising one day from an agreeable *tête-à-tête* over the dinner-table, two or three of the men considered it nothing more than an act of politeness to invite the farmer and his family to take dinner with them the following day. "I shall certainly do so, with pleasure," was the reply. Nothing more was thought of the invitation until the next morning, near the dinner-hour, when who should make their appearance in camp but the farmer, wife, daughters, and small members of the family (as he had promised), to dine with the "boys." There was nothing prepared, and, worse than all, no provisions on hand with which to prepare a suitable dinner. The joke was soon known all over camp. The men strolled negligently about the unfortunate victims in groups, to enjoy and add to their discomfiture; and sly jokes, witticisms, and suppressed laughter greeted them on all sides, as they escorted their visitors through the encampment. They determined not to be the subject of fun for the whole regiment; so, "*nil desperandum,*" with commendable zeal a portion of the mess made preparations for dinner, while the remainder " played the agrèeable." By dint of borrowing and begging, a really nice meal was served up, consisting of the following bill of fare : corn-bread, hominy, with some rancid blue beef. " Not very palatable," says the farmer, " but I take a little to prevent hunger." Now, add to this most detestable water, and the bill of fare is completed. The mess, for once in the history of the company to which they belonged, were excused from drill that day, and a fashionable meal eaten in the encampment.

The weather was dark, gloomy, and very damp, while we remained at this camp, but even that didn't keep the ladies away. They still roamed through the camp, gratifying their natural curiosity. On the morning of the 24th inst. we resumed the march in the direction of Camden; crossed the State line dividing Arkansas and Louisiana; noticed a change in the character of the country.

April 25th. Marched sixteen miles. Passed through a little town named Calhoun. After our arrival in camp, we learned that General Steele had succeeded in getting supplies from Pine Bluff.

On the morning of the 26th, we marched eighteen miles, and camped within twelve miles of Camden. Many were the surmises, rumors, and reports about Steele's army. Occasionally we would hear that General Price's army had the enemy completely surrounded, with no possible chance of escape, and momentarily expecting the surrender of Steele and his army ; and again, we heard that General Price had all the forces necessary, without the aid of Walker's Division of Texans.

General Kirby Smith's headquarters were within a few miles of our camp. After our arrival at this camp, we learned more fully the strength of our forces that were opposing the enemy, their situation, etc. We discovered, much to our surprise, that the enemy remained unmolested in Camden, sending out his cavalry scouts all over the country, and no obstacles thrown in his way to prevent him from joining his forces with Banks's army, at Alexandria. He was left perfectly unmolested, to withdraw from Camden or to advance on Shreveport at leisure. Until the arrival of Walker's Division no effort was made to check his career, except the crossing of part of our cavalry to the east side of the Ouachita River.

It is useless to deny the fact that, up to the period of the arrival of Walker's Division, no campaign was ever worse conducted. As soon as General Steele discovered the object of General Kirby Smith, he determined to evacuate Camden and fall back to Little Rock. Having cut down a number of wagons, as well as throwing the greater part of his artillery into the river, he succeeded in crossing his troops to the east side of the river, which feat he completed by sunrise on the morning of the 27th. Hearing of the evacuation of Camden, General Kirby Smith at once issued orders for the troops to pursue Steele to his fortifications at Little Rock. On our march towards Camden, we passed by the headquarters of General Price, better known as " Old Pap," so called by his troops. We arrived at Camden at 4 o'clock, P. M., and received orders to cook three days' rations. Singular to state, the evacuation of Camden was not known (or, if so, not acted on) in our army until   o'clock in the morning, notwithstanding the reports that there was no possible chance for Steele's army to escape. But he gave our generals to understand that he was too old a bird to be caught with chaff. The fortifications at Camden, constructed by General Holmes, and improved by the enemy, were not inferior to any in the Trans-Mississippi Department, and, from the appearance of the place, we should have had some difficulty in taking it, if the enemy had not left.

Being without a pontoon-train of any kind, it was necessarily a slow and difficult undertaking to cross our infantry.

On the morning of the 28th we commenced crossing the Ouachita River, on a hastily-constructed floating bridge of plank. No transportation was allowed us. The troops carried their own rations and ammunition. After getting across the river, we continued our line of march in pursuit of the flying foe, satisfied that Walker's Greyhounds would overtake the enemy before they got to Little Rock, notwithstanding they had about thirty hours start of us. Our cavalry having crossed the river, they took their position in advance. No one doubted but that the flight of the enemy would soon be checked. After marching fourteen miles, we camped for the night.

April 29th. Left camp at 3 o'clock, A. M. On we traveled, mile after mile, with no sign of the enemy, other than the blackened ruins which marked his path. Passed through the town of Princeton, and encamped on a creek two miles beyond, after marching twenty miles. During the night it commenced to rain, and partly overflowed our camp.

April 30th. Continued our march at 3 A. M. On our arrival at the town of Tulip, we were informed that the rear-guard of the enemy had passed scarce two hours before. All then became wild with excitement. The troops, although broken down with fatigue, became fired with new life and energy, and redoubled their efforts to overhaul the flying foe. The passage through the town of Tulip will long be remembered by the troops of our division. Raining as it did, the ladies rushed to the roadside, and with wild enthusiasm cheered us on to the coming struggle. On account of the severity of the march, the troops were in a wretched condition. I do not exaggerate in stating that scarcely half the effective force was in position. Between the hours of 6 and 7 o'clock, we heard the echo of cannon in advance; the skirmishers had commenced. At 8 o'clock, the rain ceased. Shortly afterwards we arrived at the enemy's camp of last night, and saw all around evidence of the morning's skirmish—trees cut half in two by cannon balls; limbs of trees torn off and lying in the road; fences down and scattered in endless confusion; old clothes and all the paraphernalia of a soldier lying in all directions; houses riddled with cannon and musket balls; negro-quarters and meat-houses broken open and rifled of their contents;—in a word, a general desolation prevailing everywhere. Onward we push, striving with every nerve to do or die in our undertaking.

CHAPTER XXX.

THE BATTLE OF JENKINS'S FERRY.

" No gorgeous banners we unfold,
    Of crimson silk and yellow gold ;
    No waving plumes, nor helmets bright,
    Nor chargers prancing for the fight;
    But men as true, and hearts as bold,
    As e'er a life for freedom sold
    At Leuctra, or Thermopylæ,
    We bring into the field to-day,
    To chase thé weir-wolf from his lair,
    Or, failing, sleep forever there."

ABOUT the hour of 12 o'clock, M., on the 30th of April, the rattling of musketry gave us to understand that at last we had overtaken the enemy, rather unexpectedly. They were in the act of crossing the Saline River, at a point known as Jenkins's Ferry, distant from the town of Camden about 55 miles. As soon as the Federal General Steele discovered that an engagement was inevitable, he recrossed such of his troops as had already crossed, and formed his line of battle in the form of a crescent around his pontoon bridge. His position was a strong one, and further strengthened by such logs as they could conveniently get at. The location was in a thickly-timbered bottom, and the ground was covered with water, from ankle to knee deep, precluding the possibility of using artillery.

On arriving within about two miles of Jenkins's Ferry, Walker's Division filed off to the right, taking a road that apparently had not been used for years. At this place we beheld our favorite leader, General Walker, mounted on his iron-gray war-horse, awaiting to address a few remarks of encouragement to each regiment as they passed him by. His presence alone on this occasion was enough to inspire his troops with the highest patriotism and love for their old chieftain ; cheer after cheer was freely given him, as they passed by him. They had implicit confidence in his judgment, and that he would not tolerate any useless sacrifice of life in the forthcoming battle. The greatest vivacity and enthusiasm prevailed throughout the whole division. Already a rattling fire of musketry was heard in our front, plainly indicating that General Price's command was in action. At first a few scattering shots were heard ; quickly, volleys of platoons succeeded, and soon the fire extended and increased, until the rolling reports of long lines of musketry could be distinctly recognized. General Kirby Smith notified General Walker that the Arkansas and Missouri troops were at it, hot and heavy, and to press on the Texans, to support them. The Texans moved forward with alacrity, rushing headlong into action. The 3d Brigade of the Division, commanded by General Scurry, dashed up gallantly on the right, using their muskets quite soldierly, and, in the language of General Walker, sustained the fight, without assistance, against 7,000 of the enemy, for forty minutes.

The 2d Brigade, commanded by General Waul, went into action on their arrival, like old veterans.

The 1st Brigade, commanded by General Randall, was ably led by that distinguished officer into action. He seemed ubiquitous as he screamed his orders here and there, always urging his men on the foe. An incessant roar of musketry prevailed for about six hours. During this time the tide of battle ebbed and flowed—now advancing, then receding ; but at no time did the ground fought over vary more than two hundred and fifty yards. Owing to the dense fog and the dense clouds of smoke which hung in the thick woods, many times, opposing lines could only be discovered by the flash of their muskets. The firing on both sides grew more terrific every moment ; even the elements were terribly convulsed. They seemed to groan with the heavy burden of storms which had been gathered from the hemispheres, to pour upon the heads of God's erring children the vial of wrath, as an admonition to both armies to stay their bloody hands. But we continued fighting, irrespective of the storm. In the midst of the battle, our gallant general (General Walker) could be seen galloping along the lines, cheering his men forward. He was accompanied by his chief of staff, Major McClay.

General Kirby Smith likewise was indefatigable, riding from line to line, cheering on the men. Seeing some of the Arkansas troops falling back, he rallied them by dismounting from his horse, and, taking a gun from one of the soldiers, he took his place in the ranks as a private. The troops, seeing him thus exposing his life, rallied to his support, and kept in line until the close of the battle. To see the commanding general of the Trans-Mississippi Department, wielding the destinies of a great fight, with its cares and responsibilities upon his shoulders, performing the duty of a private soldier, in the thickest of the conflict, is a picture worthy of the pencil of an artist.

About 4 o'clock P.M. the enemy endeavored to turn our right flank, by extending their lines, which they were able to do by reason of their great numbers. This was unfortunate for us, as it required a corresponding extension of our lines, to prevent their extreme left from outflanking us—a movement, on our part, which weakened the force of resistance along our whole line of battle, which finally extended over a space of three miles. It also rendered it the more difficult to reinforce the left of our army, as the further the enemy extended his left, the greater the distance our forces had to travel over the impenetrable swamp, covered with briers, brambles, and water ; and all without the least knowledge of our locality, which proved insurmountable barriers to our success. There was no time to be lost to counteract the enemy's movement. The enemy made every possible effort to turn our flank, for one long weary hour, during which time the tide of battle ebbed and flowed along the entire line with alternate fortunes. The enemy's column continued to stretch away to the left, like a huge anaconda, seeking to envelop us within its mighty folds, and crush us to death ; and at one time it really looked as if they would succeed.

The moment General Walker discovered the enemy's order of battle, he dispatched orders to General Kirby Smith for reinforcements, to turn the enemy's flank. In the mean time, General Walker was on the alert in watching the enemy's programme. Notwithstanding all of his generals had been wounded, he was still confident that the battle would end in our favor. He advanced his division in an oblique direction, continuing to keep up a heavy firing on the enemy, expecting every moment reinforcements ; but, alas ! the reinforcements came too late. Had General Walker received reinforcements when he asked for them, he would have destroyed the enemy, and perhaps have captured their entire army. Attacked in front, on the flank, and in the rear, they could not possibly have escaped ; and if they did escape, it would be with the loss of thousands of prisoners, and all his artillery and wagons, while the field would have been strewed with his dead. A few minutes before the battle was over, Parsons's Division of Missourians, reached our right. They dashed on the enemy's flanks with loud shouts, and in the most gallant style. Meanwhile, General Price rallied the left for the final struggle. General Kirby Smith kept the center well up, while Walker's Division dashed into the fight with a shout that seemed to shake the very earth. The result of this maneuver drove the enemy back ; they commenced to retreat, first in good order, and finally in much confusion. The Federal troops fought well, and were handled in a masterly manner, until they were about to be flanked.

Before crossing the river, the enemy destroyed everything in the shape of transportation. They threw their artillery and wagons into the Saline River, and left their dead and wounded on the field. Having crossed the river, they destroyed their pontoon bridge, rendering further pursuit on our part impossible. Our troops having exhausted almost the last cartridge, they were unable to reap much advantage, except the glory of the battle-field.

A few minutes after the battle was over, General Fagan's Cavalry Corps, composed of Arkansians and Missourians, arrived on the battle-field. They had come from the neighborhood of Benton, distant about thirty miles from Jenkins's Ferry. They had anticipated meeting the enemy at or near Benton, but hearing the sound of cannon, and believing that the battle had taken place, they rode in a gallop the entire distance, in order to have the pleasure of participating with us in whipping the foe. On their arrival, many of their officers beseeched General Kirby Smith to allow their commands to swim the river in pursuit of Steele's army. General Smith believed that the risk the cavalry would have to undergo in swimming the river, without the infantry being able to cross, was too great. As it was, he was satisfied with the laurels he had already won; consequently he allowed Steele's army to return to Little Rock, his base of operations, unmolested.

General Steele's loss was very severe. But a few months previous, he marched proudly from Little Rock towards Shreveport, with 20,000 men, 1,000 wagons, and 30 pieces of artillery. He returned, having lost 800 wagons, 16 pieces of artillery, and 12,000 men, demoralized and burdened with his sick.

Our loss was very severe. We numbered amongst our dead some of the most gallant men of the division. Generals Scurry and Randall died a few days after the battle.

" Hope for a season bade the world farewell,
And freedom shrieked when Scurry and Randall fell."

The loss in the Missouri and Arkansas Divisions was equally severe, and many a true heart, which in the morning beat with high hope, at night lay cold in death.

Having alluded to General Fagan's Corps of Cavalry, it is proper to give some account of them. Much blame was attached to General Fagan, in failing to check the enemy's march before they got to the Saline River. Many hard things were said about him. Amongst the various rumors I heard, and which seems probable, was, that the enemy had succeeded in arresting one of General Price's couriers, carrying a dispatch from General Price to General Fagan, informing General Fagan of the evacuation of Camden by the enemy, and that the enemy would probably cross the Saline River, near the town of Benton. General Steele, upon reading General Price's dispatch, at once had one of his own couriers dressed in the captured courier's clothes, and sent a dispatch to General Fagan, signing General Price's name, for him to hold the crossing of the Saline River, near Benton, at all hazards, until his infantry arrived.

But admitting the above rumor to be false, it appears mysterious to the mind of any sane person, that General Fagan failed to leave scouts behind him, to watch the movements of the enemy, instead of leaving a vacancy of some thirty miles between his forces and those of the enemy, without even a solitary picket to inform him of the whereabouts of the enemy. Most singular to relate, General Fagan's command encamped at Jenkins's Ferry the night previous to the battle, and took up their march from there at two o'clock in the morning, the very day of the battle. It was an unfortunate occurrence, and can only be excused on the ground that General Fagan, being in front, was necessarily cut off from the commanding general, and was consequently without correct information.

Soon after the battle ended, a detail of men were employed in burying the dead. Armed with shovel, pickaxe, and spade, they proceeded along the battle-ground to complete this mournful task, which the enemy were unable to accomplish. The ground was thickly strewn with the ghastly and mangled forms. The effluvium from the swollen, festering forms was too horrible for human endurance. No conception of the imagination, no power of human language, could do justice to such a horrible scene.

Faint rays of the sinking sun now peered through broken clouds upon the blood-stained waters of the Saline. Our camp-ground was selected about two miles from the battle-ground. Shortly after our arrival in camp, rations were issued to us from the commissary, consisting of two ounces of bacon and one ear of corn to each man, with which we had to be satisfied, as there was nothing else to be had to satisfy our appetites. The following morning found us wet and cold, hungry and broken down in spirits. About eight o'clock the rain ceased, for the first time in three days ; the sun came out in all its glory, and one of the most bright and lovely of summer days smiled upon Jenkins's Ferry. The skies ceased to weep, and the veil of clouds was withdrawn, as if God would allow the angels to look down and witness this awful spectacle of man's inhumanity to man.

Rambling over the battle-field and witnessing the newly-dug graves, surrounded by water, I felt like calling to memory the dying words of our Revolutionary heroes, and applying them to those gallant heroes before me, who sleep the sleep that knoweth no waking. " If you are victorious, and our country emerges free and independent from the contest in which she is now engaged, but the end of which we are not permitted to see, bury us in our beloved State, and engrave our names on the monument you shall erect over us, as victims who willingly surrendered their lives as a portion of the price paid for your liberties ; and our departed spirits will never murmur, nor regret the sacrifices we made to obtain for you the blessing we hope you may enjoy."

CHAPTER XXXI.

THE BURIAL OF GENERALS SCURRY AND RANDALL.

"For oh, how grand they sink to rest,
Who close their eyes on victory's breast."

N the morning of May 1st, we heard the melancholy news of the death of General Scurry; he died during the night. His remains were escorted by the entire division to the town of Tulip, distant about eight miles. He was buried the following day with military honors. Generals Smith, Price, Walker, Churchill, Parsons, Hawthorne, and Tappan, were present. On our return to camp after the burial of General Scurry, we learned that the gallant General Randall had breathed his last, having expired an hour after the burial of his comrade-in-arms; he was buried the following day, with military honors.

The following beautiful obituary notice, written by Captain W. G. Weaver (of the 16th Dismounted Cavalry) *in memoriam* of the death of General Scurry, is very appropriate, and, without his permission, I take the liberty of applying it to both Generals Scurry and Randall:

" 'Our leaders have fallen!' Brigadier-Generals William R. Scurry and Horace Randall are dead. They fell on the field of battle, in the arms of victory, the place where heroes died. But oh! the price of victory! The precious offering of noble, generous, and heroic heart's-blood has brought mourning to their conquering brigades. How difficult it is to realize that they are numbered with the heroic dead of the world's grand revolutions, the illustrious hosts of Freedom's martyrs!

"But a few days since we saw their bold forms towering above the lines of battle. At Mansfield and Pleasant Hill we heard their words of gallant cheer to the soldiers who loved them. We saw them fearlessly lead the desperate charge which wreathed our banners with victory's laurels. At Pleasant Hill, in the face of the foe, ten times our strength in number, a hundred times in position, they led their decimated brigades through torrents of grape, hurricanes of shells, and showers of bullets; and though they saw destruction before them, still their calm and open faces wore the same undaunted look, and their old, familiar smiles played there as sweetly as in moments of hilarity around the camp-fire.

> ' Cannon to the right of them,
> Cannon in front of them,
> Cannon to the left of them,
> Volleyed and thundered.'

Still those clear, sonorous tones rang through the forest: 'Charge them, boys!' but these words will never ring along the line of battle again; no more will they sound at the head of their columns. They are gone to the warrior's grave, the soldier's rest! and for nobility, kindness, and sincerity of heart, for unfaltering courage, constant moderation as commanders, unvarying patience, unalloyed cheerfulness, and genial humor, there live not their superiors, but their names will still be the soldier's watchword, glory's legacy, our country's honor. The dying words of these noble heroes were, that they were content to die, since they received their death-wounds while doing their duty on the battle-field. Could the devotion of their brigades, the confidence and respect of their superior officers, and the kindness of friends have saved them, they would not have died.

> ' The path of glory leads but to the grave.'

Over their coffins let us alternately strew clusters of myrtle and cypress—emblems in life of delight; garlands of affection in death."

17

"Multiplied words can add nothing to their fame. It is eternal as the granite hills. Their bodies moulder in soldiers' graves. The emerald sward, and, doubtless, sweet flowers planted there by living hands, cover their honored remains. Of all the martyrs' graves that dot the southern hillsides and valleys, none contain the remains of nobler souls and more fearless and chivalric spirits, more efficient commanders, more idolized chieftains, than those which hold the mortal remains of Generals Scurry and Randall."*

* Private soldier's remarks.

CHAPTER XXXII.

RETURN TO CAMDEN.—GENERAL KIRBY SMITH'S ADDRESS TO THE SOLDIERS
OF THE TRANS-MISSISSIPPI DEPARTMENT.—EN ROUTE FOR ALEXANDRIA.
—PROMOTIONS.—GENERAL TAYLOR'S ADDRESS TO THE CAVALRY AND
POLIGNAC DIVISION.—CAMP NEAR ALEXANDRIA.

ON the morning of May 3d, the whole army was ordered back to Camden. This place, for the present, was to be our base-line of defense, in consequence of the difficulty of obtaining supplies east of the Ouachita River. After marching twelve miles we arrived at the same camp-ground we left on the morning of the 30th of April.

The-sick list of the division was very large, owing to the result of late hardships. Comfortable hospitals were provided for our sick and wounded at Camden. The patriotic ladies of Camden were untiring in their endeavors to ameliorate the sufferings of the brave soldiers that were brought to their city.

At dress-parade, in the evening, the following congratulatory address of General Kirby Smith was read to us:

" SOLDIERS OF THE TRANS-MISSISSIPPI DEPARTMENT : The campaign inaugurated at Mansfield, on the day of national fast and supplication, has, under Providence, been crowned with most glorious and brilliant success. You have defeated a foe three times your own number. The fields of Mansfield, Pleasant Hill, Cloutierville, Poison Springs, Marks's Mills, and Jenkins's Ferry, attest your devotion. 8,000 killed and wounded, 6,000 prisoners, 34 pieces of artillery, 1,200 wagons, one gunboat, and three transports, are already the fruits of your victories. The path of glory is still open to you. Permanent security to your homes is before you. Call together your comrades, and, shoulder to shoulder, we will yet free the soil of our beloved country from the invaders' footsteps. Soldiers of Arkansas, Missouri, Texas, and Louisiana! you have the thanks of a grateful people. Your living will be respected, and your dead honored and revered. While in the midst of our victory we are called upon to mourn the heroic dead. Generals W. R. Scurry and Horace Randall have fallen upon the field of honor. At Jenkins's Ferry they offered themselves up precious victims on the altar of liberty. Mouton and Green are gone! Scurry and Randall have followed on the same glorious path. Be it ours to emulate their virtues and valor, and to act as men not unworthy to associate with such heroes. The colors of their respective brigades will be draped in mourning for thirty days."

On the morning of the 4th we left camp at sunrise. A long, weary march of seventeen miles brought us to camp, worn out and exhausted.

May 5th. Marched seventeen miles, over a new road that our pioneers made, and camped within three miles of Camden. Owing to the continued rains, the streams were very much swollen, and often we waded the mud knee-deep. Roads were repaired, and bridges built. Then we were water-bound. It seemed as if all the tortures and sufferings of years were being poured upon us from one huge vial of wrath. We remained at this camp until the morning of the 8th. The night previous, orders were received from General Kirby Smith for General Walker to move his division in the direction of Campti, on Red River, or to any other convenient point that General Taylor might select.

On the morning of the 8th, the entire division was ready for marching. About 9 o'clock, A. M., we commenced crossing the Ouachita River, at the Lone-Pine Ferry, situated about a mile north of Camden. After all the troops had crossed we continued our march, passing through Camden, and struck camp about a mile from Camden, on the Shreveport road. During the evening we learned that the orders issued for the division to march to Campti were countermanded; the town of Alexandria was selected as the place we were to march to.

On the morning of the 9th we left camp at daylight, for Alexandria, to which place Banks's army had retreated after the battle of Pleasant Hill, in order to be under the protection of their gun-boats. On their retreat from Pleasant Hill they were hotly pursued by Green's Cavalry, under the command of General Wharton, and Polignac's Division of Infantry. We arrived in camp late in the evening, after marching fifteen miles. Shortly after our arrival, the Arkansas and Missouri Divisions arrived and camped alongside of us.

May 10th. Marched sixteen miles. A heavy shower of rain commenced pouring down upon us, completely saturating us. On we marched through the silent and gloomy pine woods, entertaining each other with jokes, and all manner of witty fusilades.

May 11th. Marched twenty miles; crossed the State-line dividing Arkansas from Louisiana. Shortly after arriving in camp it ceased raining.

May 12th. Marched sixteen miles. At this camp Colonel R. Waterhouse, of the 19th Infantry, and Major R. P. McClay, of General Walker's staff, were promoted to Brigadier-Generals, by order of General Kirby Smith. A few weeks afterwards, Colonel King, of the 18th Regiment, was promoted Brigadier General, on the resignation of General Waul.

General McClay was assigned to the command of the 1st Brigade ; General King was assigned to the command of the 2d Brigade, and General Waterhouse was assigned to the command of the 3d Brigade.

On the 13th we marched seventeen miles, passing through the towns of Homer and Athens.

May 14th. Marched twenty-one miles. Passed through the town of Mount Lebanon. At this town was established one of the best hospitals in the Trans-Mississippi Department, in charge of Doctor Powell, one of the most scientific doctors south of Mason and Dixon's line. Many of the Texas troops were under his kind treatment. The troops marched through the town by companies, in columns, presenting a handsome appearance. The sidewalks were filled with ladies, and many highly palatable gifts were distributed by them to the soldiers. After our arrival in camp it commenced to rain, pouring down in torrents. During the night a courier arrived in camp, with dispatches for General Walker, from General Taylor, urging General Walker to hasten his division forward to Alexandria. He reported that the enemy was still in possession of Alexandria, making every exertion to get their fleet over the falls, and if our division could possibly get opposite the town, with the assistance of artillery we would be able to destroy their fleet.

On the 15th we marched fifteen miles. The Arkansas and Missouri troops were ordered back to Camden.

May 16th. Marched twenty-one miles. Our march to-day was severe on the men as well as on the teams. A company of men from each regiment was detailed to accompany the wagon-train, to help them out when they became stuck in the mud. Heard that the enemy was engaged in fortifying Alexandria.

May 17th. At an early hour we were again in motion. After marching twenty miles we bivouacked for the night. No further news from Alexandria.

May 18th. Marched eleven miles. The march to-day was truly a pleasant change from our previous tedious marches. The scenery on either side of the route was magnificent, and doubly recompensed a lover of nature for any annoyances occasioned by the trip.

May 19th. Marched eighteen miles. After our arrival in camp, General Walker was notified by General Taylor that the enemy had evacuated Alexandria, leaving it a mass of ruins. He also informed General Walker that the troops of our division that had been captured at Pleasant Hill had been exchanged, and were doing guard-duty at Natchitoches. This was glad tidings to their old comrades in arms.

May 20th. Marched fifteen miles, and camped near a running creek. Many of the troops enjoyed themselves, after their long and tedious marches, by swimming and bathing in the limpid waters. At this camp the following address was read to the troops, on dress-parade, by order of General Taylor:

"The Major-General commanding desires to express to Major-General Wharton, commanding Cavalry Corps, and Major-General Polignac, commanding 2d Infantry Division, and the officers and men of their commands, his high appreciation of their gallantry and conduct displayed in the action of the 16th and 18th instant, at Mansura and Norwood. At Mansura the enemy's whole army was kept back for five hours, his charges repulsed, and, at the proper time, our forces were withdrawn from his front to be thrown upon his flank and rear.

"At Norwood, a superior force of fresh troops was beaten after a stubborn resistance, and driven from the field, leaving their dead in our hands. Here fell Colonel Stone, commanding 2d Brigade, Polignac's Division, whose gallantry at Mansfield and Pleasant Hill had endeared him to this army.

"The skillful dispositions made by General Wharton, commanding in the field, in both these engagements, stamped him as a soldier of high capacity, and equal to any position."

On the 21st we resumed our march, traveling through a poor, piny section of country, and arrived at camp after a march of fourteen miles.

May 22d. Marched fourteen miles, and encamped near Pineville, opposite Alexandria. We remained at this place until the 4th of June. Apparently to keep in good walking trim, we had to march six miles every morning, in addition to going through the routine of company and brigade drills every day. The summer days were hot, hotter, hottest, and fleeted rapidly away, while the men employed the time as best they could, lying 'neath the shadow of the pines, indulging in speculative fancies, yet interested spectators of the fierce struggle for supremacy between the contending hosts. The gentle summer air would swell into thunder-toned voices, borne from the mountains and valleys, from Virginia and Georgia, mingled with the triumphant shouts of victory. Aye! victory, radiant, triumphant, would poise, like the incarnation of beauty, upon the Southern banner, and point to the obscurity which shrouded the future, as if it contained the germs of white-winged peace and final success. The rainbow of hope, with every tint of its exquisite coloring, would stand out in bold relief against the dark war-cloud that hung over the land, and was fast sinking into the horizon of the past; its dark setting rendering all the more beautiful the soft hues. It seemed then as if the sun of peace was tinging with its parting beams the jagged edges of the storm-cloud, as with a silver lining. Thus it seemed as if the Southern hosts were striding forward towards the goal of their hopes, the prize for which they contended so stubbornly, and gave so freely the priceless treasure of their rich, red blood.

Thus, while the men indulged in their speculations, they were actually suffering both for clothing and shelter. Our rations consisted chiefly of corn-meal and poor beef, and not in large quantities. We were without tents, and usually slept on pine brush, in the open air, protected from the night-dews only by shelters of brush.

CHAPTER XXXIII.

THE ENEMY'S RETREAT FROM PLEASANT HILL.—FORTIFYING AT GRAND-
ECORE.—VINDICATION OF GENERAL KIRBY SMITH.—DESTRUCTION OF
THE COUNTRY.—CRITICAL POSITION OF THE ENEMY AT ALEXANDRIA.—
BURNING OF ALEXANDRIA.—FIGHTING AT YELLOW BAYOU.

DURING our march in pursuit of General Steele in Arkansas, we heard no particular details of Banks's army in Louisiana, until we arrived at Pineville, opposite Alexandria. Here we learned that the enemy fell back from Pleasant Hill, towards Grand-Ecore on Red River, where they would be under the protection of their gun-boats. At this place the enemy commenced fortifying, to protect them from an attack in their rear. The prisoners they had captured from us at Pleasant Hill were exchanged. The enemy was compelled to do so in order to have all their available force (without the extra charge of guarding prisoners), in order to reach the Mississippi River with safety. Much blame was attached to General Kirby Smith in withdrawing the division from Louisiana, in order to pursue General Steele in Arkansas, before Banks's army was annihilated in Louisiana. For him to act otherwise than rendering the same aid to the people of Arkansas as he did to the people of Louisiana, would have stamped him forever unfit for the office he held as Department Commander. Taking the field in person, he displayed military skill in defeating two of the best disciplined armies of the enemy that they had in the field, in the short period of twenty-two days.

Our cavalry felt the loss of their gallant commander, General Tom Green, to lead them on to victory, as he had done before on many a bloody battle-field. If he had been alive, the enemy never would have crossed Cane River, much less the double bridges, without they had done so as prisoners of war.

The enemy, after remaining a few days at Grand-Ecore, behind their fortifications, took up their line of march for Alexandria, distant about one hundred miles. Their entire route could be traced by the melancholy monuments of their devastating march; it could be distinguished by tall chimneys standing solitary and alone, and blackened embers lying at their feet as it were. Every fine residence, every corn-crib, smoke-house, cotton-gin—all that could give comfort to men— were committed to flames. Dead animals—horses, mules, cows, calves, and hogs, slain by the enemy, were scattered along the road.

After they arrived at Alexandria, they commenced fortifying the town; here they remained a few days awaiting the arrival of their fleet, commanded by Admiral Porter. His fleet was above the falls, about two miles above Alexandria. The fleet was in a critical position above the falls, and it was generally believed that they would have to abandon it altogether, from the fact of Red River falling so rapidly, while they were loading their transports with stolen cotton. A few days elapsed before they were released from their awkward position. The fleet succeeded in getting over the falls in the following manner: There was a large sugar-house a short distance from the falls, which they pulled down, and out of the materials made a dam of some six hundred feet across the falls, which enabled their fleet to pass. If proper disposition had been made of our forces, it would have been impossible for them to have saved their fleet. On the arrival of their fleet at Alexandria, their land forces prepared to evacuate the town, but not before they set fire to the town. The town was fired in several places by their negro troops; the flames soon burst forth, and the streets were quickly crowded with helpless women and children. Agonized mothers, seeking their children, all affrighted and terrified, were rushing on all sides from the raging flames and falling houses. Invalids had to be dragged from their beds, and lay exposed to the flames and smoke that swept the streets. Drunken negro soldiers, as well as white ones, rushing from house to house, emptying them of their valuables and then firing them; contraband negroes carrying off piles of booty, and grinning at the good chance, and exulting, like so many demons; officers and men reveling on the wines and liquors, until the burning houses buried them in their drunken orgies.

> " Through solid curls of smoke the bursting fires
> Climb in tall pyramids above the spires,
> Concentrating all the winds, whose forces, driven
> With equal rage from every point of heaven,
> Wheel into conflict, round the scantling pour
> The twisting flames, and through the rafters roar;
> Suck up the cinders and send them sailing far,—
> *They warn the country of the raging war.*"

Maddened in his disappointment to subdue the " rebels," General Banks was determined to lay the country waste for revenge. After leaving Alexandria, he marched for Simmsport on the Atchafalaya Bayou, closely pressed by our cavalry and infantry. At Yellow Bayou, near Simmsport, the enemy made a final stand, but was repulsed again by our forces, destroying the bridge over Yellow Bayou to prevent further pursuit from our troops. They crossed the Atchafalaya Bayou at Simmsport, and made a hasty march to the mouth of Red River, where transports were awaiting to convey them to New Orleans.

General Banks certainly must have come to the conclusion that the people of Louisiana, outside of New Orleans, were not as loyal as he expected to find them. They only recognized Governor H. Allen as the executive officer of Louisiana. Notwithstanding the bombastic proclamation of his military satrap, Mr. Hahn, styling himself Governor of Louisiana, ordering the people of Louisiana to lay down their arms, and to show no resistance to Banks's expedition, an army which had advanced in all the pomp and pride of war, was now returning to New Orleans more like a disorderly mob than an organized army. Thus closed Banks's second Red River expedition.

CHAPTER XXXIV.

MARCH FROM PINEVILLE TO SNAGGY POINT.—STORM IN CAMP.—GENERAL
WALKER LEAVES THE DIVISION.—ORGANIZATION OF THE ARTILLERY.
—MARCH TO THE MISSISSIPPI RIVER.—GENERAL WALKER'S ORDERS
TO GENERAL KING.—PREPARATIONS TO CROSS THE MISSISSIPPI RIVER.
—GENERAL TAYLOR'S PLAN THWARTED.—FAILURE TO CROSS THE MIS-
SISSIPPI RIVER.

ON the morning of June 4th we left camp, at Pineville, for Snaggy Point, on Red River. Marched twelve
miles down the east bank of Red River, and camped.

June 5th. Marched ten miles, and arrived at Snaggy Point.
Preparations were at once made to cross the river to the
west bank. A detail of one hundred men were employed in
cutting down the river bank, so that our wagons could cross.
After everything was ready, the order was countermanded.
We remained encamped at Snaggy Point until the morning of
the 11th. On the evening of the 7th, a tremendous storm took
place, flooding the camp with water, which flowed in a minia-
ture river through its center, sweeping away tin pans, plates,
etc. Amid the lightning's vivid flash, and the deep roll of
thunder, could be heard the shouts of the men, their exclamations and expletives, as they were literally drowned out of
their quarters. " Knee deep ! " one would shout ; " Quarter less
twain! " came from another direction ; " Quack, quack, quack ! "
answered a third—thus displaying an indifference to their
inconveniences, and commendably endeavoring to make sport
out of each other's mishaps. It rained every day while we
remained at this camp. The men were lying in mud and
water, oblivious to all their troubles, curled up like snakes,
and actually making pillows of their knapsacks.

On the morning of the 11th it ceased raining ; we moved

four miles, to a dryer camp-ground, where we remained until the morning of the 13th, when we took up the line of march, back again, in the direction of Pineville. Marched ten miles and struck camp, our wagons failing to arrive until late in the night. After eating supper, we lay down on our blankets, to think of our loved ones at home, and when the cruel war would be over. On the morning of the 14th we left camp about 9 o'clock. Marched fifteen miles, leaving Pineville to the left. Reported in camp, that General Dick Taylor was ordered across the Mississippi River, to take command of the defenses of Mobile.

June 15th. Marched twelve miles, through the pine hills. The weather was unusually fine. We finally struck camp on Bayou Flaggon, within three miles of Holloway's prairie.

June 16th. Marched seven miles, and encamped near Taylor's hospital, about fifteen miles from Alexandria. For the last two days we marched in a semicircular form, hunting a good camp-ground.

On the morning of the 17th we learned, much to our surprise, that our favorite leader, Gen. Walker, was assigned to the command of the District of Western Louisiana, thereby relieving Gen. Taylor. About noontime, on the 18th, General Walker bade farewell to his "Old Division." Although he did not take each officer and soldier by the hand, his countenance, and the countenances of his men, sufficed to express the feeling he entertained for them and they for him. Oftentimes have we seen Gen. Walker dash along the road, followed by his staff, when, meeting some soiled and uncouth-looking private, wearily marching down the road, he would bend forward gracefully in his saddle, and, lifting his hat from his brow, salute the soldier with all the polished ease and elegance of manner so indicative of the high-toned gentleman, with a soldierly politeness worthy a superior, and not as if the object of his deference and marked attention was the private soldier of his division. No wonder the men loved him and disliked to part with him!

" We had seen him on the fierce field of battle,
Firm as the granite, while the musket's sharp rattle,
The cannon's deep roar, the charge of the foes,
Told where thickest the fight—where fiercest the blows.
We had seen him, on march, long, toilsome, and dreary,
Encourage the men, travel-worn, weak, and weary ;
Amid the quiet of camp, on the showy review,
Always affable, kind, brave, courteous, and true,—
Ever cherished, remembered, wherever thou mayest go,
Brave Gen. John G. Walker, we bade thee adieu."

After Gen. Walker had been relieved of command of the division, Brig.-General King took command of the same, in the absence of Brig.-Gen. Waul (senior general), who was absent in Texas, suffering from the wound he received at the battle of Jenkins's Ferry. General King remained in command of the division until the arrival of Major-General John H. Forney, who arrived from east of the Mississippi River shortly after General Walker was relieved.

Nothing unusual transpired in camp until the morning of the 30th, when we moved camp a few miles, to a new camp, which might be safely called Camp Vermin. At this camp, we were annoyed, day and night, with mosquitoes, red-bugs, ticks, etc., and last, though not least, with blue beef. Shortly after our arrival at this camp, all of the light artillery in the District of Western Louisiana was formed into three battalions, commanded by Col. J. L. Brent; afterwards, with a slight alteration, by Major G. W. Squires. They were composed as follows :

1st BATTALION.

Captain W. G. MOSELEY'S Horse Artillery.
    "   M. V. McMAHON'S   "   "
    "   T. D. NETTLES'S (Valverde) Horse Artillery.
    "   J. A. A. WEST'S   "   "
Commanded by Major O. J. SEMMES.

2d BATTALION.

Captain H. C. WEST'S   Light Artillery.
    "   WM. G. GIBSON'S   "   "
    "   B. F. WINCHESTER'S "   "
    "   THOMAS BOONE'S   "   "
Commanded by Major G. W. SQUIRES.

3D BATTALION.

Captain T. O. BENTON's   Light Artillery.
J. T. M. BARNES's   "   "
M. T. GORDEY's   "   "

Commanded by Major T. A. FARIES.

We remained at this camp until the morning of the 23d of July, when we received orders to proceed, with all possible haste, to the Mississippi River, the location to be at or near Waterloo Landing.   After marching fifteen miles, we arrived at camp on the edge of Cathoulia Lake.

July 24th. Marched twenty miles.   We traveled through a section of country that was entirely deserted by man and beast.

July 25th. Marched ten miles, and camped on the bank of Black River, about two miles below the mouth of Trinity River.   We remained at this camp until the 27th, when we crossed over Little River on a pontoon bridge, and camped on Bird Creek (about four miles from Harrisonburg), after marching twelve miles.   We remained at this camp until the 26th of August.   While remaining at this camp, General King received a letter of instruction from General Walker, relating to transfer of cotton, etc., etc., in the following patriotic words :

" GENERAL :—You are instructed to prevent all intercourse with the enemy at Natchez, or elsewhere, for the purpose of trade, or upon any pretext whatever.   You will warn persons who are or have been in the habit of visiting places occupied by the enemy, that such visits will be treated as cause of arrest, and the confiscation of any goods that they may introduce within our lines.   You will see that these instructions are strictly enforced.   The habit of permitting such intercourse has demoralized the people, and depreciated our currency, and it must be prevented.   Similar instructions have been sent to the commander of the cavalry."

This was gratifying news to the troops, coming from their old commander.   Although shoeless and coatless, they preferred it, rather than to wear any ill-gotten goods from their oppressors. On the evening of the 25th, we received orders to be ready to cross the Mississippi River. This order created some dissatisfaction amongst the troops. Quartermasters were busily engaged in sending off all baggage. All baggage was ordered to be sent to Shreveport for "safe keeping." Only one wagon and one ambulance were allowed to each regiment.

On the morning of the 26th, we took up the line of march again ; crossed the Washita River at Harrisonburg, on a pontoon bridge. Harrisonburg looked rather the worse for wear. But few houses were left standing in the place. The town was destroyed by the Federals when they took possession of the place. After crossing the Washita River, we continued our march in the direction of the Tensas River. We arrived in camp late in the evening, after marching eighteen miles.

Aug. 27th. Marched twelve miles, and camped on the banks of the Tensas River. Shortly after our arrival in camp, the pontoon-train from Alexandria, accompanied by General Polignac's Division, arrived. The boats were placed across the Tensas River, to swell them, so as to make them watertight before we would attempt to cross the Mississippi River in them. In the mean time, detachments of cavalry were sent along the bank of the Mississippi River, to watch the movements of the enemy's gun-boats. We were distant from Waterloo Landing, on the river, about five miles. Some few of the troops deserted, in order to escape crossing the river, but the mass of the troops were ready to embark at a moment's warning. Some reflections had been cast on the division for not going across, when, in fact, they were never ordered to make the attempt, nor even allowed the pleasure of seeing the river at this place. For the information of the many, I will state, from good authority, that General Taylor failed in his well-laid plan. It was not his intention to attempt to cross any troops over the Mississippi River until he was able to negotiate with two of the gun-boat commanders for buying them and their gun-boats, for a certain amount of cotton, then stored at Brownsville. His plan was for the two

18

gun-boats to come alongside of the river-bank, where our men were prepared to board them. Dressing our men in the Yankee uniform, at the same time knowing the enemy's signals, he would send one of the gun-boats up the river, and the other down the river. It seemed very probable he would be able to capture all the gun-boats on the Mississippi River. This he expected to accomplish, after he succeeded in getting their private signals. If successful in this undertaking, he could readily cross his troops over the river, without being molested.

It is well enough known that the two captains were afraid of one another. These remarks I make by way of an explanation, as the real cause of the non-crossing of our division. General Taylor, having failed in his plans, took a final adieu of the division. During the night, he crossed the river, to take charge of the defenses of Mobile.

CHAPTER XXXV.

THE MARCH.—GENERAL FORNEY TAKES COMMAND OF THE DIVISION.—
ARRIVAL AT MONTICELLO.—GRAND REVIEW.—MARCH FROM MONTI-
CELLO TO CAMDEN.—FORTIFYING CAMDEN.—MARCH FROM CAMDEN TO
CAMP SUMTER.—MARCH FROM CAMP SUMTER TO CAMP MAGRUDER.—
WINTER QUARTERS.—DESCRIPTION OF CAMP MAGRUDER.—AMUSEMENTS
IN CAMP.—ANECDOTES, ETC.—SHAM BATTLE.—GENERAL REVIEW.

AUG. 29th. Having abandoned all hopes of crossing the river, for the present, we fell back some twelve miles from the river, and camped to await further orders.

On the morning of the 30th of August, accompanied by General Polignac's Division, we took up our line of march for Monticello, Arkansas. This movement was made through the intercession of General Magruder to General Kirby Smith. He informed General Kirby Smith that the Federal general (General Steele) at Little Rock had been reinforced by the 16th Army Corps, under command of General A. J. Smith. The Federal general, anticipating that Walker's and Polignac's Divisions had crossed the Mississippi River, had contemplated making a reconnoissance towards Monticello. The expedition was to start from Pine Bluff. When about ready to start, they heard of the arrival of our forces at Monticello. Consequently they had to abandon their contemplated raid, on hearing of our advance. After marching eight miles, we camped on Turkey Creek.

Aug. 31st. Marched sixteen miles, and camped near Bœuff Prairie. On arriving in camp, the commissary department, to be up and doing, issued us four ounces of "hard tack," and three-quarters of a pound of flour. The next day we rested, to eat our "hard tack."

Sept. 2d. Marched eight miles, in the direction of Monroe.

Sept. 3d. Marched fifteen miles, over a dry, sandy road ; water was very scarce along the route. Shortly after our arrival in camp, our new division commander, Major-General John H. Forney, of Vicksburg fame, arrived in camp, accompanied by his respective staff officers, as follows, viz. :

Major S. CROOM, *A. A. General.*
"   H. B. ADAMS, *Quartermaster.*
"   H. W. WILLIAMS, *Paymaster.*
"   J. M. DOUGLAS, *Assist. Commissary.*
Surgeon—D. PORT SMITH.
Med. Inspector—J. C. NIDELET.
Lieut. R. L. UPSHAW, *A. A. and Inspector-General.*
"   J. M. AVERY, *Ordnance Officer.*
"   J. M. WYLEY. *Aid-de-Camp.*
"   R. R. JONES, *Aid-de-Camp.*

Major-General John H. Forney was an old United States army officer ; a graduate of West Point. He was a strict disciplinarian. He commanded a division of Alabama troops, east of the Mississippi River, and participated in pretty much all the battles east of the river, from the battle of Manassas to the fall of Vicksburg. After being paroled at Vicksburg, he returned to his home in Alabama for a short period of time. Having been exchanged, he was assigned to the command of all the Vicksburg paroled soldiers. Afterwards, he was ordered to report to Lieut.-General E. Kirby Smith, for duty. On reporting to General Smith, he was assigned to the command of late Walker's Division.

On the 4th, we marched fourteen miles, over a dry, sandy road. The day was clear and warm. The constant daily march over the sandy roads began to exhibit its effects on the men. They were physically worn out, and much reduced in flesh.

Sept. 5th. Marched eleven miles. On our arrival in camp, blankets were stretched in tent form, to keep the scorching rays of the sun from us.

Sept. 6th. Marched eight miles. Passed through the town of Monroe again, and camped about half-a-mile north of the town, at an old camp-ground, known by the name of Bluff Springs, where we remained until the morning of the 14th, when we took up the line of march in the direction of Bayou Bartholomew; marched fourteen miles and camped for the night.

Sept. 15th. Left camp at 4 o'clock, A. M., and marched eighteen miles. Apparently for recreation, a new style of tactics was adopted by General Forney, which consisted in having roll-call every time we rested. What his object was I am unable to say, unless it was to shorten the period of resting. No sooner was the roll called than we would be on the march again.

Sept. 16th. Marched twenty miles. Passed through the town of Bastrop, and camped a few miles from the town.

Sept. 17th. Marched twenty-four miles. Roll-call as usual. Crossed Bayou Bartholomew on a pontoon-bridge. Crossed the State-line dividing Louisiana and Arkansas. Passed through a little village called Berlin, and arrived in camp near the town of Hamburg, where we remained until the morning of the 19th, when we were on the march again. Passed through the town of Hamburg, and marched sixteen miles.

Sept. 20th. Marched seventeen miles, and encamped near the town of Monticello, the place of our destination for the present. From the 21st till the 24th, we were employed in cleaning our camp-ground. On the evening of the 25th, at dress-parade, we received orders to be ready the next day for a grand review, to be held by General Magruder, then commanding the State of Arkansas.

Sept. 26th. Having dressed ourselves in our best apparel, we left camp at 9 o'clock, A. M., and arrived at the parade-ground, situated north of Monticello. After we took our position, we stacked arms, and awaited the presence of General Magruder. General Forney was soon notified that the commanding-general of the State of Arkansas would shortly make his appearance on the field. Presently, the command "Attention," was given; then, "Take arms." Drawing our breath, and casting our eyes to the right, we perceived, at a distance, something resembling a *comet*, with a long tail, advancing towards us. Further investigation plainly told us that what we took for a *comet* was nothing more nor less than the bunch of ostrich-feathers in General Magruder's hat. He approached General Forney, and the two saluted each other. The bands struck up the tune " Hail to the Chief." General Magruder then took his position alongside a number of carriages filled with ladies. Presently, General Forney gave the command, " Prepare for inspection." " To the rear, open order." After the lines were dressed, and the guides had taken their position, General Magruder passed along the lines, mounted on his war horse "Cincinnatus," who appeared to keep time to the national air of " Dixie." As he passed before us, I believe there was not an officer or soldier in the division who did not eye the hero of the peninsula, Malvern Hill, and last, though not least, the hero of Galveston, in such a manner that, even if he dressed himself in mask apparel, he could be easily recognized by any soldier of the division. After getting through his inspection, he took his former position alongside the carriages. The command was given, " Close order, march!" " Prepare to pass in review by companies, left wheel, column forward, guide right, march!" After passing in review, we took our former position. Afterwards, General Magruder drilled us for half an hour, to please the ladies. He expressed himself highly pleased with our division, and remarked that he would soon settle the dispute between him and Steele, the Federal commander, viz., whether he or Steele was the legal commander of Arkansas. The divisions of Polignac, Churchill, and Parsons were also on the parade-ground. After the review was over we returned to our old camp, where we went through the regular routine of camp-life. Nothing unusual transpired in camp until the morning of the 30th, when the Missouri Cavalry, under command of General Price, crossed the Arkansas River, on their way to their own State, to create a general havoc among the loyal folks wherever they went.

On the morning of the 30th, we received orders to get ready to march for Camden, on the Ouachita River.

On the morning of October 2d, we took a final adieu of Monticello, and marched off in the direction of Camden. The roads were miserably bad, owing to the incessant rains. We arrived in camp late in the evening, after marching only twelve miles. Our wagons did not arrive until midnight.

October 3d. Marched thirteen miles. The country we traveled through was remarkably fertile, but the most of the farms were lying waste, without fences; while briers, and weeds, and young saplings encumbered the rich soil, in place of the golden grain, and rich harvests of corn. In addition to want, there was deep mourning in every house we passed, for dear ones who had bravely laid down their lives in the cause they believed was just.

October 4th. Marched fourteen miles, tramping over puddly roads and wading through the creeks. To-day's march was over roads deserted, almost covered in with overhanging woods, bleak, black, and dismal looking. About four o'clock in the evening we arrived in camp.

October 5th. Marched eleven miles. The sun was up, and looked bright and cheerful throughout the day.

October 6th. Marched twenty miles, and encamped near Camden, where we remained, drilling and fortifying the place, until the morning of the 15th, when we were ordered to cross the Ouachita River, at the Lone-Pine Ferry, situated about two miles north of Camden. After crossing the river we camped about half a mile from the town. At dress-parade, in the evening, we were ordered to be ready to commence fortifying the following morning. Our division was assigned the duty of fortifying the water-front of Camden; Parsons's the south-east; Polignac's, the south-west; and Churchill's, the north-west lines.

On the evening of the 16th, we witnessed the melancholy performance of shooting Captain John Guynes, Company F, 22d Texas Infantry. He was accused of encouraging his men to desert, when we were expected to cross the Mississippi River. He was a man about fifty years old, and very much admired by his men, and well liked by the officers of his brigade. Every effort was made to have him reprieved, but all without avail.

On the evening of the 8th, General King was relieved from duty with the division, and assigned to the Texas Brigade of Polignac's Division. Nothing unusual transpired in camp until November 3d, when a regiment from each brigade went on picket on the Princeton road, about twelve miles from Camden, for what purpose I am unable to say, as there was no enemy nearer than Pine Bluff, some eighty miles distant. After completing the fortifications around Camden, we took up the line of march for Camp Sumter (named by the Missouri troops), on Red River, north of Shreveport, near Spring Bank, on the morning of the 14th, and marched twelve miles over a very good road.

On the morning of the 15th it commenced to rain as if all the "floodgates of heaven were turned loose." Arrived in camp late in the evening, wet to the skin, after marching fifteen miles.

October 16th. Marched eleven miles. Still raining. A great many of our wagons were unable to arrive in camp last night.

October 17th. Marched twelve miles, over a stiff red clay road, the rain still pouring down in torrents, with no prospect of its clearing up soon. It was almost impossible to march over the roads; and, to look at us on our weary and laborious march, one would judge us to be a party of "Shaking Quakers," reclining backward nearly as much as forward.

October 18th. Marched eight miles, and arrived at Camp Sumter. Shortly after our arrival in camp, the weather cleared off, with the exception of a cold norther. We remained at this camp until the morning of the 22d, when we were ordered to march for Minden, Louisiana, to go into winter quarters. About nine o'clock in the morning, we bade farewell to Camp Sumter, but not before we received four ounces of sugar from the Commissary Department—the first we had received since we left the sugar regions of Louisiana. We marched twelve miles, over a barren and rocky road.

October 23d. Marched fourteen miles. The weather was miserably cold, and a regular norther blowing.

October 24th. Marched fifteen miles, through a rich section of country. The weather cleared off about sunset.

October 25th. Marched fourteen miles, and camped on a clear, crystal-running creek.

October 26th. Marched twelve miles through the pine woods, and camped.

October 27th. Marched twelve miles over the same section of country as yesterday. After our arrival in camp, the weather cleared off, and no indication of any more rain soon.

October 28th. Marched eight miles, and camped near the town of Minden. We remained at this camp until the 1st of December, when we moved camp four miles, to a more suitable camp-ground. After our arrival in camp, we were given to understand that the present camp would be our winter quarters. Preparations were at once made by the troops to erect log cabins, which was quickly done. On the evening of the 4th, at dress-parade, we were informed that our present camp was to be known by the name of Camp Magruder, through respect to General Magruder, commanding the State of Arkansas. Many of the troops were careless in building their cabins, owing to the fact that there was no certainty of our remaining any definite period of time; but the cold weather now set in, which left them no alternative but to get into their cabins as soon as possible.

On the morning of the 8th, it commenced to sleet; during the night it commenced to freeze, and the next morning the ice was fully two inches thick. Providence seemed to have favored us until we had our quarters completed.

On the evening of the 12th, the troops received two months' wages. This was the first money we had received in two years for our services, or, in other words, the first money received since our pay was advanced from $11 to $13 per month. To prove the generosity of our paymaster, he advised the soldiers to bond their money for a period of twenty years, drawing interest at the rate of eight per cent. per annum. The greatest portion of them believed in the old adage, that " half a loaf of bread was better than none," and chose the ready cash, giving a receipt to the C. S. A., and trusting to their honor for the balance due us, viz. : two years' pay, clothing, etc., etc. Those that were unfortunate enough to trust to the bonding scheme may get the principal and interest after the ratification of the treaty of peace between the Confederate and United States. Those that received their $22 enjoyed themselves at betting at monte, poker, euchre, etc., etc., much to the amusement of the bond-holders. The greatest care as to the cleanliness of cabins was the next order of the day, and each regiment tried to excel in this particular. Time passed on as smoothly as you pleased, nothing occurring to disturb our peace of mind, except the routine of camp duties.

Camp Magruder was situated on the right of the military road leading from Shreveport to Camden, in the midst of a pine ridge. On the south-west was a deserted field, well adapted to the exercise of drilling. Of course, camps were *always* selected in view of such very *agreeable* contingencies. Our quarters were substantial log cabins, constructed of pine logs. Each cabin was fourteen by sixteen feet. The privates' quarters were in two parallel rows, facing each other, while the officers' ran perpendicular to them, forming nearly a square at one end. The men were not too much crowded, and slept in berths placed one above the other, similar to those in a state-room of a river steamer.

We have read descriptions of palaces, with their marble colonnades, tesselated floors, ceilings frescoed and embellished with carved and curious figures, adorned, ornamented and furnished with all the richness and elegance which art and genius could devise, or the skill of man produce ; yet no such picture intrudes its glare and glitter upon us at Camp Magruder. The heart wearied with long years' of suffering, danger and hardship, amid the stirring and eventful scenes of our struggle for national independence, naturally turns to an humbler scene, with all its fond associations. " Home, sweet home," is a theme which melts the heart of the sternest of our scarred veterans. Many times have we seen the tears steal down the bronzed cheeks of those who have passed unmoved amid the horrors of the battle-field, as the strains of this cherished refrain came from some saddened heart, gushing its melody from a sweet-toned voice or instrument. We remember the cottage-home embowered in trees, with the rose and honeysuckle clambering over the trellis at the ends of the porch, and the jessamine, with its sweet-scented flowers, perfuming all the summer air. We remember, too, with intense yearning, the social family-gathering in the evening, the fondly-loved sisters and brothers, the adored mother and revered father, now exiled from that cottage home, or battling in the ranks of our country's patriots. Ah! how these memories throng to the mind and bring forth long-dormant reminiscences of the past! But what have these thoughts to do with " Our Quarters " at Camp Magruder? Nothing, dear reader, save as a reverie of camp-life.

The winter wind is whispering a sighing requiem through the pine-boughs, which form a shelter near our present home. Its breath is sharp and biting. What matters it? Do not our log cabins keep Boreas at bay? Moreover, there is a comfortable fireplace at one end, with its mud chimney outside, where the fire crackles and the ruddy flame leaps joyfully upward, as if defying all old Winter's fierce attacks. We sit (my companions and myself, I mean) around this cozy fire, and laugh and chat away the laggard hours, as if stern war was not a bitter reality, and life had no aim save the enjoyment of its flitting hours. Soldiers are proverbial for their light-heartedness and reckless joviality under the most trying circumstances. Taking a ramble through the camp, you could behold a party of soldiers engaged at whist, all fours, euchre, or some other game. In another part was the game of monte, and around would be gathered a large number of betters, staking small sums upon the turn of the cards;

for all appeared to have more or less Confederate money. In still another quarter, a small party would be seen half-reclining upon their blankets, while one of them recited some story of other days and lands. Songs, too, enlivened the scene, and served to beguile the hours. We will introduce our readers to a cabin full of soldiers, who are enjoying themselves with songs, jokes, etc., etc.

"Why," asked one of them, who appeared to be the leader in the crowd, "are love and war so closely allied? I cannot see the analogy between them at all, unless it be that one leads to a future being, the other to a future world."

"Bravo, Jack! Now you have given and solved a conundrum in the same breath. It is always said and sung that

" ' None but the brave deserve the fair,' "

exclaimed the jolly C—— from a corner of the cabin.

"That may be very well," replied Jack, "but you find the dear creatures seldom trouble their heads much about a fellow if he gets an ounce of lead in the stomach ; they generally bear the thing with Christian resignation, and console themselves by picking up some sensible man who stayed at home, to look after them."

"A plague on such cowards," said another. "You are losing your gallantry ; didn't you see how they literally buried us in flowers, as we passed through Minden ? "

" All very fine ; it reminds me of a hungry man suffering at a delicious feast, while some sensible fellow walks in and enjoys the banquet."

During the time we remained at camp Magruder, there was an active campaign of amusement, and both men and officers devoted themselves with ardor to such sports as the service at all tolerated, enjoying the fleeting hours up to the time we took a final adieu, with unabated devotion to pleasure. Such was camp-life at Camp Magruder.

The utmost contentment and good feeling prevailed among the men, and all seemed determined to enjoy the days of the winter months. With abundant material for the purpose, they soon manufactured tables, shelves, and benches. Most agreeably were they disappointed at their situation and surroundings. They soon gathered about them all those little comforts and conveniences which so materially contribute to the happiness of a soldier's precarious existence.

Nothing unusual transpired in camp, until the evening of January 8th, 1865, when the troops participated in a "sham battle," under the jurisdiction of General Forney. Everything passed off pleasantly, and to the entire satisfaction of the ladies, who assembled in large numbers to witness the scene. We returned to camp late in the evening, strongly convinced that it was easier to participate in a hundred "sham battles" than one sure-enough battle. After the "sham battle" was over, nothing unusual transpired in camp until the morning of the 17th, when the commander of the Trans-Mississippi Department, Gen. Kirby Smith, arrived at camp, for the purpose of reviewing his troops; and great enthusiasm was evinced by them. He was accompanied by General Buckner, of Fort Donaldson fame, then commanding the district of Louisiana. After passing in review, and taking our former position in line, Gen. Buckner put us through Hardee's tactics for about two hours, which proved highly gratifying to the ladies who had come from all parts of the country to witness the grand review. We returned to camp late in the evening, tired and weary. We remained at camp Magruder until the morning of the 26th, when we took a final adieu of it, and took up the line of march for Shreveport. A large number of ladies from the surrounding country arrived in camp, to witness our departure, and, as the troops were moving off, " Good bye," " God bless you," was on the lips of all.

CHAPTER XXXVI.

EN ROUTE FOR SHREVEPORT.—GRAND REVIEW OF THE DIVISION.—GRAND
BARBECUE GIVEN BY THE LADIES OF LOUISIANA TO THE DIVISION.

N the evening of the 26th we arrived in camp, after getting a thorough drenching from the rain that had been falling in torrents upon us. Our march to-day was sixteen miles.

Jan. 27th. Marched eight miles. Nothwithstanding the heavy drizzling rain falling the men were all in fine spirits, and gay songs, from a hundred throats in unison, made the march a merry one.

On the morning of the 28th the march was resumed. Re-crossed Red River at Shreveport, and camped about a mile east of town, after marching four miles. On our arrival in camp, details were made from the various companies, to haul wood and water a distance of about half a mile. To add to this inconvenience, about 4 o'clock, P.M., a most terrific storm of wind, rain, and hail commenced from the north-west; the howling tempest and pelting rain blended in a continuous roar throughout the night. When the morning of the 29th began to send its pale rays across the hills, our camp presented a most lamentable spectacle. Only two tents were standing, out of all the officers' tents in the division. The men were huddled together in groups, endeavoring to keep warm. The fires, having been extinguished, could add nothing to their comfort; and the poor fellows, wet, supperless, and without the fragment of a chance for breakfast, presented a most wretched appearance indeed. Tents, blankets, and all the paraphernalia of a soldier's outfit were scattered right and left over the camp-ground. Our brave and determined troops looked as if in a dream, standing near their shelter, lamenting their lost supper and breakfast,—many of them in their shirt sleeves, regardless of the rain, and reminding one of a person invited to a feast, who could not go. Poor fellows! they looked the personification of "Patience on a monument, smiling at grief." The storm continued raging in all its fury, until the evening of the 29th, when the wind changed, and it cleared off piercingly cold.

On the 30th, apparently to warm the troops up, General Forney held a grand review of the division. The parade-ground was about five miles from our camp. On our march to the parade-ground, many of the soldiers, worn out by exhaustion, and unable to march with their companies, were picked up and placed under guard by General Forney's body-guard (consisting of a company of cavalry). On their arrival on the parade-ground, they were compelled to march a ring until the review was over. This treatment of the sick was loudly denounced by both officers and men.

On the morning of the 31st it commenced to rain again, and, in the midst of the rain, we moved camp to where wood and water were more abundant. Shortly after our arrival in camp, it ceased raining for a short period of time. In the evening it seemed as the flood-gates of heaven had been opened upon us. It continued to rain until the morning of the 6th, when once more it cleared off, and the sun came out as brilliant as ever.

On the morning of the 7th, we again moved camp, convenient to a drill-ground. The ordinary course of drills was performed each and every day. Such was camp-life near Shreveport, where we passed "awa' the small hours," regardless of sunshine or storm, contentedly smoking our pipes, or discussing the latest war news. A soldier's tent—provided he is blessed with any—is his parlor, kitchen, and bedroom; and contains, within its small and circumscribed limits, all the conveniences of his existence. How seldom do we imagine what man can endure, and still continue hopeful, healthy, and joyous. Such is a soldier's life.

We received orders on the evening of the 14th to make preparations for a grand review and barbecue, to take place on the 18th. While encamped near Shreveport we were daily visited by numbers of ladies from the surrounding country, and from the city of Shreveport, who always had pleasant smiles and cheerful words for the soldiers. The brass-band attached to the division discoursed most excellent music, and was a great feature of our camp-life, and a source of great gratification to our men. Soldiers, as a class, are passionately fond of music. Well do we remember with what deep emotions we have listened to the harmonious strains, as they floated out on the air, some still moonlight night, returning in murmuring echoes from the surrounding hills. Truthfully has the great English bard written:

> " He who hath not music in his soul,
> And is not moved by concord of sweet sounds,
> Is fit for treason, stratagem, and spoils."

Awaiting for the coming of the 18th, the troops continued performing their duties of guard mounting, morning drill, policing camp, and evening parade: such were the hours in camp. In the evening a roseate hue would tinge the western horizon, or light clouds flit lazily across the sky overhead, and camp-fires glittered for miles ; shouts, laughter, the hum of voices, mingled with songs, sentimental and religious, would float away on the still evening air. Such were some of the duties we had to perform.

Thus the days slipped away into the irrevocable past. The fierce storm-cloud swept in its fury over Virginia, Georgia, and Missouri. The result of the elections in several of the Northern States proclaimed the probability of no change in the political status of the land.

At last the day of the 18th arrived. The day was clear, beautiful, and pleasant. Thousands of spectators, of all ages, and both sexes, thronged to the grounds, early in the day. The division moved from their camp to the parade-ground, about 10 o'clock. As soon as they arrived on the parade-ground, they took their respective positions in line of battle. Shortly after the line was formed, Generals E. Kirby Smith and J. B. Magruder, accompanied by their respective staffs, arrived. Aids-de-camp were dispatched with orders, to the various brigade commanders. Everything being in readiness, the head of the column moved off, passing in review. After the review was over, the division commenced to maneuver; advanced in columns of attack, and, after deploying, broke to the rear, forming two lines of battle. After changing front to rear on the first line, they advanced to the attack. First was heard the scattering fire of the skirmishers; volleys of musketry mingled with the roar of artillery. The maneuvering was well executed, and, but for the gala appearance of the scene, a spectator would have imagined that one of those bloody dramas so frequent in those warlike days was being enacted. As it was, some fair ladies screamed, and down the cheeks of others coursed tear-drops, either of sympathy for a soldier's dangers, or from some memory brought up by this warlike scene. After the sham battle, the division was drawn up in columns of regiments, to be presented to that gallant band, the veterans of the 3d Louisiana Infantry. This command, numbering 130 men, was marched up to the division, and introduced by Gen. Forney to his troops, in a few pointed remarks, which were responded to by three hearty cheers.

The division then presented arms to the regiment, which compliment was returned. Arms were then stacked, and all repaired to the tables, where a bountiful and substantial repast was spread. Without waiting for grace to be said, we helped ourselves, in regular soldier's style, much to our own comfort and to the pleasure of the ladies, doing ample justice to the dinner, and only regretting that we had not such a dinner every day. After dinner we repaired to the speaker's stand, to enjoy a "feast of reason and a flow of soul." A letter from Governor Allen was first read, in which he expressed his regret at his unavoidable absence on this occasion. The troops were very much disappointed in not having the pleasure of hearing the gallant and defiant chieftain of Louisiana.

19

Too much praise cannot be bestowed on him while governor of Louisiana. Day and night he superintended the feeding of the hungry and the caring for the soldier's widow. The Louisiana troops adored him, while the Texas troops admired him for his patronage. At the cessation of hostilities he bade adieu to the people he loved so well, and took up his abode in a foreign country, where he breathed his last. His remains have been carried to his own State, and interred amongst the people he loved so well; and when the time arrives that each State will have the right to erect monuments over their fallen heroes, I am satisfied that the gallant sons of Louisiana will not forget their patriot governor, H. W. Allen.

But notwithstanding the absence of the governor, short and stirring addresses were delivered by Colonel L. Bush of Louisiana, and Colonels G. Flournoy and Hubbard of Texas. The whole affair passed off pleasantly, and will be long remembered by all those who participated in it. We felt grateful at this complimentary tribute to the gallantry and valor of Texans by the citizens and fair women of Louisiana. The 18th of February, 1865, will not soon be forgotten by the immense concourse assembled near Shreveport. On the 19th General Forney received orders from General Buckner to hold his division in readiness to move to Natchitoches. At dress-parade, the following address was read to us.

CHAPTER XXXVII.

GENERAL BUCKNER'S ADDRESS.—ON THE MARCH.—DISMOUNTING THE CAVALRY.—REINFORCEMENTS.—ORGANIZATION OF THE 4TH BRIGADE.— SEARCHING FOR HONEY.

THE Lieutenant-General commanding desires to caution the troops of his command against indulging in unreasonable expectations of peace. The policy of our enemy, heretofore, has been to attempt to force us to comply with dishonorable terms which they have proposed. The question should be willingly left where the Constitution of the country places it, in the hands of the President and Senate. It is our duty to abide, patiently, their action, and to continue, as soldiers, to prepare for a prolonged struggle to rescue the independence to which we are so clearly entitled. Our vigilance, energy, and determination to contend for the rights which we claim, should be in no degree relaxed.

By command of

Lieut.-General BUCKNER.

On the 21st we took up the line of march in the direction of Natchitoches ; marched ten miles, and camped near the old Mansfield road. We remained at this camp until the 6th of March. While at this camp, the following-named cavalry regiments were dismounted and attached to our division, viz. :

Colonel CHISUM's 2d Regiment, Texas Partisan Rangers.
"   J. H. CANDLE's 34th Texas Cavalry.
"   J. M. WELLS's   "
"   DeMORSE's 29th   "

After dismounting the cavalry, another brigade was organ-

ized, known as the 4th Brigade. W. H. King was assigned to
its command. It consisted of the following regiments :

16th T. V. Infantry,	commanded by Colonel Geo. Flournoy.
18th "	" " T. M. Bonner.
28th Texas Dismounted Cavalry,	" " E. H. Baster.
34th,	" " J. H. Candle.
Wells (no number),	" " J. M. Wells.

Col. DeMorse's 29th Dismounted Cavalry was attached to Waul's Brigade.
Col. Chisum's 2d Partisan Rangers was attached to Waterhouse's Brigade.

NAMES OF THE OFFICERS OF THE 2D REGIMENT TEXAS PAR-
TISAN RANGERS.

Colonel—J. Chisum.
Lieut. Col.—C. Miller.
Major—J. G. Vance.
Quartermaster—Capt. W. T. Barns.
Surgeon—J. C. Brubaker.
Adjutant—J. O. Crutchfield.

Company Officers.

COMPANY A.

Captain, J. W. Wilson.
1st Lieut., H. L. Gilbert.
2d Lieut., B. F. McBride.
2d Lieut., M. L. Payne.

COMPANY B.

Captain, A. J. Hunt.
1st Lieut., A. C. Hoyle.
2d Lieut., S. P. Bell.
2d Lieut., D. Jackson.

COMPANY C.

Captain, J. G. Williams,
1st Lieut., C. Gour.
2d Lieut., A. Brundrige.
2d Lieut., G. P. Porter.

COMPANY D.

Captain, I. Foreman.
1st Lieut., J. S. Vest.
2d Lieut., I. B. Farmer.
2d Lieut., W. D. Vance.

Company Officers.

COMPANY E.

Captain, R. L. Askew.
1st Lieut., I. Brooksier.
2d Lieut., S. Garvin.
2d Lieut., T. M. Crowder.

COMPANY F.

Captain, R. H. Scott.
1st Lieut., F. B. Lilly.
2d Lieut., J. Walker.
2d Lieut., —— ——.

COMPANY G.

Captain, J. W. Lane.
1st Lieut., J. W. Tregg.
2d Lieut., T. H. Williams.
2d Lieut., J. P. Wallace.

COMPANY H.

Captain, J. D. Stratten.
1st Lieut., A. A. Thomas.
2d Lieut., A. G. Jackson.
2d Lieut., J. A. Jackson.

COMPANY I.	COMPANY K.
Captain, R. H. Harding.	Captain, C. L. James.
1st Lieut., W. S. Murrell.	1st Lieut., J. O. Heath.
2d Lieut., (vacant.)	2d Lieut., W. V. Moore.
2d Lieut., (vacant.)	2d Lieut., J. G. Gibbs.

NAMES OF THE OFFICERS OF THE 29TH REGIMENT OF TEXAS DISMOUNTED CAVALRY.

Colonel—CHAS. DeMORSE.
Lieut.-Colonel—OTIS G. WELCH.
Major—JOSEPH A. CARROLL.
Surgeon—R. W. REED.
Assistant Surgeon—E. B. ROCHILLE.
Quartermaster—JOHN CARROLL.
Adjutant—L. C. DeMORSE.

Company Officers.

COMPANY A.

Captain, J. W. Dougherty.
1st Lieut., A. A. Miller.
2d Lieut., W. I. McNeil.
2d Lieut., J. J. Smoot.

COMPANY B.

Captain, Nick Wilson.
1st Lieut., A. Z. Bone.
2d Lieut., Eli Tibbets.
2d Lieut., (vacant.)

COMPANY C.

Captain, W. T. Gunn.
1st Lieut., G. W. Pierce.
2d Lieut., R. D. Hancock.
2d Lieut., J. W. Hardison.

COMPANY D.

Captain, W. H. Hooks.
1st Lieut., Eli Gaffney.
2d Lieut., G. W. Mitchell.
2d Lieut., Rufus Mann.

Company Officers.

COMPANY E.

Captain, (vacant.)
1st Lieut., A. J. Zonnet.
2d Lieut., J. W. Robinson.
2d Lieut., H. Tritt.

COMPANY F.

Captain, E. R. Oliver.
1st Lieut., P. Fulbright.
2d Lieut., Jno. A. Franklin.
2d Lieut., Jno. A. Hooker.

COMPANY G.

Captain, W. I. T. Littlejohn.
1st Lieut., D. W. Mosley.
2d Lieut., V. Buyless.
2d Lieut., I. E. Byrd.

COMPANY H.

Captain, (vacant.)
1st Lieut.,   "
2d Lieut., F. M. Bonds.
2d Lieut., —— ——.

COMPANY I.

Captain, (vacant.)
1st Lieut., R. P. Duty.
2d Lieut., W. C. Rainey.
2d Lieut., J. G. Attoway.

COMPANY K.

Captain, Thos. R. Wilson.
1st Lieut., W. I. Walker.
2d Lieut., R. E. D. Smith.
2d Lieut., (vacant.)

NAMES OF THE OFFICERS OF THE 34TH REGIMENT TEXAS CAVALRY DISMOUNTED.

Colonel—JOHN H. CANDLE.
Lieut.-Colonel—WM. M. BRUSH.
Surgeon—FRANCIS D. CASH.

Company Officers.

COMPANY A.

Captain, Ed. Baldwin.
1st Lieut., B. F. Martin.
2d Lieut., J. H. Hallford.
2d Lieut., J. H. Byas.

COMPANY B.

Captain, E. T. Morris.
1st Lieut., W. C. Hightower.
2d Lieut., A. Gray.
2d Lieut., (vacant.)

COMPANY C.

Captain, L. D. Ross.
1st Lieut., M. V. Devitt.
2d Lieut., D. L. Ritchey.
2d Lieut., (vacant.)

COMPANY D.

Captain, A. H. R. Bryant.
1st Lieut., W. J. Lewilling.
2d Lieut., (vacant.)
2d Lieut., (vacant.)

COMPANY E.

Captain, A. J. Duckworth.
1st Lieut., J. R. Zourie.
2d Lieut., (vacant.)
2d Lieut., (vacant.)

Company Officers.

COMPANY F.

Captain, W. Metcalf.
1st Lieut., B. B. Meders.
2d Lieut., (vacant.)
2d Lieut., (vacant.)

COMPANY G.

Captain, W. N. Brush.
1st Lieut., J. M. Fox.
2d Lieut., W. G. Barnes.
2d Lieut., (vacant.)

COMPANY H.

Captain, T. J. Dove.
1st Lieut., H. Wheeler.
2d Lieut., Thomas Grant.
2d Lieut., J. N. Steel.

COMPANY I.

Captain, J. H. Roderick.
1st Lieut., J. H. Kincaid.
2d Lieut., W. T. James.
2d Lieut., (vacant.)

COMPANY K.

Captain, E. B. Titus.
1st Lieut., J. M. Blain.
2d Lieut., D. H. Bearden.
2d Lieut., (vacant.)

NAMES OF THE OFFICERS OF "WELLS'S REGIMENT" OF TEXAS CAVALRY DISMOUNTED.

Colonel—J. W. WELLS.
Lieut.-Col.—C. GOOD.
Major—S. E. GILLETT.
Quartermaster—W. R. WARREN.
Commissary—J. R. McDONALD.
Surgeon—G. G. DUGGINS.
Assistant Surgeon—D. W. SWIGGART.
Adjutant—R. W. MATTHEWS.

Company Officers.

COMPANY A.

Captain, Julius Harshaw.
1st Lieut., F. H. Dun.
2d Lieut., J. B. Reagan.
2d Lieut., J. E. Jones.

COMPANY B.

Captain, L. F. Cook.
1st Lieut., J. M. Kennedy.
2d Lieut., G. W. Thompson.
2d Lieut., T. C. Marsh.

COMPANY C.

Captain, D. M. Vanter.
1st Lieut. W. C. Jones.
2d Lieut., R. R. White.
2d Lieut., P. H. Lacy.

COMPANY D.

Captain, J. J. Edwards.
1st Lieut., J. J. Whittington.
2d Lieut., (vacant.)
2d Lieut., (vacant.)

COMPANY E.

Captain, J. T. Parrish.
1st Lieut., Robert Edwards.
2d Lieut., (vacant.)
2d Lieut., (vacant.)

Company Officers.

COMPANY F.

Captain, R. H. Chapman.
1st Lieut., D. J. Marsh.
2d Lieut., A. R. Brown.
2d Lieut., A. D. Wallace.

COMPANY G.

Captain, (vacant.)
1st Lieut., D. J. Bear.
2d Lieut., P. H. Cross.
2d Lieut., S. M. Weems.

COMPANY H.

Captain, T. A. Perkins.
1st Lieut., J. D. Williams.
2d Lieut., J. S. Cross.
2d Lieut., (vacant.)

COMPANY I.

Captain, A. P. Ryan.
1st Lieut., T. P. Lockhart.
2d Lieut., J. P. Gatlin.
2d Lieut., (vacant.)

COMPANY K.

Captain, J. N. Daniel.
1st Lieut., A. J. Ward.
2d Lieut., S. S. Syday.
2d Lieut., (vacant.)

After the dismounting of the cavalry, everything passed off quietly in camp. The reason assigned for the dismounting of so many cavalry regiments, by order of General Kirby Smith, was owing to the scarcity of corn and fodder to feed the animals; and, besides, the cavalry branch of the service was larger in proportion than all the infantry and artillery combined, in the Trans-Mississippi Department.

While remaining at this camp, near Mansfield, an amusing and laughable incident occurred in camp. On the evening of the 4th, some soldiers paid a visit to Mr. ——'s residence, situated a few miles from camp. Mr. —— devoted his leisure time to the raising of bees. In close proximity to his house were some dozen of bee-hives. A few of the soldiers attracted the attention of Mr. —— in telling yarns of their exploits in the war, while the balance of them were engaged in helping themselves to his honey. The following morning he missed some of his bee-hives, and at once reported the facts to the field-officer of the day. The field-officer of the day, as a matter of course, sympathized with him in the loss of his honey. He told him he would give him the privilege of making a thorough search throughout the entire camp, and, if he discovered the honey, to report the facts to him and he would punish the guilty parties.

As he proceeded from mess to mess, throwing the cooking utensils about, the uproar and crowd increased, hollowing at the top of their voices, "Here's your honey." Unmercifully they made the intruder the subject of witticisms and sly jokes, making honey the theme of it all, until he could stand the assault no longer.

Turning upon his persecutors with a lugubrious expression of features laughable to behold, and raising his stick aloft, he exclaimed: "Gentlemen, some parties took three bee-hives, and not satisfied in doing that, they broke into my store-room and took a basket containing three bottles of honey, which I had engaged to one of my neighbors. I care not for the honey that the thieving rascals stole; and they haven't the manliness to acknowledge it. I want them to give me my basket, if not the honey. Men, the basket they stole belonged to my brother. He's in the Southern army, and I hate to lose it. Give me my basket," hollowing at the top of his voice. "No you don't, old fel," said a voice; "you want somebody to bring you the basket, and then take him up for stealing your honey. No you don't. ' 'Lasses is sweet, but honey am sweeter.'"

Stooping to enter a tent, he was assaulted by a full dose of corn meal (scarce as it was), from the mischievous occupant. As he suddenly emerged, sputtering and blowing the meal from his mouth and nostrils—a serio-comic spectacle—a new uproar greeted him. "Take him out," said one; "hunting honey is a pretense; he is trying to steal some one's 'blue beef.'" Thus, this seeker, after having lost his sweetness, was assailed on all sides with a thousand absurd suggestions how to find his honey, until, almost crazed, he fled to the officers' quarters, cursing the Texans, and swearing that there wasn't an honest man among all the Texas troops. He withdrew from camp, still hearing the ringing voices of the men, "Here's your honey."

On the evening of the 5th, General Forney received orders from General Smith, for his division to proceed to Hempstead, Texas.

CHAPTER XXXVIII.

HOMEWARD BOUND.—RETROGRADE MOVEMENT.—LINE OF MARCH.—GENER-
ALS SMITH, MAGRUDER, AND FORNEY'S ADDRESS TO THE SOLDIERS.—
NEGOTIATIONS FOR THE SURRENDER OF THE TRANS-MISSISSIPPI DEPART-
MENT.—ARRIVAL AT HEMPSTEAD.—DISBANDING OF THE TROOPS.—
FAREWELL PARTING.

ON the morning of the 6th, the division was formed in
line. The command was given to "about face." We
marched back the same road we came, and camped
after marching ten miles. The whole command was exceedingly rejoiced in returning to their beloved State. But, as the
old proverb says, "Never hollow until you are out of the
woods." Such was the case on this occasion; as, the following morning, we "about-faced" again and marched eleven
miles back the same road we marched over yesterday—the
rain pouring down in torrents. Many were the murmurs and
curses of the men, at being disappointed in not getting to
Texas.

On the 8th marched thirteen miles; passed through the
heroic town of Mansfield, where the ladies were, as usual, glad
to see the "Greyhounds."

March 9th. Marched thirteen miles. After arriving in camp
we were visited by a heavy hail-storm.

March 10th. After resting until about 4 o'clock, P. M., we
took up the line of march, and marched six miles. We remained at this camp until the morning of the 12th, when we
once more took up the line of march for Texas. Marched
fourteen miles, through a cold and drizzling rain. The morning of the 13th was bitterly cold, yet the troops traveled merrily along through the pine woods, entertaining each other

with jokes and all manner of witty fusilades. Arrived in camp late in the evening, after marching thirteen miles. After our arrival in camp we learned that the enemy was fitting out a large expedition at New Orleans, for the purpose of invading Texas. We also received information that all of General Bee's Cavalry was ordered to be dismounted. Two of his regiments were ordered to report to General Forney, at the crossing of the Sabine River, but failed to report.

On the 14th we marched through the town of Keatchie. The troops were hailed with enthusiasm by the citizens. Every door, window, and house-roof was crowded with eager spectators. We arrived in camp early in the day, after marching six miles.

March 15th. Marched ten miles ; crossed the State-line, and camped in Texas once more. Went to sleep with lighter hearts than we did since we left our beloved State, some three years ago.

March 16th. Marched fifteen miles, and camped on the banks of the Sabine River.

On the 17th we crossed the Sabine River at Grand Bluff, in Panola County. At the point of crossing, the river was some fifty yards wide, the water running over a bed of sand between six and seven feet deep. By keeping the ferry-boat in rapid motion, the passage was made without difficulty. After crossing the river we marched three miles from the river-bank and camped.

March 18th. Moved camp two miles further, and camped at a stream of pure water, fringed on either bank with large cotton-wood trees. We remained at this camp until the morning of the 20th. Game was in abundance, and the boys enjoyed themselves a-hunting.

On the 20th we took up the line of march again. The weather was now delightfully cool in the morning and evening, while the heat of the sun at noonday was tempered by a fresh breeze from the south. We marched thirteen miles, through a thickly-timbered and well-watered country. Of timber there is a sufficiency for all ordinary purposes, and the day must come when this section will support a thriving population. We camped about four miles from a village called Rake Pocket, a suitable name when Confederate money was at stake, as the money basis of the country.

Early on the morning of the 22d, we took up the line of march. After marching fifteen miles we arrived at camp. As soon as our wagons arrived, the animals were turned out to graze until dark, when they were brought back to camp under guard. They appeared to improve very much, owing to the abundance of the mesquite grass.

March 23d. Our march to-day was nearly due west. Game was abundant. In the distance, looking west, a line of high bluffs had been seen, supposed to be the hills that border the town of Rusk, in Cherokee County. We arrived in camp early in the day, after marching ten miles.

On the 24th, while pursuing a westerly course, with the high hills in plain sight before us, we reached a swift-running creek, where we camped for the night, after marching thirteen miles.

March 25th. After marching four miles, we arrived at the neatly-located town of Rusk. The town is located between two hills. The scenery is delightful. The population consisted of about 2,000 people. After passing through the town, we struck camp on a small creek, about one mile southwest of town.

At an early hour on the morning of the 26th we were on the march. The atmosphere was delightfully cool, after recent rains which had fallen. We continued our march in a southwesterly direction. We arrived at a beautiful valley, where wood and water were plentiful. A beautiful stream of water, some twenty feet wide and six inches deep, ran through the valley. We camped at this creek of water, after marching fourteen miles.

As usual, on the morning of the 27th, we were once more on the march, still marching in a southwesterly course. After marching several miles, we arrived at an elevated ridge. From the top of this ridge you could behold, at some distance off, the roads leading to the towns of Henderson, Crockett, and Palestine. The country we traversed to-day was a poor, unfertilized, barren country, hardly suitable for man or beast to live in. The soil was a red clay, mixed with gravel. Dwelling houses were few and far between. In fact, there could be no comparison between it and the poor, sandy soil of Arkansas. This was the first section of country lying west of the Sabine River that we came across not suitable for agricultural purposes, but very well adapted for manufacturing purposes. We arrived in camp late in the evening, after marching fourteen miles over a rocky and hilly road.

March 28th. Marched fourteen miles. Shortly after our arrival in camp a heavy thunder-storm took place, wetting our clothes and extinguishing our camp-fires. We had no means of shelter to keep even our provisions dry; consequently, the following morning we took up the line of march, wet and hungry. Marched twelve miles; passed through the town of Crockett, and camped two miles from town, where we remained until the morning of April 2d. While remaining at this camp, General Forney ordered company drill twice a day. This order seemed not to give satisfaction, and led to cries all over camp of "Beef, beef, and no drill." Orders were soon issued from division headquarters to regimental commanders, to have all the soldiers that hollowed for beef arrested; consequently, the cry of "beef" was stopped amongst the troops for the present. The company-drill exercise, no doubt, would have been proper, provided we had been in a permanent camp; but, under the circumstances, a little rest was more preferable. However, the duty of the private soldier was to obey orders, whether right or wrong.

On the morning of the 2d we took up the line of march again, traveling in the direction of the Trinity River. Marched fifteen miles, and camped on some table-land adjoining the bottom-land of the Trinity River.

April 3d. Crossed the Trinity River, and continued our march about twelve miles. Our wagons didn't arrive in camp until about midnight.

April 4th. Marched five miles, and camped convenient to a pond of dirty water, which we were compelled to use, as there was no other within a long distance of our camp.

April 5th. Marched fourteen miles, over a miserably poor country. Although the immediate bottom of the Trinity River is good soil, of a dark and sandy mould, yet, a short distance from the river-banks, the soil is generally poor.

April 6th. Marched fifteen miles. Our march to-day was more pleasant than yesterday's march. We traveled over a country of picturesque and varied scenery, broken into rocky hills of singular shapes; little valleys, with pure crystal water here leaping swiftly along, and there losing itself in the sands; timber of different kinds—everything to give it a varied beauty, except game.

April 7th. Marched ten miles. The weather was pleasant and cool. The country we traveled over was extremely beautiful. The farms were well cultivated.

The morning of the 8th opened clear and beautiful, and the troops seemed anxious to get to Piedmont Springs, to drink of its famous waters. We arrived at camp, situated near the springs about noontime. The springs are situated alongside of a running creek, beautifully timbered, which sweeps closely around, shutting up the springs in a kind of a cove. The water has a very agreeable taste, resembling that of the famous Seltzer Springs, in the grand duchy of Nassau, a country famous for wine and mineral waters; and it is almost entirely of the same character, though still more agreeable than that of the famous Bear Springs, near Bear River of the Great Salt Lake. We remained at the springs, apparently for the benefit of our health, until the morning of the 13th, when we took up the line of march for Hempstead. Marched eight miles, and arrived in camp.

April 14th. Marched fifteen miles, and camped near Groce's Retreat.

April 15th. Marched fifteen miles, and camped near Camp Groce, about two and a half miles from Hempstead. We remained at this camp, awaiting further orders. The troops appeared to be in buoyant spirits ; many of their friends came from distant parts of the State, to welcome them back once more to their beloved State.   But, alas ! the sad news of all the Confederate troops east of the Mississippi River, seemed for the time being to crush their spirits ; but, notwithstanding the various rumors afloat, the troops of the division continued to do their duty in a cheerful manner.   Many of them believed the war would be continued west of the river, and that we would be reinforced from across the Mississippi River.   Their patriotism was irreproachable, notwithstanding they had heard that the armies of Generals Lee, Johnston and Taylor had surrendered.   They awaited patiently to hear General Kirby Smith's programme.   But, alas ! they were soon given to understand that General Kirby Smith considered that any further resistance on his part would be in vain.   He was willing and ready to surrender the Trans-Mississippi Department at any moment.

In the mean time, stirring addresses were made to the troops to stand by their colors to the last moment, by Generals Smith, Magruder, Walker, Forney, etc., etc., as follows :

GENERAL SMITH'S ADDRESS.

SOLDIERS OF THE TRANS-MISSISSIPPI ARMY :

The crisis of our revolution is at hand.   Great disasters have overtaken us.   The army of Northern Virginia and our Commander-in-Chief are prisoners of war.   With you rest the hopes of our nation, and upon your action depends the fate of our people.   I appeal to you in the name of the cause you have 'so heroically maintained—in the name of your firesides and families, so dear to you—in the name of your bleeding country, whose fate is in your hands.   Show that you are worthy of your position in history.   Prove to the world that your hearts have not failed in the hour of disaster, and that, at the last moment, you will sustain the holy cause which has been so gloriously battled for by your brethren east of the Mississippi River.

You possess the means of long resisting invasion. You have hopes of succor from abroad. Protract the struggle, and you will surely receive the aid of nations which already deeply sympathize with you.

Stand by your colors; maintain your discipline. The great resources of this department, its vast extent, the numbers, the discipline, and the efficiency of the army, will secure to our country terms that a proud people can with honor accept, and may, under the providence of God, be the means of checking the triumph of our enemy, and of securing the final success of our cause.

GENERAL MAGRUDER'S ADDRESS.

The Major-General commanding the District of Texas, New Mexico, and Arizona, deems it proper, in view of recent events, to call upon the army and patriotism worthy of the holy cause of liberty and independence, and of the great efforts heretofore made by the army and the people of Texas to advocate and uphold it.

The enemy threatens our coast, and will bring his great, undivided resources for a successful invasion of the State. Let him be met with unanimity and Spartan courage, and he will be unsuccessful, as he has been in Texas.

Let him be met at the water's edge, and let him pay dearly for every inch of territory he may acquire. Six hundred Frenchmen, under the first Napoleon, recaptured France from her enemies.

Forty-two Irish soldiers, on our soil, drove fifteen thousand men to sea.

The army of the Trans-Mississippi Department is larger, in finer order, and better supplied than ever. There are no navigable streams in Texas; therefore the enemy will be divested of the great power of steam, which he has elsewhere relied upon.

Crops have been bountiful. Our armies can therefore be supplied in almost any part of Texas.

There is no reason for despondency; and, if the people of

Texas will it, they can successfully defend their territory for an indefinite period.

The Major-General commanding therefore exhorts the soldiers of the army to stand firmly by their colors, and obey the orders of their officers; and recommends to the citizens, that they devote themselves still more fully to the cultivation of breadstuffs; for, should our armies be unsuccessful in the East, every gallant soldier will rally to the banner of the Confederacy, which will still float defiantly west of the Mississippi River.

GENERAL FORNEY'S ADDRESS.

After having been so long and so arduously engaged in the service of your country, I know that the news from the other side of the Mississippi River is calculated to depress your spirits, and I therefore desire to say to you a few plain words. And I call upon you to listen to me, as one that has the same interest at stake as yourselves. You should recollect that all the news we have received is from Northern telegrams, direct from the hands of our enemies, who would much rather whip us by dispatches than any other way. They tell us that our friends in the East are whipped, have surrendered, and are conquered. Some of it may be true, but a good deal of it is, doubtless, false. In this uncertainty, let us hope for the best, but be prepared for the worst. At the same time, I conjure you to stand firm.

Let us wait to hear from our own side of the question. Of course the news is far from cheering. We all feel depressed. We all feel that it is time to consider well how to act. But it grieves me to learn that some of you, I cannot think many, are willing to sacrifice the fair renown of the division by leaving it now; and it is to them that I am speaking.

But why are you acting thus? Think! are you acting honorably, nobly, wisely? It is full a thousand miles to the scene of action in Virginia and North Carolina. Shall the great State of Texas quail before the enemy has come within sight of her shores? And shall the proud men of Texas throw down

20

their arms, and run cowardly home, before the enemy has set foot in the State, or they have even been asked to surrender? Should the worst come to the worst, you certainly can make better terms and stipulations banded together as an army and with arms in your hands than you can scattered and dispersed all over the country. Should the enemy invade this country in large force, you surely cannot believe that your generals would be guilty of the madness of sacrificing your lives, without a strong probability of success, and unless there was some great end to be obtained. In conclusion, I appeal to you as men and soldiers—I ask you for the honor of your State and your honor ; in the name of your wives and children ; in the name of those gallant Texans who have fought and toiled on every battle-field of this war—to do your duty orderly and quietly, till the proper authorities shall say when and on what terms we shall be discharged. My interest is the same, and is identified with yours. My only object is now, and will be, to do what I conceive to be the best for you and the country at at large.

Be firm and irreproachable. When we get to our homes, let it be with honorable discharges in our hands.

On the morning of May 1st, a Federal officer, named Colonel Sprague, arrived at the mouth of Red River, with dispatches from General Canby to General Smith. General Smith sent Colonel Flóurnoy, of the 16th Texas Infantry, and Colonel Alston, of his staff (under flag of truce), to meet Colonel Sprague, and learn the nature of his dispatches. On meeting with Colonel Sprague, he informed them that he was sent by General Canby to demand of General Smith the surrender of the Trans-Mississippi Department. It appears that Colonels Flournoy and Alston did not have the authority to act for General Smith ; consequently, they returned to Shreveport, bearing the dispatches to General Smith, for him to act according to his judgment. The troops hearing that General Kirby Smith was about to surrender, confusion worse confounded reigned everywhere, among the troops and citizens.

The soldiers were gathered in groups everywhere, discussing the approaching surrender. Curses, deep and bitter, fell from lips not accustomed to use such language; while numbers, both officers and men, swore fearful oaths never to surrender. It was such a scene as one seldom cares to witness. The depth of feeling exhibited by compressed lips, pale faces, and blazing eyes, told a fearful story of how bitter was the hopeless surrender of the cause for which they had fought, toiled, suffered for long years. The humiliation was unbearable. For nearly four years had "Walker's Division" battled for the South, homes, and freedom; for nearly four years of horrors, suffering, toil, and bloodshed, they had trod the soil of Arkansas and Louisiana, and left their heroic dead upon the hills and plains of those States; and now, once more in their native State, they are to witness the final overthrow of the Confederate government. They must relinquish their arms, and see their proud banner trailed in the dust, never more to be raised by mortal hands. What a torturing reality for their brave and noble spirits!

The morning of the 19th found the majority of the troops gone or preparing to leave. They were allowed to take a wagon to each company. On the evening of the 20th, the balance of the troops that remained were furloughed, or, more properly, discharged from the Confederate army. The parting among the troops was most affecting. Many put their arms around each other's necks, and sobbed like children; others gave the strong grasp of the hand, and silently went away with hearts too full for utterance; while still others would mutter a huskily-spoken "Good-bye" or deep oath. Such were some of the farewell scenes. Together in battle or camp, in sunshine and in storm, in suffering and pleasure, in sorrow and joy, on the weary and toilsome march, no wonder that their hearts were linked together in bands of steel, with ties unspeakable, inexpressible. No wonder the parting—perhaps for years, perhaps forever—wrung their souls with torturing agony.

CHAPTER XXXIX.

THE "PERSONNEL" OF THE DIVISION, AND HOW THEY ACCEPT THE
SITUATION.

IN events of unusually startling nature, the mind naturally investigates causes, reasoning from these to the effect produced. Thus, in reading the history of this gallant organization, the peruser inquires, "Who and what were these men?" Let us answer. The members of Walker's Texas Division were principally men of high social standing at home; intelligent, refined, young,—the fires of youth glowing in their stalwart forms, voluntarily offering their services to their country. They were actuated by a firm conviction of the justice of their cause. From workshop and counter, from cottage and mansion, from the lordly plantation and the crowded city they came, standing side by side in defense of a common cause. Look at them! the fire of a fixed determination glowing in their clear, bright eyes; the strength of a settled purpose evinced in their firm tread and upright carriage.

No wonder that they distinguished themselves on the battle-field, covering themselves with an imperishable glory. There is not to-day a man living who ever doubted the courage and gallantry of the whole division. Thus they fought through the stirring scenes of the whole war, and when the inevitable decrees of fate decided against them, they accepted the issue as brave men only could.

If they were gallant soldiers, now they are good citizens, and can be implicitly trusted in their fealty to the government. They feel that they have been overpowered, and accept the situation as brave and honorable men—such men as Generals T. N. Waul, W. H. King, R. Waterhouse, and Colonels

Overton Young, O. M. Roberts, James H. Jones, John H. Burnett, W. A. Crawford, Ed. Clarke, Wm. Byrd, Geo. Flournoy, James E. Shepard, Wm. Fitzhugh, E. P. Gregg, T. P. Allen, Geo. W. Jones, E. W. Taylor, W. L. Crawford, D. B. Culbertson, Thos. R. Bonner, R. B. Hubbard, J. J. Cannon, E. H. Baxter, R. S. Gould, etc.

They are considered the most trustworthy of citizens. Many of them have held some of the highest offices of this State. Yet they were the first to answer to the bugle-call. These are all true men. In financial and commercial circles, at the bar, in the workshop, at the bench and counter, in the fields, they are striving to rebuild their fallen fortunes— striving to regain the loss inflicted during the war. They are neither despondent nor despairing, but work with alacrity and cheerfulness, to repair the many ravages of the conflict. Such are the positions of men who gave fortunes and staked their lives on the issue of the war. The heroism displayed in accepting their defeat is not less praiseworthy than their undaunted bearing in the deadly battle-field.

CHAPTER XL.

SURRENDER OF THE TRANS-MISSISSIPPI DEPARTMENT.

ERMS of a military convention, entered into this 26th day of May, 1865, at New Orleans, between General E. Kirby Smith, commanding the department of Trans-Mississippi, and Major-General E. R. S. Canby, U. S. Army, commanding the army and division of West Mississippi, for the surrender of the troops and public property under the control of the military and naval authorities of the Trans-Mississippi Department.

I. All acts of war and resistance against the United States, on the part of the troops under General Smith, shall cease from this date.

II. The officers and men to be paroled, until duly exchanged, or otherwise released from the obligations of their parole, by the authorities of the Government of the United States. Duplicate rolls of all officers and men paroled to be returned by each officer, as may be designated by the parties hereto, officers giving their individual paroles, and commanders of regiments, battalions, companies, and detachments signing a like parole for the men of their respective commands.

III. Artillery, small arms, ammunition, and other property of the Confederate States Government, including gun-boats and transports, to be turned over to the officers appointed to receive the same on the part of the Government of the United States, duplicate inventories of the property to be surrendered to be prepared, one copy to be retained by the officer delivering, and the other by the officer receiving, for the information of their respective commanders.

IV. The officers and men paroled under this agreement will

be allowed to return to their homes, with the assurance that they will not be disturbed by the authorities of the United States, as long as they continue to observe the conditions of their parole, and the laws in force where they reside ; except that persons residents in the Northern States,.and not excepted in the amnesty proclamation of the President, may return to their homes on taking the oath of allegiance to the United States.

V. The surrender of property will not include the side-arms, or private horses, or baggage of officers.

VI. All horses which are in good faith the private property of enlisted men will not be taken from them. The men will be permitted to take such with them to their homes, to be used for private property only.

VII. The time, mode, and place of paroling and the surrender of property will be fixed by their respective commanders, and it will be carried out by commissioners appointed by them.

VIII. The terms and conditions of this surrender to extend to all officers and men of the army and navy of the Confederate States, or any of them, being in or belonging to the Trans-Mississippi Department.

IX. Transportation and subsistence to be furnished at public cost for the officers and men, after parole, to the nearest practicable point to their homes.

(Signed,) S. B. BUCKNER,
Lieut. Gen. and Chief of Staff, for Gen. E. K. SMITH.

P. J. OSTERHOUSE,
Major-General and Chief of Staff, for Major-Gen. CANBY.

APPENDIX.

I CANNOT close this volume without a special acknowledgment of my indebtedness to my friends for their interest in my labors, and for furnishing me the necessary funds to have my book published, as well as furnishing me with valuable documents and papers. I sincerely trust that they may feel repaid by a perusal of its pages.

J. P. BLESSINGTON.

CONCLUSION.

In closing this chronicle, I regret that many a noble deed and daring act, done by the men of "Walker's Division," should be left unnoticed; but the necessity of keeping my record within reasonable limits has compelled brevity in all my narrations, and what I have considered a judicious selection, under all the circumstances, of the facts that are contained in this book. There has been no necessity with me to draw on the imagination in order to be able to fill a certain number of pages. The only trouble has been to give such facts as would portray the courage and consistency of our men. Indeed, it needed not the potent aid of fiction, as in many other accounts of warlike events, to preserve the name of "Walker's Division."

I have thus briefly sketched the services of the gallant troops, during the late war. I have labored to be as correct and impartial as possible, and if I have in any way failed in the prosecution of this important task, it has been through no feeling of partiality of mine. I trust that my readers, one and all, and I know many of the gallant members of my old division, at least, will believe me, when I say that my object in putting this work before the public has not been of a sordid nature; and if I, by my publication, keep from oblivion the deeds of the fathers of the future generations of Texas, my desire is accomplished—my most ardent wish gratified.

Let the veil of obscurity fall over the deeds of those who often were misled during moments of excitement, or blindly followed their own wishes in preference to military orders. The curtain falls upon the bloody drama of war; the foot lights have been extinguished ; the actors have all departed ; the audience of the world's wondering nations turned to other scenes. The pen which has dotted these reminiscences through long and weary years is laid aside, as white-winged *peace*, all radiant with joy, settles down once more upon the land of Columbia.

> "How vain, how frail, how transitory
>   This world, with all its pomp and show !
>   Its mighty names renowned in story,
>   They've gladly left them all below."

Index